W9-CQZ-479

Microsoft Office XP

SIMPLY VISUAL

Perspection, Inc.

SYBEX®

San Francisco ◆ Paris ◆ Düsseldorf ◆ Soest ◆ London

Associate Publisher: Cheryl Applewood
Contracts and Licensing Manager: Kristine O'Callaghan
Acquisitions & Development Editor: Bonnie Bills
Managing Editor: Steve Johnson
Authors: Elizabeth Eisner Redding and Kathryn Toyer
Editors: Barbara Waxer and Christy Parrish
Production Editor: Marian Hartsough
Technical Editors: Beth Teyler and Kristy Thielen
Book Designer: Maureen Forys, Happenstance Type-O-Rama
Electronic Publishing Specialist: Marian Hartsough
Proofreaders: Holly Johnson and Shirley Todd
Indexer: Michael Brackney
Cover Designer: Daniel Ziegler
Cover Illustrator: Ziegler Design

Library of Congress Card Number: 2001090111

ISBN: 0-7821-4004-1

*To our spouses
who held us together and
our children who missed us
during the lengthy process.*

Perspection

Perspection, Inc., is a software training company committed to providing information and training to help people use software more effectively in order to communicate, make decisions, and solve problems. Perspection writes and produces software training books, and develops multimedia and Web-based training. This incorporates Perspection's training expertise to ensure that you'll receive the maximum return on your time. With this straightforward, easy-to-read reference tool, you get the information you need to get the job done.

We invite you to visit the Perspection Web site at:

www.perspection.com

Acknowledgments

The task of creating any book requires the talents of many hardworking people pulling together to meet almost impossible demands. For their effort and commitment, we'd like to thank the outstanding team responsible for making this book possible: the writers, Elizabeth Eisner Reding and Kathryn Toyer; the editors, Barbara Waxer and Christy Parrish; the technical editors, Beth Teyler and Kristy Thielen; the production editor, Marian Hartsough; the proofreaders, Holly Johnson and Shirley Todd; and the indexer, Michael Brackney.

At Sybex, we'd like to thank Jordan Gold and Cheryl Applewood for the opportunity to undertake this project, Bonnie Bills for her editorial support, and Amy Changar, Judith Hibbard, and Cheryl Hauser for their direction and guidance with the printing process.

Perspection

Contents

Contents

Contents

Introduction

This book offers a simple visual approach to learning Microsoft Office XP. Designed for the beginner who may find the complexity of the Office programs intimidating, Microsoft Office XP Simply Visual uses a highly visual, step-by-step format to present the fundamental tasks that any new user needs in order to get "up and running" as quickly as possible on the Office XP programs that are the industry standard.

How This Book Is Organized

Microsoft Office XP Simply Visual is designed to be an easy-to-read and easy-to-use reference tool that helps you get your work done quickly and efficiently in a straightforward way. Each chapter is organized by tasks. Each task gives you information that is essential to performing the task. For each operation, you'll see what commands to enter and which options to select.

This book contains sixteen chapters. In Chapter 1, you'll learn the essentials for getting started with the Office XP programs. Chapters 2 and 3 describe tools and features in every Office XP program. Chapters 4–6 cover tasks for creating, formatting, and enhancing documents with Microsoft Word 2002. Chapters 7 and 8 cover tasks for creating and designing spreadsheets with Microsoft Excel 2002. Chapters 9 and 10 cover tasks for creating and delivering presentations with Microsoft PowerPoint 2002. Chapters 11 and 12 cover tasks for planning, creating, and modifying databases with Microsoft Access 2002. Chapters 13 and 14 cover tasks for managing information with Microsoft Outlook 2002. Chapter 15 guides you through the process of creating and modifying Web pages with Office XP programs. Chapter 16 shows you how to share information between the Office XP programs.

How to Make Good Use of This Book

We recommend using this book as a kind of beginner's reference. Use the index or table of contents to find the command or feature you want to learn about and go directly there. Each basic operation is presented as a step-by-step procedure, with illustrations to guide you. Simple but realistic examples allow you to try out most procedures on your own. As key terms are introduced, you'll find capsule definitions in the margin. (These definitions are also gathered into a Glossary at the end of the book, so you can look up a term at any time.) Margin notes also provide alternative methods to accomplish particular steps and summarize important concepts.

Every reader should begin with the first chapter, especially if you are not at all familiar with Office XP. After that, you can jump to any of the chapters that meet your needs. Keep the book near your workstation for quick access as you work on your projects. If a command or procedure confuses you, you can easily flip to the two or three pages that describe it.

We hope this book serves you as a useful guide as you learn and use Office XP.

1 Getting Started with Office XP

As we manage our business and personal worlds, we continually need to accomplish more, faster, and better. Microsoft Office XP provides you the tools to do all this and more. Each of its programs—Word, Excel, PowerPoint, Access, Outlook, Publisher, and Internet Explorer—has a special function, yet they all work together so you can combine word processing, spreadsheets, presentations, databases, scheduling, publications, and Internet communication. The results are professional, dynamic, and effective documents for every occasion. Every Office program uses the same structure of windows, menus, toolbars, and dialog boxes, so you can focus on creating the best document rather than struggling with how each program works. Office programs have personalized menus and toolbars that display only the commands and toolbar buttons you use most frequently, which saves space and increases your efficiency. In addition, you can perform your most basic actions the same way in every program. For example, in each Office program, you open, save, and close documents with the same buttons or commands. When you have a question, the identical help feature is available throughout Office programs.

Starting an Office Program

The quickest way to start an Office program is from the Start menu on the taskbar. Office lets you customize your work area and switch from program to program with the click of a button.

> **NOTE** You can get Office information on the Web from within any Office program. Click the Help menu, and then click Office On The Web. Your Web browser opens, displaying the Microsoft Office Update Web site.

Start an Office Program from the Start Menu

1. Click the **Start** button ![Start] on the taskbar.

2. Point to **Programs**.

3. Click the Office XP program that you want to open.

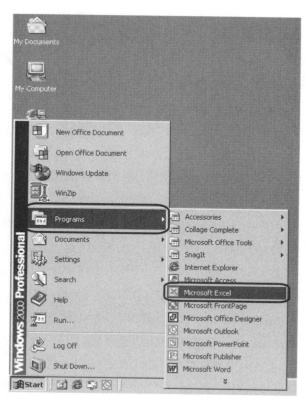

Start an Office Program and Open a New Office Document

1. Click the **Start** button 🔁 Start on the taskbar, and then click **New Office Document**. The New Office Document dialog box opens.

2. Click the tab for the type of document you want to create.

3. Click a document icon, and then click the **OK** button to start the program and open a new document.

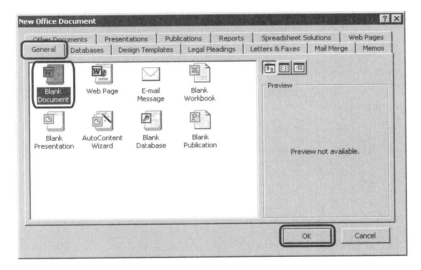

Opening an Existing File

Before you can begin working, you need to open a document. You can open the file (and its program) at one time, or you can start the program and then open the file from within the program.

NOTE   You can quickly open a copy of a file. When you open a file from the Open dialog box, click the Open button drop-down arrow, and then click Open As Copy. The Office program creates a new copy of the file in the same folder with the filename *Copy of [Filename]*.

Open an Existing File from the Start Menu

1. Click the **Start** button [Start] on the taskbar, and then click **Open Office Document**.

2. Click an icon on the **Places bar** to open a frequently used folder.

3. If necessary, click the **Look In** drop-down arrow, and then click the drive where the file is located.

4. Double-click the folder in which the file is stored.

5. Double-click a filename to start the program and open the file.

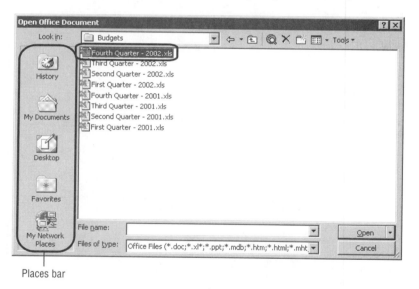

Places bar

Open an Existing File from Within an Office Program

1. Click the **Open** button on the Standard toolbar.

2. Click an icon on the **Places bar** to open a frequently used folder.

3. If necessary, click the **Look In** drop-down arrow 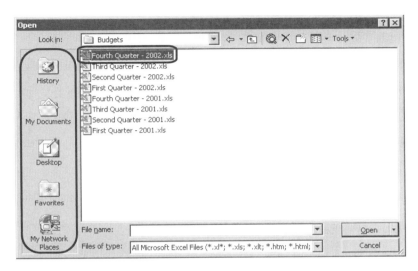 , and then click the drive where the file is located.

4. Double-click the folder in which the file is stored.

5. Double-click the file you want to open.

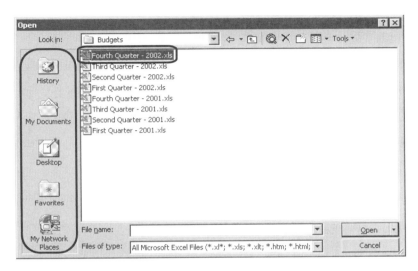

NOTE You can delete or rename any closed file from the Open or Save As dialog box. Click the file, click the Tools drop-down arrow, and then click Delete or Rename.

Saving a File

Frequently saving your files ensures that you don't lose work during an unexpected power loss. The first time you save a file, specify a filename and folder in the Save As dialog box. The next time you save the file, Office saves it with the same name in the same folder. If you want to change a file's name or location, you can use the Save As dialog box to create a copy of the original file.

TIP What's the difference between the Save and Save As commands? The Save command saves a copy of your current document to a previously specified name and location. The Save As command creates a copy of your current document with a new name, location, or type.

NOTE   When you name a file, you do not have to type the filename extension. Each Office program automatically adds the correct filename extension to files.

Save a File for the First Time

1. Click the **Save** button 🖫 on the Standard toolbar.

2. Click an icon on the Places bar to open a frequently used folder.

3. If necessary, click the **Save In** drop-down arrow ▾, and then click the drive where you want to save the file.

4. Double-click the folder in which you want to save the file.

5. Type a name for the file, or use the suggested name that appears in the **File Name** box.

6. Click the **Save** button.

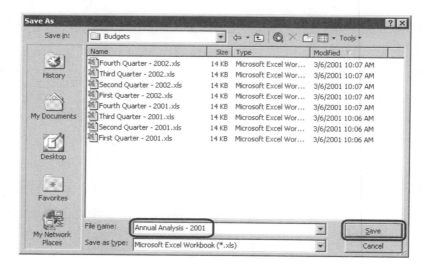

TIP   To modify your default save settings, choose Tools ➤ Options, click the Save tab, click the options you want, and then click the OK button.

Save a File with Another Name

1. Click the **File** menu, and then the **Save As** command (**File ➤ Save As**). The Save As dialog box opens

2. Click an icon on the Places bar or click the **Save In** drop-down arrow ▼, and then click the drive or folder where you want to save the file.

3. Type a new filename in the **File Name** box.

4. Click the **Save** button.

Choosing Menu and Dialog Box Options

Menu

A list of associated commands or options, located beneath the title bar (at the top of the window). You can choose a command or option by pointing to it and the clicking the mouse, or by highlighting it, and then pressing the Enter key on the keyboard.

Shortcut menu

A menu that lists commands when you right-click a word or object. To customize shortcut commands, choose Tools ➤ Customize ➤ Toolbars.

Dialog box

A window that displays onscreen that you use to enter or select information.

A **menu** is a list of related commands. For example, the Edit menu contains commands for editing a document, such as Delete and Cut. A **shortcut menu** opens when you right-click a word or object while you're working and contains commands related to a specific object. Clicking a menu command followed by an ellipsis (...) opens a **dialog box**, which is where you choose various options and provide information for completing the command. As you switch between programs, you'll find that all Office menus and dialog boxes look similar and work in the same way.

| TIP | When you first open a menu, the commands you used most recently appear first. Point to the Toolbar Options drop-down arrow to display the full menu. |

Choose Menu Commands

1. Click a menu name on the menu bar, or right-click an object (such as a toolbar, spreadsheet cell, picture, or selected text).

2. If necessary, click the double arrow to expand the menu and display more commands.

3. Click a menu command you want, or point to the arrow to the right of the menu command to display a submenu of related commands, and then click the command you want.

TIP Toolbar buttons and shortcut keys are faster than menu commands. You can learn the toolbar button equivalent of a menu command by using the toolbar button icon to the left of a menu command. Keyboard shortcuts appear to the right of their menu commands. To use a keyboard shortcut, hold down the first key (such as Ctrl), press the second key (such as V), and then release both keys (such as Ctrl+V).

NOTE The most common dialog box buttons are the OK button, which confirms your selections and closes the dialog box; and the Cancel button, which closes the dialog box without accepting your selections.

Choose Dialog Box Options

All Office dialog boxes contain the same types of options, including the following:

Tabs. Click a tab to display its options. Each tab groups a related set of options.

Option buttons. Click an option button to select it. You can usually select only one.

Spin box. Click the up or down arrow to increase or decrease the number, or type a number in the box.

Check box. Click the box to turn the option on or off. A checked box means the option is selected; a cleared box means it's not.

List box. Click the drop-down arrow to display a list of options, and then click the option you want.

Text box. Click in the box and type the requested information.

Button. Click a button to perform a specific action or command. A button name followed by an ellipsis (...) opens another dialog box.

Preview box. Many dialog boxes display an image that reflects the options you select.

Option button   Check box

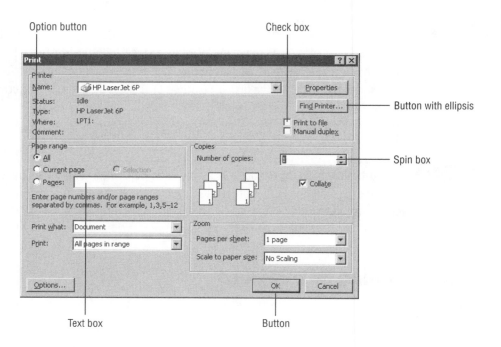

Button with ellipsis

Spin box

Text box   Button

Tab   List box

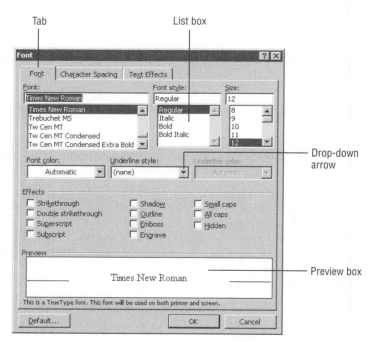

Drop-down arrow

Preview box

Working with Toolbars

Each Office **toolbar** contains a collection of buttons that you click to select frequently used menu commands. Most programs open by placing the Standard toolbar (which contains commands such as Save and Print) and the Formatting toolbar (which contains commands for selecting fonts and sizes) side by side. You can also display toolbars designed for specific tasks, such as drawing pictures, importing data, or creating charts. The Office program you're in will personalize the toolbars as you work, showing only the buttons you use most often. Additional toolbar buttons are available by clicking the Toolbar Options drop-down arrow at the end of the toolbar.

Toolbar
A collection of buttons that represent tools and that have equivalent commands on a related menu.

Display and Hide a Toolbar

1. Right-click any visible toolbar.

2. Click the name of the toolbar you want to display or hide.

Move and Reshape a Toolbar

You can modify the look of a toolbar in any Office program.

Docked

A toolbar that is attached to one edge of the window.

Floating

A toolbar that has a visible title bar and that you can move.

- ❖ To move a toolbar that is **docked** (attached) or **floating** (unattached) over the window, click the gray bar on the left edge of the toolbar, and then drag it to a new location.

- ❖ To return a floating toolbar to its previous docked location, double-click its title bar.

- ❖ To change the shape of a floating toolbar, drag any border until the toolbar is the shape you want.

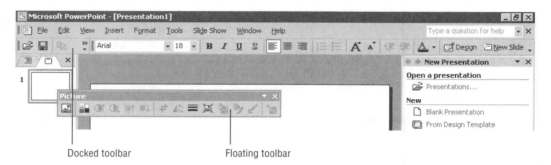

Docked toolbar   Floating toolbar

TIP   When you first open a toolbar, the buttons you used most recently display. Click the Toolbar Options drop-down arrow to display any other toolbar buttons. To display the full toolbar, double-click the gray bar on the left edge of the toolbar.

Display Toolbar Options on a Toolbar

To display more buttons on a toolbar, click the Toolbar Options drop-down arrow at the right end of the toolbar.

Arranging Windows

Every Office program and document open inside a **window**, which contains all the program commands and is where you create and edit your documents. Most often, you'll probably fill the entire screen with one window. Other times, when you may want to move or copy information between programs or documents, it's easier to display several windows at once. You can arrange simultaneously on the screen two or more windows from one program or from different programs. However, you must make the window active before you can work in it. You can also click the document buttons on the taskbar to switch between open Office documents.

Resize and Move a Window

All windows contain the same sizing buttons:

Maximize button. Click to make a window fill the entire screen.

Restore button. Click to reduce a maximized window to approximately half its full size.

Minimize button. Click to shrink a window to a taskbar button. To restore the window to its previous size, click the appropriate taskbar button.

Close button. Click to shut a window.

Window
An onscreen box that contains a title bar, menus, toolbars, and a work area.

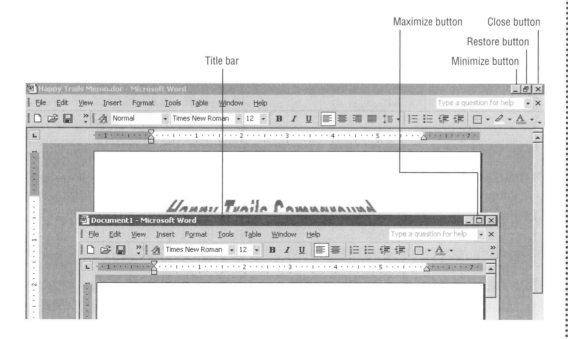

Maximize button   Close button

Restore button

Minimize button

Title bar

You can move a window to any location on the screen by clicking its title bar and dragging the window to a new location. Release the mouse button when the window is where you want it.

> **TIP**
> You can use shortcut keys to open and close windows, and quickly switch between windows. To close the active window, hold down the Ctrl+W keys on the keyboard. To switch to the next window, hold down the Ctrl+F6 keys on the keyboard, and to switch to the previous window, hold down the Ctrl+Shift+F6 keys on the keyboard.

> **TIP**
> Only one window can be active at a time. You can tell whether a window is active by the color of its title bar. By default, an active window's title bar is blue and the inactive title bar is gray. To make an inactive window active, click anywhere in the window.

Switch Between Document Windows

Each open Windows file or document displays its own button on the Windows taskbar. You can click the buttons on the taskbar to switch between open files.

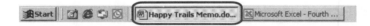

Choosing Templates and Wizards

Template
A file that defines the styles, fields, formatting, and layout of a document.

Wizard
A utility that leads you through steps to produce a product or accomplish a task.

Office makes it easy to create many common documents based on a template or using a wizard. A **template** opens a document (such as a letter) with predefined formatting and placeholder text that specifies what information you should enter (such as your name or address). A **wizard** walks you through the steps to create a finished document tailored to your preferences. The wizard asks you for information, and then, when you click the Finish button, it creates a completely formatted document based on the options and content you entered. You use a template to add information to a designed document, and you use a wizard to add a design to information you supply.

Choose a Template

1. Click the **Start** button [🎇 Start] on the taskbar, and then click **New Office Document**, or choose **File ➢ New**. The New Office Document dialog box opens.

2. Click the tab for the type of document you want to create.

3. Click the template you want to use.

4. Check the Preview box so you verify that the template will create the right style of document.

5. Click the **OK** button.

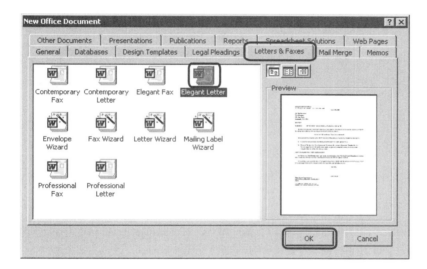

6. Type text for placeholders such as *[Click here and type your letter text]*.

TIP　If you create a Word document using a wizard, Word bases the document on the Normal document template. However, the styles Word uses in the document reflect the formatting options that you select when responding to the wizard.

Choose and Navigate a Wizard

1. Click the **Start** button 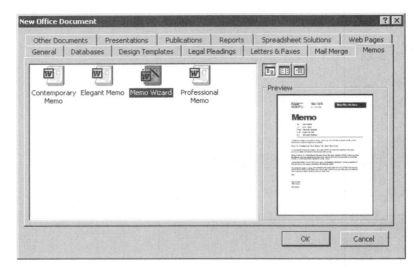 on the taskbar, and then click **New Office Document**, or choose **File ➢ New**. The New Office Document dialog box opens.

2. Click the tab for the type of document you want to create.

3. Double-click the icon for the wizard you want to use.

4. Read and select options (if necessary) in the first wizard dialog box.

5. Click the **Next** button to progress to the next wizard dialog box. Each wizard dialog box asks for different information.

6. Continue to select options, and then click the **Next** button.

7. When you reach the last wizard dialog box, click the **Finish** button.

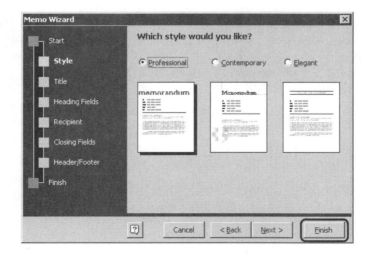

Getting Help in an Office Program

At some point, you will have a question or two about the program you're using. The Office online Help system provides the answers you need. **ScreenTips** show toolbar names and short descriptions about anything you see on the screen or in a dialog box. If you need help while you work, you can use the Ask a Question box to quickly get help. You can also search an extensive catalog of Help topics by an index or a table of contents to locate specific information.

ScreenTips

Descriptive text that displays when you hold the mouse pointer over a button.

Get a ScreenTip

1. Place the mouse pointer over a toolbar button. The name of the button, or the **ScreenTip**, appears below the button.

> **NOTE** To hide ScreenTips, choose Tools ➢ Customize ➢ Options, click the Show ScreenTips On Toolbars check box to clear it, and then click the OK button.

Get Help While You Work

1. Click the **Ask a Question** box `Type a question for help` on the menu bar, type a question, press the Enter key, and then click a topic.

Getting Help from the Office Assistant

Often the easiest way to learn how to accomplish a task is to ask someone who knows. Now, with Office, that knowledgeable friend is always available in the form of the Office Assistant. Tell the Office Assistant what you want to do in the same everyday language you use to ask a colleague or friend, and the Office Assistant walks you through the process step by step. If the personality of the default Office Assistant—Clippit—doesn't appeal to you, you can choose from a variety of other Office Assistants.

TIP You can open the Office Assistant by clicking the Help button. If the Office Assistant is already turned on, you will see the Office Assistant at the top of your screen. If the Office Assistant is turned off, the Help pane appears where you can get search for help by topic.

Ask the Office Assistant for Help

1. Click the **Help** button ![?] on the Standard toolbar, or click the **Office Assistant** to turn on the Office Assistant.

2. Type your question about a task with which you want help.

3. Click the **Search** button.

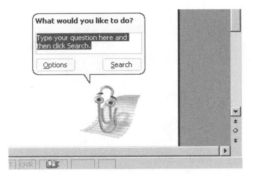

4. Click the topic in which you're interested.

5. Read and follow the directions. After you're done, click the **Close** button ![X] on the Help window.

6. Click the **Help** button ![?] on the Standard toolbar to hide the Office Assistant.

NOTE Get useful tips from the Office Assistant. When a light bulb appears above the Office Assistant, click the Office Assistant to see a tip for a simpler or more efficient way to accomplish a task.

Choose an Office Assistant

1. Right-click the **Office Assistant** and click **Options**, or click the **Options** button in the **Office Assistant** window. The Office Assistant dialog box opens.

2. Click the **Gallery** tab.

3. Click the **Next** button and the **Back** button to preview different Office Assistants.

4. Display the Office Assistant that you want to use.

5. Click the **OK** button. If the Office program prompts you to insert the Office XP CD-ROM in your drive, insert the CD-ROM, and then click the **OK** button.

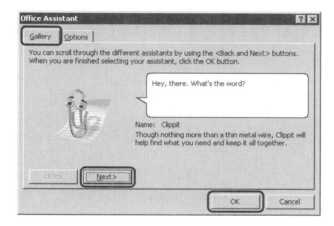

Turn Off the Office Assistant

1. Right-click the **Office Assistant** and click **Options**, or click the **Options** button in the Assistant window.

2. Click the **Options** tab.

3. Click the **Use Office Assistant** check box to clear it.

4. Click the **OK** button.

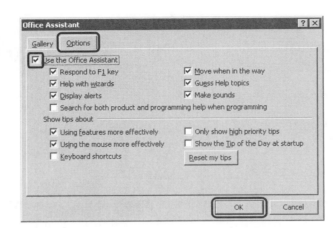

Displaying the Office Shortcut Bar

The Office Shortcut Bar provides quick access to all the programs on your computer. You can display one or more toolbars and customize buttons on the Office Shortcut Bar. The Office Shortcut Bar itself can be floating, not attached to any part of your screen, or docked, attached to the left, right, or top edge of your screen.

1. Click the **Start** button ![Start], point to **Programs**, point to **Microsoft Office Tools**, click **Microsoft Office Shortcut Bar.**

2. Install the component if necessary.

3. Click **Yes** to start the Office Shortcut Bar automatically whenever Windows is started.

TIP   To customize the Office Shortcut Bar, right-click anywhere on the Office Shortcut Bar (except the title bar), click Customize, click the Buttons tab, click to select or clear the buttons you want to show or hide on the toolbar, and then click the OK button.

Close the Office Shortcut Bar

1. Click the **Office** icon on the title bar.

2. Click **Exit**.

3. If prompted, click the **Yes** or **No** buttons to instruct Windows to display the Office Shortcut Bar the next time you open Windows.

Closing a File

To conserve your computer's resources, close the files and programs that you are not currently working in. You can close open documents one at a time, or you can use one command to close all open files without closing the program. Either way, if you try to close a document without saving your final changes, a dialog box appears, prompting you to do so.

> **TIP**   When two or more documents are open in a program, the document window contains one Close button. The Close button closes the document without exiting the program. You might need to click a Word document button on the taskbar to make it active before you click the Close button.

Close One File

1. Click the **Close** button ⊠ on the title bar in the upper-right corner.

2. If necessary, click the **Yes** button to save your changes.

Quitting an Office Program

When you decide to stop working for the day, before you shut down your computer, you must quit any running programs. All open documents close when you quit. If you haven't saved your final changes, a dialog box appears, prompting you to do so.

TIP Access automatically compresses a database when you close the file. Choose Tools ➢ Options ➢ General tab, click the Compact On Close check box to select, and then click the OK button.

Quit an Office Program

1. Click the **Close** button ⊠, or choose **File** ➢ **Exit**.

2. If necessary, click the **Yes** button to save any changes you made to your open documents before the program quits.

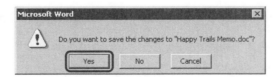

2 Using Shared Office XP Tools

The Microsoft Office XP programs are designed to work together so that you can focus on what you need to do, rather than how to do it. In fact, the Office programs share tools and features for your most common tasks so that you can work uninterrupted and move seamlessly from one program to another. All the Office programs work with text and objects in the same way. As a result, once you learn how to move, find, correct, and comment on text in one program, you can perform these tasks in every program. If you know how to perform a task in Word, you already know how to perform the task in Excel, Access, and PowerPoint. If an Office XP program begins to malfunction, it can detect and fix the problems in its program so that your work can continue uninterrupted.

Editing Text

Select

Highlighting text so that you can modify it.

Before you can edit text, you need to highlight, or **select**, the text you want to modify. Once you select the text, you can delete, replace, move (cut), or copy it within a document or between documents, even if they're in different programs. In either case, the steps are the same. Unlike the Windows Clipboard, which only stores a single piece of information at a time, the **Office Clipboard**, a temporary storage area, collects and stores up to 24 selections, any or all of which you can paste to a new location. You can also move or copy selected text without storing it on the Clipboard by using **drag-and-drop editing**.

Office Clipboard

A temporary area that holds up to 24 pieces of copied information and is available from within any Office program.

Drag-and-drop editing

A method of copying or moving selections without using the Windows Clipboard or the Office Clipboard.

Select and Edit Text

1. Move the mouse pointer to the left or right of the text you want to select.

2. Drag the mouse pointer to highlight the text you want to select.

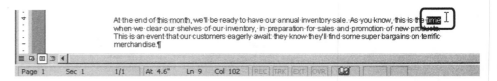

At the end of this month, we'll be ready to have our annual inventory sale. As you know, this is the time when we clear our shelves of our inventory, in preparation for sales and promotion of new products. This is an event that our customers eagerly await: they know they'll find some super bargains on terrific merchandise.¶

Page 1   Sec 1   1/1   At 4.6"   Ln 9   Col 102   REC TRK EXT OVR

3. Type to replace the selected text, or press the Delete or Backspace keys on the keyboard to erase the selected text.

Move or Copy Text

1. Select the text you want to move or copy.

2. Click the **Cut** button or **Copy** button on the Standard toolbar.

3. If you want to collect multiple selections, repeat steps 1 and 2.

To Delete	Press /Hold Down
One character at a time to the left of the insertion point	Backspace
One word at a time to the left of the insertion point	Ctrl+Backspace
One character at a time to the right of the insertion point	Delete
One word at a time to the right of the insertion point	Ctrl+Delete
Selected text	Backspace or Delete

4. Click in the document where you want to insert the text.

5. Click any icon on the Clipboard task pane to paste a selection, or click the **Paste All** button on the Clipboard task pane to paste all the selections at once.

If the Office Clipboard is not visible, choose Edit ➤ Office Clipboard to display it.

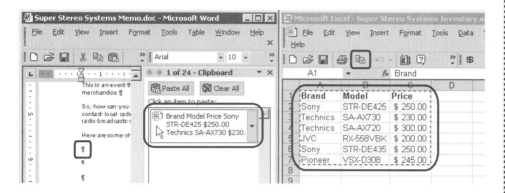

After you paste an item, the Paste Options button appears next to the item. You can click the Paste Options button to display a list of options on the shortcut menu. This button, known as a smart tag, allows you to immediately adjust how information is pasted or how automatic changes occur.

> **TIP** To turn on or off Paste Options, choose Tools ➤ Options, click the Edit tab, click the Show Paste Options Buttons checkbox to select or clear it, and then click the OK button.

6. When you're done, click the **Close** button ☒ on the Clipboard toolbar.

> **TIP** You can remove some or all the selections stored on the Office Clipboard. To clear all the entries, click the Clear All button on the Office Clipboard. To erase an individual entry from the Office Clipboard, click that entry's list arrow, and then click Delete.

Move or Copy Text Using Drag and Drop

1. If you want to drag text between programs or documents, display both windows.

2. Select the text you want to move or copy.

3. Point to the selected text, and then hold down the mouse button.

4. Drag the selected text to the new location, and then release the mouse button (and the Ctrl key, if necessary). If you want to copy the text to a new location, hold down the Ctrl key and the mouse button. A plus sign (+) appears in the pointer box, indicating that you are dragging a copy of the selected text. Release the Ctrl key when you release the mouse button.

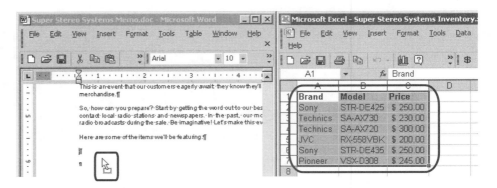

Finding and Replacing Text

The Find and Replace commands make it easy to locate or replace specific text or formulas in a document. For example, if you're working with a long report, you might want to find each figure reference to verify that the proper graphic and caption appears. Or, you might want to replace all the references to cell A3 in your Excel formulas with the data contained in cell G3. The Find and Replace dialog boxes vary slightly from one Office program to the next, but the commands work essentially the same.

> **TIP** You can use wildcards to help you search. When you click the Use Wildcards check box to select it, click the Special button to see the wildcards you can use. To enter a wildcard in the Find What or Replace What box, click Special, and then click a wildcard. For example, enter "ran*" to find "ranch," "ranger," and so on.

Find Text

1. Click the beginning of the document.

2. Choose **Edit ➢ Find**. The Find and Replace dialog box opens.

3. In the **Find what** box, type the text you want to locate.

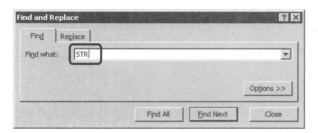

4. If necessary, click the **Options** button, then select other options as appropriate.

5. Click the **Find Next** button until you highlight the text you want to locate. You can click the **Find Next** button repeatedly to locate each instance of the text.

6. When a message box appears when you reach the end of the document, click the **OK** button.

7. When you're done, click the **Close** button or the **Cancel** button.

NOTE   In a Word document, you can search for and replace special characters (such as a bullet) and document elements (such as a tab character). Click the Options button, click the More button in the Find and Replace dialog box, click the Special button, and then click the item you want from the menu.

TIP   In a Word document, you can search for and replace text with specific formatting features, such as font and font size. Click the Options button, click the More button in the Find and Replace dialog box, click the Format button, click the formatting option you want, and then complete the corresponding dialog box.

Replace Text

1. Click the beginning of the document.

2. Choose **Edit** ➤ **Replace**. The Find and Replace dialog box opens.

3. In the **Find what** box, type the text for which you want to search.

4. In the **Replace with** box, type the text you want to substitute.

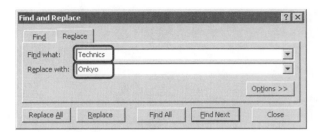

5. Select other options as appropriate. In Word, click the **Options** button, and then click the **More** button to display the additional options.

6. Click the **Find Next** button to begin the search and select the next instance of the search text.

7. Click the **Replace** button to substitute the replacement text, or click the **Replace All** button to substitute text throughout the document. You can click the **Find Next** button to locate the next instance of the search text without replacing it.

8. When a message box appears when you reach the end of the document, click the **OK** button.

9. When you're done, click the **Close** button or the **Cancel** button.

Correcting Text Automatically

Since the dawn of typing with a typewriter, people have consistently mistyped certain words or letter combinations. How many times do you misspell *and* or press and hold down the Shift key one character too long? **AutoCorrect** fixes common misspellings and incorrect capitalization as you type. It also replaces typed characters, such as - - (two hyphens), with typographical symbols, such as — (an em dash). In addition, you can add your personal problem words to the AutoCorrect list. In most cases, AutoCorrect corrects errors after you press the Enter key or the Spacebar on the keyboard.

TIP To reverse an AutoCorrect change, click the Undo button on the Standard toolbar as soon as AutoCorrect makes the change or point to the corrected text to display a blue box, click the AutoCorrect Options button, and then click Undo or any of the other options.

Replace Text as You Type

- ✧ To correct capitalization or spelling errors automatically, continue typing until AutoCorrect makes the required correction.

- ✧ To replace two hyphens with an em dash, turn ordinals into super-scripts (such as *1st* to *1st*), or stack a fraction (such as ½), continue typing until AutoCorrect makes the appropriate change.

- ✧ To create a bulleted or numbered list, type **1.** or * (for a bullet), press the Tab key or Spacebar on the keyboard, type any text, and then press the Enter key. AutoCorrect inserts the next number or bullet. To end the list, press the Backspace key to erase the unnecessary bullets.

TIP You can specify abbreviations and terms that you don't want AutoCorrect to correct. In the AutoCorrect dialog box, click the Exceptions button and add these items to the list of exceptions.

NOTE To prevent automatic corrections, choose Tools ➤ AutoCorrect, click the Replace Text As You Type check box to clear it, and then click the OK button.

Type of Correction	If you Type	AutoCorrect Inserts
Capitalization	cAP LOCK	Cap Lock
Capitalization	TWo INitial CAps	Two initial caps
Capitalization	betty Sue	Betty Sue
Capitalization	microsoft	Microsoft
Capitalization	thursday	Thursday
Common typos	acommodate	accommodate
Common typos	can;t	can't
Common typos	windoes	windows
Superscript ordinals	3rd	3rd
Smart quotes	" "	" "
Em dashes	New York--excluding its big cities--has rural communities	New York—excluding its big cities—has rural communities.
Symbols	(c)	©
Symbols	(r)	®
Hyperlinks	www.microsoft.com	www.microsoft.com

Add or Edit AutoCorrect Entries

1. Choose **Tools** ➢ **AutoCorrect Options**. The AutoCorrect dialog box opens.

2. Click the **AutoCorrect** tab. To edit an AutoCorrect entry, select the entry you want to change.

3. Type the incorrect text that you want AutoCorrect to correct.

4. Type the text or symbols that you want AutoCorrect to use as a replacement.

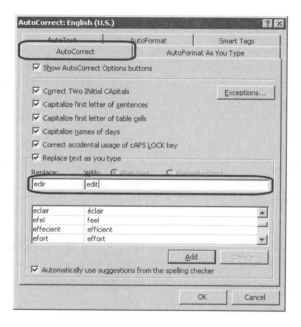

5. Click the **Add** button or the **Replace** button.

6. When you're done, click the **OK** button.

TIP   To delete an AutoCorrect entry, choose Tools ➢ AutoCorrect Options, click the AutoCorrect tab, select the AutoCorrect entry you want to delete, and then click the Delete button.

NOTE   You can use AutoComplete to complete your words. As you enter common text, such as your name, today's date, and some ordinary salutations and closings, Word prompts you with the rest of the text in a ScreenTip. Press the Enter key on the keyboard to accept the AutoComplete entry.

Making Corrections

Everyone changes their mind at some point, especially when creating or revising a document. With Office, you can instantly correct typing errors by pressing a button. You can use the Undo button to reverse more complicated actions, such as typing an entire word, formatting a paragraph, or creating a chart. If you change your mind, you can just as easily click the Redo button to restore the action you reversed.

Undo or Redo an Action

◆ Click the **Undo** button on the Standard toolbar to reverse your most recent action, such as typing a word, formatting a paragraph, or creating a chart.

◆ Click the **Redo** button on the Standard toolbar to restore the last action you reversed.

◆ Click the **Undo** button drop-down arrow on the Standard toolbar, and then select the consecutive actions you want to reverse.

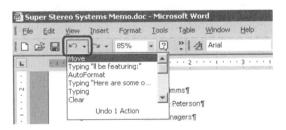

◆ Click the **Redo** button drop-down arrow on the Standard toolbar, and then select the consecutive actions you want to restore.

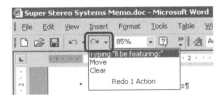

Inserting Comments

Comments

Text you insert that is tagged with your initials. A comment is visible only when you place the mouse pointer over your initials.

When you review an Office document, you can insert comments that will be visible to yourself, the author, or to other reviewers. **Comments** are like electronic adhesive notes tagged with your name. They appear as small yellow boxes in PowerPoint, as red triangles in Excel, or as yellow selected text in Word. You can use comments to solicit feedback or leave yourself a note.

> **TIP** To move to the previous or next comment, click the Previous Comment or Next Comment button on the Reviewing toolbar.

Insert a Comment

1. Click where you want to insert a comment.

2. Choose **Insert ➢ Comment**, or click the **Insert Comment** button or **New Comment** button on the Reviewing toolbar.

> **TIP** To display the Reviewing toolbar, right-click any toolbar, and then click Reviewing.

3. Type your comment in the comment box or pane.

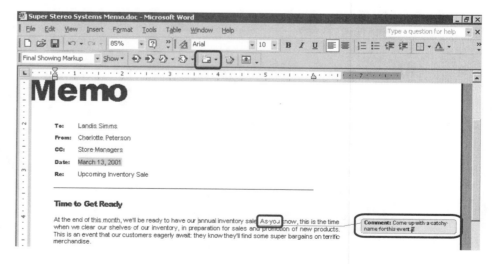

4. When you're done, click anywhere in the document.

Read a Comment

1. Point to a red triangle in Excel; read the comment in the margin in Word; position the mouse pointer over the comment indicator in PowerPoint, or click the **Show/Hide Comment** button 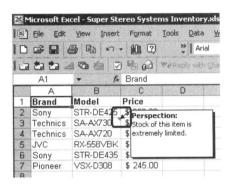 on the Reviewing toolbar.

2. Read the comment.

Delete a Comment

1. Click the selected word, the cell with a red triangle, or the comment box on a slide.

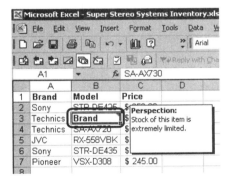

2. Click the **Delete Comment** button 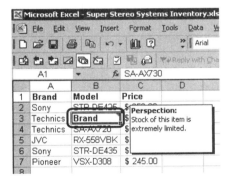 on the Reviewing toolbar, or select the comment, and then press the Delete key or the Backspace key.

Using Track Changes

When multiple people are involved in the editing and preparation of a document for publication, the Track Changes feature will note who made any particular correction and save a record of all such changes for everyone who works on the document later. Each change can be either accepted or rejected by the person who has authority over the final form of the document.

1. In Excel, choose **Tools** ➢ **Track Changes** ➢ **Highlight Changes**. The Highlight Changes dialog box opens. Click the **Track changes while editing** check box to select it, and then click the **OK** button.

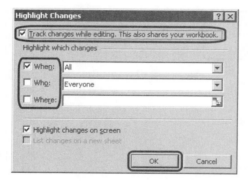

In Word, choose **Tools** ➢ **Track Changes**, or double-click **TRK** on the status bar to turn tracking on and off. The **Track Changes** button on the Reviewing toolbar is active.

2. Make changes to the document.

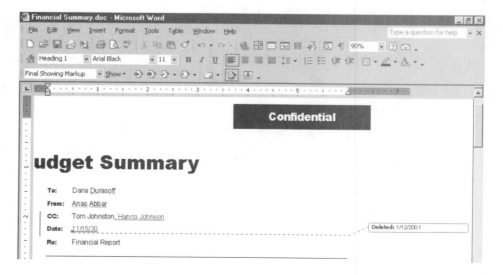

NOTE To see who made each change, on the Reviewing toolbar, click the Reviewing Pane button to open a new window below the main document that displays each change, the person who made it and the time and date that the change was made. Comments (see the next section) also appear in the Reviewing Pane.

Comparing and Merging Documents

You can compare documents to graphically indicate changes between different versions of a document. The changes can be merged into one document or viewed for comparison.

1. Open an edited document (as an example, it can be any newer version of a document where the older version has also been saved and not overwritten by the updated version).

WARNING In Excel, you need to share the workbook before you can merge it with another workbook. Choose Tools ➢ Share Workbook, click the sharing check to select it, and then click OK.

2. Choose **Tools** ➢ **Compare and Merge Documents** (Word) or **Compare and Merge Presentations** (PowerPoint) or **Compare and Merge Workbooks** (Excel). The Compare and Merge dialog box opens.

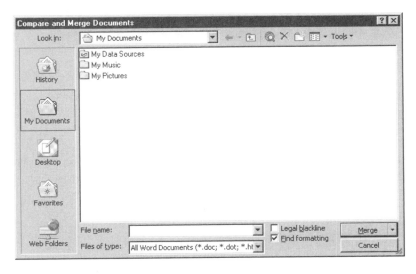

3. Select the document you want to compare and merge.

4. Click the **Merge** button or the **OK** button. In Word, you can also click the **Merge** button down arrow, and then do one of the following:

◇ To display the comparison results in the original document (the unedited version for example), click **Merge**.

◇ To display the comparison results in the newer document that is currently open (the edited version), click **Merge Into Current Document**.

◇ To display the comparison results in a new document, click **Merge Into New Document**.

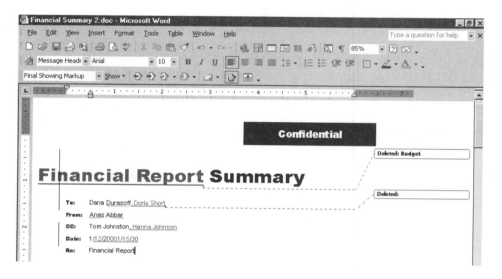

NOTE When you compare or merge documents, the text that differs between the two versions will be highlighted in a different color.

Automating Your Work

Macro
A sequence of commands and entries that can be activated collectively by clicking a toolbar button, clicking a menu command, typing a key combination, or clicking the Run command in the Macros dialog box.

Complicated keyboard sequences can be recorded and saved as a **Macro**. For example, if you routinely create tables for your document of a certain size and width, why not create the table structure once, record it as a Macro, then invoke it the next time by either using a keyboard shortcut that you assign, or by clicking the Run command in the Macros dialog box.

1. Choose **Tools ➢ Marco ➢ Record New Macro**. The Record Macro dialog box opens.

2. In the **Macro Name** box, assign a name to the Macro.

3. In the **Store Macro In** box, click the template (or document) in which you wish to save the macro.

4. In the **Description** box, enter a description of the macro.

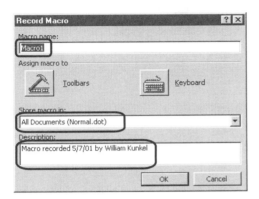

> **TIP**   To assign macros to shortcut keys, click the Keyboard button in the Record Macro dialog box.

5. Unless you intend to assign the macro to a menu, toolbar, or shortcut keys (which is covered below), click the **OK** button. You now begin recording the macro.

6. Perform the steps in sequence that are required to complete the action, and then click the **Stop Recording** button ■ on the Macro toolbar.

> **TIP**   Accuracy is more important than speed when recording macros.

Run a Macro

If you created a macro but did not assign it to a shortcut key, you can still invoke the macro via the Macros dialog box.

1. Click to position the insertion point in the document where you want the output of the macro to appear.

2. Choose **Tools** ➢ **Macro** ➢ **Macros**. The Macros dialog box opens.

3. Click the macro you want to run.

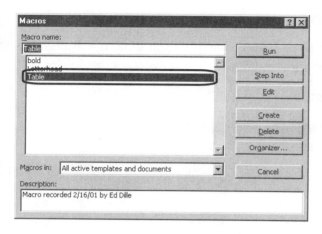

4. Click the **Run** button. The macro is now inserted into the document.

Delete a Macro

When a Macro outlives its usefulness, it is time to delete it and make room for new Macros on the list.

1. Choose **Tools** ➢ **Macro** ➢ **Macros**. The Macros dialog box opens.

2. Select the macro you want to remove.

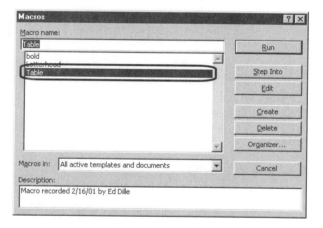

3. Click the **Delete** button. An alert box appears, confirming that you wish to delete the macro.

4. Click the **Yes** button. The alert box closes and the macro is deleted.

5. Click the **Close** button.

Controlling Programs with Your Voice

The Office Language toolbar allows you to dictate text directly into your document and also to control buttons, menus and toolbar functions by using the Voice Command option. When you first install an Office XP program, the Language toolbar will appear at the top of your screen. To minimize the toolbar, click the minus sign at the right end of the toolbar. The Language toolbar will dock in the System taskbar at the bottom right of the screen, near the system clock. If you are using English as the default language, the toolbar will be denoted by the letters EN (other languages have appropriate abbreviations as well). To restore the toolbar to the top of the screen, click the icon and select Show the Language toolbar from the pop-up menu.

Before you can use the Language toolbar for either dictation or voice commands, you must first train your computer to your voice using the Speech Recognition Wizard.

1. Click the **Microphone** button on the Language toolbar. The Welcome to Office Speech Recognition dialog box opens.

2. Click the **Next** button, read the instructions, ensure you are in a quiet environment, and then click the **Next** button again.

3. Read the sentence provided to automatically set the proper volume of the microphone, and then click the **Next** button.

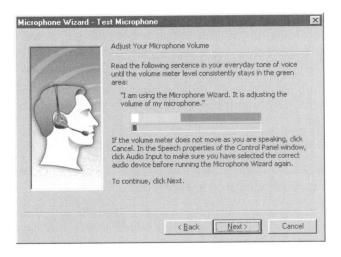

4. Read the text with hard consonants, to help determine whether or not the microphone is positioned too closely to your mouth. Repeat the process, adjusting your microphone as needed until you have a clear, distinct audio playback, and then click the **Next** button.

5. You are reminded to ensure that your environment is suitable for recording again, read the instructions and then click the **Next** button.

6. You are given a series of dialog boxes to read. As you read each paragraph, the words onscreen are highlighted as the computer recognizes them. As each dialog box is completed, the program will automatically move to the next one and the progress meter will update accordingly.

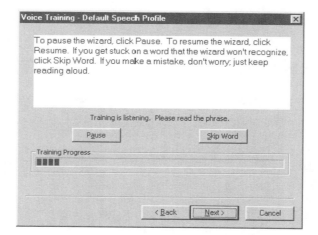

> **TIP** It is easier for an Office XP program to recognize complete sentences in context than individual words, so don't pause between each word and wait for the program to display it onscreen.

7. At the end of the training session, your voice profile will be updated and saved automatically.

> **NOTE** You are not limited to this one training session. The more that you train, the more accurately an Office XP program will recognize your voice.

Execute Voice Commands

The two modes, Dictation and Voice Command, have been designed to be mutually exclusive of one another. You do not want the word *File* typed, for example, when you are actually trying to open the File menu or, conversely, have the menu open instead of the word *File* being typed when you are in the middle of a sentence. As such, you must manually click on either mode on the Language toolbar to switch between them.

The Voice Command mode allows you to talk your way through any sequence of menus or toolbar commands, simply by reading the appropriate text from them as you would when clicking on them, but letting your words do the work. For example, if you wanted to print the current page of the document you were working on, you would simply say File, Print, Current Page, OK (without saying the commas between the words as written here). You need not worry about remembering every command sequence because as you say each word in the sequence, the corresponding menu or submenu appears onscreen for your reference.

1. Click the **Microphone** button on the Language toolbar. The toolbar expands so that the Voice Command button becomes available on the toolbar.

2. Click the **Voice Command** button to shift into that mode.

3. Type the body text of your document normally. When you are ready to issue a command, simply speak the sequence just as you would click through it were you using the menus or toolbars normally (ie: with the mouse, or via keyboard shortcuts, whichever your preference).

Dictate Text

Dictating the text of a letter or other document using Office XP's speech recognition functions may be easier for some users than typing, but don't think that it is an entirely hands free operation. For example, you must manually click on the Voice Command button when you want to format anything that has been input, and then click again on Dictation to resume inputting text. Additionally, the Dictation function is not going to be 100% accurate, so you will need to clean up mistakes (such as inputting the word *Noir* when you say or) either when they occur, or subsequently. Finally, although you can say punctuation marks like comma and period to have them accurately reflected in the document, all periods are followed by double spaces (which may not be consistent with the document formatting you wish between sentences) and issues of capitalization remain as well. Nevertheless, it is fun and freeing to be able to get the first draft of any document on paper simply by speaking it.

1. Click the Microphone button on the Language toolbar. The toolbar expands so that the Dictation button becomes available on the toolbar.

2. Click to position the insertion point inside the document where you want the dictated text to appear and begin speaking normally into your microphone. As you speak, the words will appear on the page.

3. When you have finished dictating your text, click the second Microphone button again to make the speech recognition functions inactive.

WARNING If you fail to turn off the Language toolbar functions while continuing to work in an Office XP program, distractions in the room like phone calls, even the sound of your keyboard clicking as you type, can introduce errors into your document.

Recognizing Handwriting

Although entering information into an Office XP document through the keyboard is fast and efficient, you may find that you need to enter information in handwritten form. Office provides handwriting recognition to help you convert handwriting into text. Before you can insert hand written text into a document, you need to have a third party electronic stylus, handwriting tablet, or mouse attached to your computer. Although you can use the mouse, for best results, you should use a handwriting input device.

When you insert handwritten text into a document that already contains typed text, the handwritten text is converted to typed text, and then inserted in line with the existing text at the point of the cursor. The program recognizes the handwriting when there is enough text for it to do so, when you reach the end of the line, or if you pause for about two seconds. In addition, the converted text will take on the same typeface attributes as the existing text. When you insert text into a blank document, the text is placed at the beginning of the document.

> **NOTE** If the handwriting recognition feature is installed correctly, you'll find the Language toolbar in the upper-right corner of your Office XP program window.

Insert Hand Written Text in a Document

When you click the Handwriting button on the Language toolbar and then click the Write Anywhere option, a dialog box similar to the Writing Pad dialog box opens, except there is no writing area within that dialog box. You use this feature just as you would the Writing Pad feature, except that you do your "writing" right on the Word document that is behind the dialog box.

1. Open the document you want to insert hand written text.

2. Click the **Handwriting** button on the Language toolbar, and then click **Write Anywhere**.

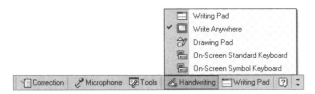

The Write Anywhere bar opens on your screen, and the Text button is selected by default.

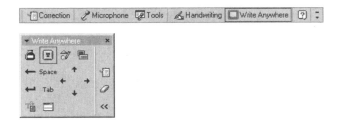

3. Move the mouse over a blank area of your document, and then write your text. The handwritten words are converted to text on your screen.

Insert Hand Written Text on a Writing Pad

When you click the Handwriting button on the Language toolbar and then click the Writing Pad option, a Writing Pad dialog box opens on your screen. Within that dialog box is another toolbar. It has the same options that are available through the Handwriting button on the Language toolbar. In addition, it has the following buttons: Ink, Text, Backspace, Space, directional cursors, Enter, Tab, Recognize Now, and Write Anywhere. You use these buttons to control the input into Word.

To use the basic features of the Writing Pad, click the Text button, and then move your mouse over the writing area within the dialog box. At that point, the mouse cursor turns into a pen. You then write with that "pen" just as you would write with a physical pen. After recognition, the characters that you write appear in the Word document that is open behind the dialog box. You use other buttons with the dialog box to manipulate the position of the cursor in the Word document itself.

1. Open the document you want to insert hand written text.

2. Click the **Handwriting** button on the Language toolbar, and then click **Writing Pad**. The Writing Pad dialog box opens on your screen.

3. Move the mouse cursor over the writing area of the Writing Pad dialog box, write your text. The new text is inserted into the document.

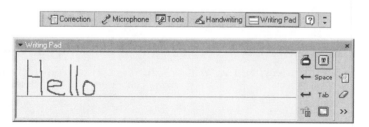

Using Multiple Languages

International Microsoft Office XP users can change the language that appears on their screen by changing the default languages settings. Users around the world can enter, display, and edit text in all supported languages, including European languages, Japanese, Chinese, Korean, Hebrew, Arabic, to name a few. You'll probably be able to use Office programs in your native language. If the text in your document is written in more than one language, you can automatically detect languages or designate the language of selected text so the spelling checker uses the right dictionary.

NOTE To use dictionaries for other languages, you must have the dictionaries for the languages installed on your computer for Office programs to detect and apply its spelling and proofing tools.

Add a Language to Office XP Programs

1. Click the **Start** button ▓ Start on the taskbar, point to **Programs**, point to **Microsoft Office Tools**, and then click **Microsoft Office XP Language Settings**. The Microsoft Office Language Settings dialog box opens.

2. Select the language you want to use.

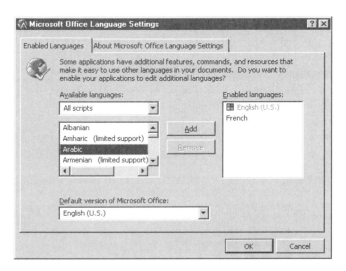

3. Click the **Add** button.

4. Click the **OK** button, and then click the **Yes** button to quit and restart Office.

> **TIP** After you enable editing for another language, you might need to install the correct keyboard so you can enter characters for that language.

Mark Text as a Language

1. Start Word or PowerPoint.

2. Select the text you want to mark.

3. In Word, choose **Tools** ➢ **Language** ➢ **Set Language**. In PowerPoint, choose **Tools** ➢ **Language**. The Language dialog box opens.

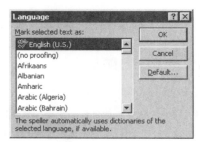

4. Click the language you want to assign to the selected text.

5. Click the **OK** button.

> **TIP** To detect languages in Word, choose Tools ➢ Language ➢ Set Language, click the Detect Language Automatically check box to select it, and then click the OK button.

> **TIP** Office XP supports an AutoCorrect list for each language to make corrections as you type in multiple languages. For example, the English AutoCorrect list capitalizes all cases of the single letter "I," but in Swedish this is a preposition.

Repairing Office Programs

Despite your best efforts or computer hardware, there will be times when an Office program stops working for no apparent reason. All the Office programs are self-repairing, which means that Office checks if essential files are missing or corrupt as a program opens and fixes the files as needed. You may never even realize there was a problem. Other times, Office starts fine but might have another problem, such as a corrupted font file or a missing template. These kinds of problems used to take hours to identify and fix. Now Office does the work for you with the **Detect And Repair** feature, which locates, diagnoses, and fixes any errors in the program itself. If the Office program still doesn't work properly, you can use the Microsoft Office Application Recovery program to restart or stop an Office program. If you need to add or remove features, restore the Office installation, or remove Office entirely, you can use Office Setup's maintenance feature.

Detect and Repair
A feature that allows Office to fix missing or corrupted program files.

Detect and Repair Problems

1. Choose **Help** ➢ **Detect And Repair**. The Detect And Repair dialog box opens.

2. Click the **Start** button. Insert the Office CD in your CD-ROM drive.

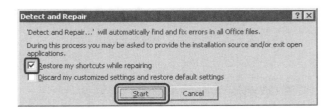

3. If necessary, click **Repair Office**, and then click the **Reinstall Office** or **Repair Errors In Your Office Installation** option button.

4. Click the **Finish** button.

Recover an Office Program

1. Click the **Start** button ![Start] on the taskbar, point to **Programs**, point to **Microsoft Office Tools**, and then click **Microsoft Office Application Recovery**. The Microsoft Office Application Recovery dialog box opens.

2. Select the application you want to recover.

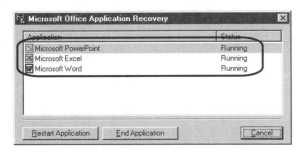

3. Click the **Restart Application** button or the **End Application** button.

Perform Maintenance on Office Programs

1. In Windows Explorer, double-click the Setup icon on the Office CD.

2. Click one of the following maintenance buttons.

- ◆ Repair Office to repair or reinstall Office.

- ◆ Add Or Remove Features to determine which and when features are installed or removed.

- ◆ Remove Office to uninstall Office.

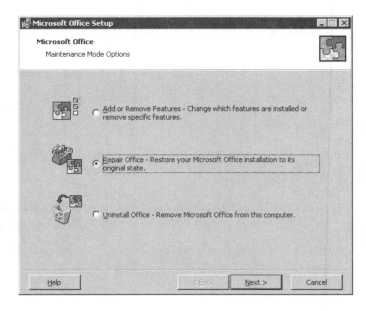

3. Follow the wizard instructions to complete the maintenance.

3 Adding OfficeArt to Office XP Documents

Microsoft Office XP comes with common drawing and graphics tools that you can use with any of the Office programs. You can draw and modify shapes and lines, and insert several different types of graphics, such as pictures, clip art, stylized text, an organization chart, a diagram, and a Graph chart. Once you insert a graphic, you can modify it to create the look you want. All the Office programs work with drawing and graphics in a similar way, so once you learn how to draw a shape or insert a graphic in one program, you know how to perform the same task in another program.

Selecting, Moving, and Resizing Objects

Object

A picture or graphic image you can insert in a file.

Clip art

Graphic art that comes with Office or that you create and insert in a file.

Handles

Small circles or squares that surround an object when it is selected.

As you learn to use each Office program, you'll want to enhance your documents beyond just text and formulas with graphics and other images. To do so, you can insert an object. An **object** is a picture or graphic image you create with a drawing program or insert from an existing file of another program. For example, you can insert a company logo that you have drawn yourself, or you can insert **clip art**—copyright-free pictures that come with Office. To work with an object, you need to select it first. Then you can resize or move it with its selection **handles**, the little squares that appear on the edges of the selected object.

Select and Deselect an Object

◆ Click an object to display its handles.

◆ To select more than one object at a time, hold down the Shift key on the keyboard as you click each object. You can also drag a selection rectangle around the objects, and then release the mouse button.

◆ Click elsewhere within the document window to deselect a selected object.

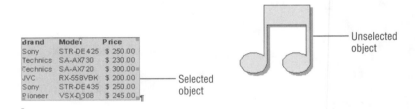

Selected object

Unselected object

Move an Object

1. Click an object to select it.

2. Drag the object to a new location indicated by the dotted outline of the object.

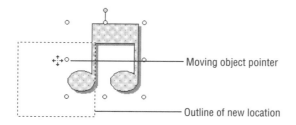

Moving object pointer

Outline of new location

3. Release the mouse button to drop the object in the new location.

Resize an Object

1. Click the object you want to resize.

2. Resize the object by dragging a sizing handle.

◇ Vertically or horizontally: drag a top, bottom, left, or right sizing handle.

◇ Proportionally in both the vertical and horizontal directions: drag a corner sizing handle.

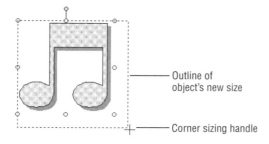

Outline of object's new size

Corner sizing handle

Drawing and Enhancing Objects

Drawn objects, such as curved lines or lightning bolts, can enliven your document, help make your point, or just reflect your individuality. You can use the options on the Drawing toolbar to draw numerous objects without leaving your current program. After you add an object to your document, you can enhance it with a host of colors and special effects. Select the object you want to enhance, and then select the effect you prefer. To make your documents easy to read, take care not to add too many lines, shapes, or other objects to the same slide, spreadsheet, or page.

> **TIP** You can draw perfect squares, circles, or straight lines. Click the Rectangle button, Oval button, or Line button on the Drawing toolbar, and then hold down the Shift key on the keyboard while you draw.

Draw Lines and Shapes

1. Display the Drawing toolbar, if necessary. Choose **View** ➢ **Toolbars** ➢ **Drawing** to display the Drawing toolbar.

2. Click the **AutoShapes** button on the Drawing toolbar, point to **Lines** or **Basic Shapes** or any other option, and then click the line or shape you want.

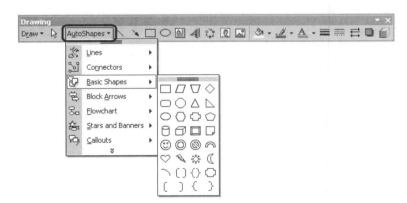

TIP You can also insert AutoShapes using the Insert menu. Choose Insert ➤ Picture ➤ AutoShapes.

3. Click in the document window, drag the mouse pointer until the line or shape is the size you want, and then release the mouse button. When you draw some curvy lines, you need to click the mouse button once for every curve you want, and then double-click to end the line.

4. If you make a mistake, press the Delete key while the line or shape is still selected, and try again.

TIP To display the Drawing toolbar, right-click any toolbar, and then click Drawing on the shortcut menu. If a check mark appears next to the toolbar name, the toolbar is already displayed.

NOTE Click the Draw button on the Drawing toolbar to use commands to group, reorder, align or distribute, and rotate or flip objects.

Add Color, Shadows, Line Styles, and 3-D Effects

1. Display the Drawing toolbar, if necessary. Choose **View** ➤ **Toolbars** ➤ **Drawing** to display the Drawing toolbar.

2. Select the object in which you want to add an effect, and then select an option.

❖ To fill a shape with color, click the **Fill Color** button drop-down arrow 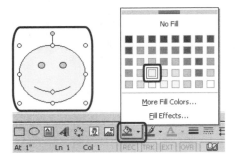 on the Drawing toolbar, and then select the color you want.

❖ To change the line color, click the **Line Color** button drop-down arrow on the Drawing toolbar, and then select the color you want.

❖ To change the line style, click the **Line Style** button or the **Dash Style** button on the Drawing toolbar, and then select the style you want.

❖ To change the line arrow style, click the **Arrow Style** button on the Drawing toolbar, and then select the style you want.

❖ To add a shadow, click the **Shadow** button on the Drawing toolbar, and then select the shadow you want.

❖ To change an object to 3-D, click the **3-D** button on the Drawing toolbar, and then select the 3-D effect you want.

Adding WordArt

You can add visual pizzazz to your documents by adding a WordArt object to your document. **WordArt** is a Microsoft Office program that allows you to add visual enhancements to your text that go beyond changing a font or font size. You can select a WordArt style that stretches your text horizontally, vertically, or diagonally. You can also change the character spacing and reshape the text. Like many enhancements you can add to a document, WordArt is an object that you can move, resize, and even rotate. WordArt is a great way to enhance a newsletter or resume, jazz up an invitation or flyer, or produce a creative report cover or eye-catching envelope.

WordArt
Program that lets you enhance text by stretching, skewing, and applying special effects to it.

Create WordArt

1. Display the Drawing toolbar, if necessary. Choose **View** ➢ **Toolbars** ➢ **Drawing** to display the Drawing toolbar.

2. Click the **Insert WordArt** button on the Drawing toolbar. The WordArt Gallery dialog box opens.

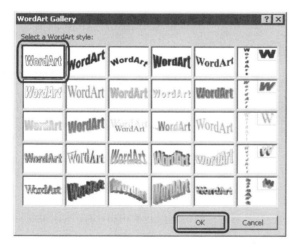

3. Click the style of text you want to insert from the WordArt Gallery menu and then click the **OK** button. The Edit WordArt Text dialog box opens.

4. Type the text you want in the Edit WordArt Text dialog box.

5. Click the **Font** drop-down arrow, and then select the font you want.

6. Click the **Size** drop-down arrow 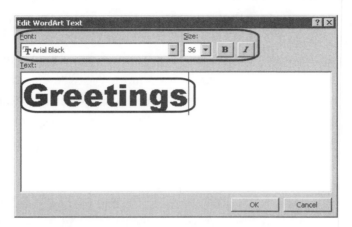, and then select the font size you want, measured in points.

7. If you want, click the **Bold** button **B**, the **Italic** button *I*, or both.

8. Click the **OK** button.

TIP You can fill a WordArt object with a pattern or special effect. Click the Fill Color drop-down arrow on the Drawing toolbar, click Fill Effects, and then click the fill effect you want.

NOTE You can change the WordArt fill color to match the background. Click the WordArt object, click the Format WordArt button, click the Color and Lines tab, click the Fill Color drop-down arrow, click Background, and then click the OK button.

---

9. With the WordArt object selected, drag any handle to reshape the object until the text is the size you want.

10. Use the WordArt toolbar buttons to format or edit the WordArt. Refer to the table below for additional information about WordArt toolbar buttons.

Icon	Button Name	Purpose
	Insert WordArt	Create new WordArt
Edit Text...	Edit Text	Edit the existing text in a WordArt object
	WordArt Gallery	Choose a new style for existing WordArt
	Format WordArt	Change the attributes of existing WordArt
Abc	WordArt Shape	Modify the shape of an existing WordArt object
	Text wrapping	Change the way text appears around existing WorkArt object
Aa	WordArt Same Letter Heights	Make uppercase and lowercase letters the same height
ab	WordArt Vertical Text	Change horizontal letters into a vertical formation
	WordArt Alignment	Modify the alignment of an existing object
AV	WordArt Character Spacing	Change the spacing between characters

11. Drag the WordArt object to the location you want.

12. Click outside the WordArt text to deselect the object and close the WordArt toolbar.

Adding Media Clips

You can insert clips from Microsoft's Clip Organizer or from your own folders. Images or pictures, sounds, and motion clips enhance any Office document. You can also insert files you've scanned or created in a drawing program from within any Office program or from the Microsoft Office Document Scanning tool.

TIP You can connect to the Web for access to additional clip art. Click the Clips Online button to open your Web browser and connect to a clip art Web site to download files.

NOTE Find the exact clip you want by typing a keyword in the Search For Clips box, and then pressing the Enter key. All of the related clips from each category that match the keyword appear.

Insert Clip Art

1. Click where you want to insert clip art.

2. Choose **Insert ➢ Picture ➢ Clip Art**. The Insert Clip Art task pane appears on the right-side of the window.

3. In the **Search text** box, type the word or phrase that describes the clip art you want to find.

4. Click the **Search** button in the Insert Clip Art task pane. Clip art appear in the task pane.

5. In the **Results** box, click the clip art image you want to insert.

6. In the Clip Art task pane, click the **Close** button ✕.

Insert a Picture

1. Click where you want to insert a picture.

2. Choose **Insert** ➣ **Picture** ➣ **From File**. The Insert Picture dialog box opens.

3. Click the **Look In** drop-down arrow ▾, and then select the location where your picture is stored.

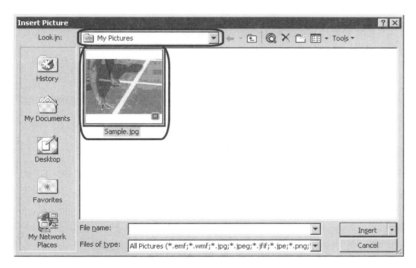

4. Double-click the image you want to use, or click the **Insert** button.

Insert a Picture from a Scanner or Camera

1. Choose **Insert** ➣ **Picture** ➣ **From Scanner Or Camera**. The Insert Picture from Scanner or Camera dialog box opens.

2. Click the **Device** drop-down arrow ▾, and select the device connected to your computer.

3. Select the resolution (the visual quality of the image).

4. Click the **Insert** button or the **Custom Insert** button.

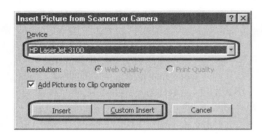

Scan a Picture

1. Click the **Start** button 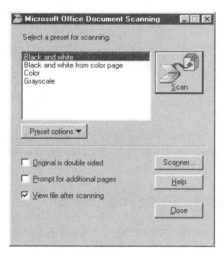 on the taskbar, point to **Programs**, point to **Microsoft Office Tools**, and then click **Microsoft Office Document Scanning**. The Microsoft Office Document Scanning dialog box opens.

2. Select a preset scanner option, or click the **Preset options** button, and then click **Create New Preset** to create one of your own.

3. Click the **Scanner** button, select a scanner, and then click the **OK** button.

4. Place the page you want to scan on the scanner, and then click the **Scan** button to scan the page.

5. Click the **Close** button.

Modifying Media Clips

After you insert clip art or a picture, you can **crop**, or cut out, a section of the image. You can also change the clip's default colors to grayscale, black and white, or **washout** (text or graphics that appear over or behind existing text).

NOTE You can change an image's brightness and contrast. Select the image, and then select the desired effect by clicking the More Brightness or Less Brightness button on the Picture toolbar, or by clicking the More Contrast or Less Contrast button on the Picture toolbar.

TIP Set an image color to transparent. Select the image, and then click the Set Transparent Color button on the Picture toolbar.

Crop a Picture

1. Click the picture or clip art image.

2. Click the **Crop** button on the Picture toolbar.

3. Drag the sizing handles until the borders surround the area you want to crop.

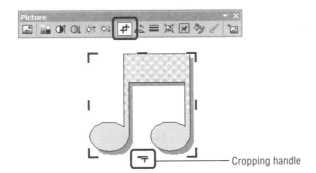

Cropping handle

Choose a Color Type

1. Select the object whose color type you want to change.

2. Click the **Color** button on the Picture toolbar.

3. Click one of the Color options.

- ◇ Automatic (default coloring)
- ◇ Grayscale (whites, blacks, and grays)
- ◇ Black & White (white and black)
- ◇ Washout (whites and very light colors)

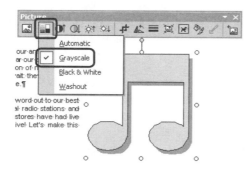

Creating an Organization Chart

Organization chart
Series of boxes that depicts an organization's structure.

Chart boxes
Individual boxes into which individual's within an organization are entered.

An **organization chart** shows the personnel structure in a company or organization. You can create an organization chart, also known as an *org chart*, in any Office document with Microsoft Organization Chart. When you insert an org chart, **chart boxes** appear into which you enter the names and titles of company personnel. Each box is identified by its position in the chart. For example, Managers are at the top, Subordinates are below, Lateral Coworkers are to the sides, and so on.

> **TIP** To edit an org chart, click the organization chart, and then click the chart title or chart box you want to edit.

Create a New Org Chart

1. Choose **Insert ➤ Picture ➤ Organization Chart**. The organization chart appears in the document.

2. Click a chart box, and then type a name.

3. Click the chart box to which you want to attach the new chart box, click the **Insert Shape** button drop-down arrow on the Organization Chart toolbar, and then click a shape option.

4. Select the placeholder text, and then type a name or other text.

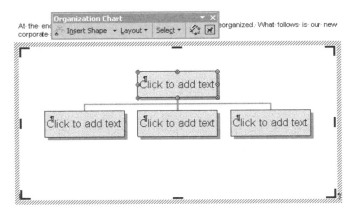

5. Click anywhere outside of the org chart to return to the document.

Open and Format an Org Chart

1. Click the org chart in the document.

2. Click the items you want to format.

3. Click the **Layout** button on the Organization Chart toolbar, and then click a layout option.

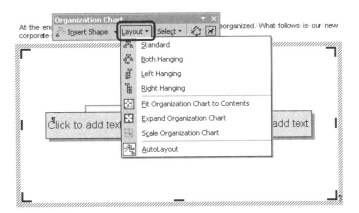

Creating a Diagram

Diagram
A collection of shapes that illustrates conceptual material.

A **diagram** illustrates conceptual material. Office offers a variety of built-in diagrams from which to choose, including pyramid, cycle, radial, and Venn diagrams as well as organization charts. Using built-in diagrams makes it easy to create and modify charts without having to create them from scratch.

> **TIP**   You can also click the Insert Diagram or Organization Chart button on the Drawing toolbar to insert a diagram.

Create a New Diagram

1. Choose **Insert** ➤ **Diagram**. The Diagram Gallery dialog box opens.

2. Select a diagram.

3. Click the **OK** button. The diagram appears in the document.

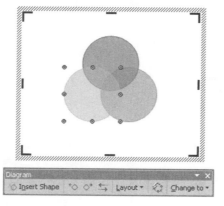

4. Select a diagram elements, and use the Diagram toolbar to format the diagram with preset styles, add color and patterns, change line styles, add elements, and move them forward or backward.

5. Click anywhere outside of the diagram to return to the document.

| TIP | To edit a diagram, click the diagram, and then click the element you want to edit. |

Creating a Graph Chart

A chart often makes numerical data more visual and easier to grasp. With Microsoft Graph, you can create a chart in Office XP programs. Just enter your numbers and labels in the **datasheet**, a spreadsheet-like grid of rows and columns that holds your data in cells (intersections of rows and columns), and watch Graph create the **chart**, a graphical representation of the data. The chart has an X-axis (horizontal axis) and a Y-axis (vertical axis), which serve as refer-ence lines for the plotted data. (In a 3-D chart, the vertical axis is the Z-axis.) Each **data series**, all the data from a row or column, has a unique color or pattern on the chart. The chart is made up of different elements that help display the data from the datasheet. You can format **chart objects**, individual elements that make up the chart, such as an axis, legend, or data series, to suit your needs.

Datasheet
A place to store chart data that is composed of individual cells in rows and columns.

Chart
A graphical representation of the data in the datasheet.

Data series
A group of related data points in a datasheet.

Chart objects
Individual items within a chart that you can select and modify.

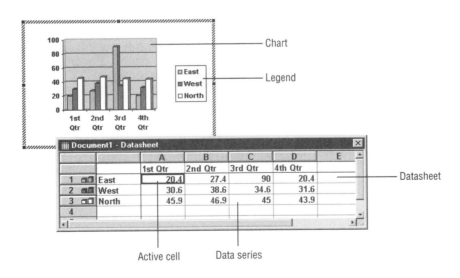

Chart

Legend

Datasheet

Active cell   Data series

Active cell

A selected cell in the data-sheet that has a heavy border around it.

To perform most tasks on the datasheet, you must first select a specific cell or range of cells. A selected cell, called the **active cell**, has a heavy border around it. When more than one cell is selected, the active cell is highlighted with a heavy border, and all other selected cells are highlighted in black. To enter data into the datasheet, you can perform one or more of the following: type your own data into the datasheet, import information directly from another program, such as Microsoft Excel, or copy and paste a specified range of data or a complete worksheet into Graph. Once the data is entered into the datasheet, you can easily modify and format the associated chart. Graph comes with a gallery that lets you change the chart type and then format the chart to get the results that you want. There are 14 chart categories, containing both two-dimensional and three-dimensional charts.

Create a New Graph Chart

1. Start Microsoft Graph. The Graph chart appears in the document.

    ❖ Choose **Insert ➤ Object**, and then click **Microsoft Graph**.

    ❖ In Word, choose **Insert ➤ Picture ➤ Chart**.

    ❖ In PowerPoint, choose **Insert ➤ Chart**.

2. Click the datasheet's upper-left button to select all the cells, and then press the Delete key to erase the sample data.

3. Enter new data in each cell, or click the **Import File** button 🖱 on the Standard toolbar to insert data from another source, such as Excel.

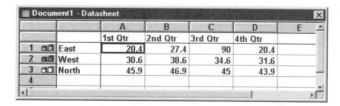

4. Edit and format the data in the datasheet as you like.

5. Click the **Close** button ☒ on the datasheet to close it.

6. Click anywhere outside of the chart to return to the document.

Format a Chart Object

1. Click the chart in the document you want to format.

2. Double-click the chart object you want to format, such as an axis, legend, or data series.

3. Click the tab (Patterns, Scale, Font, Number, or Alignment) corresponding to the options you want to change.

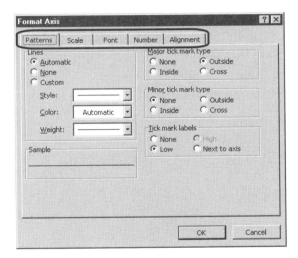

4. Select the options you want to apply.

5. Click the **OK** button.

Customize a Chart

1. Click the chart in the document you want to customize.

2. Choose **Chart** ➤ **Chart Options**. The Chart Options dialog box opens.

3. Click the tab (Titles, Axes, Gridlines, Legend, Data Labels, or Data Table) corresponding to the chart object you want to customize.

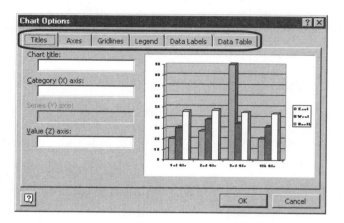

TIP To change the chart type, select the chart, click the Chart Type drop-down arrow, and then click a chart type. You can also choose Chart ➤ Chart Type, click the Standard or Custom tab, select a 2-D or 3-D chart type, and then select a chart sub-type if necessary.

4. Make your changes.

5. Click the **OK** button.

4 Creating a Document with Word

Whether you're typing a carefully worded letter, creating a professional resume, or producing a can't-miss promotional newsletter for your business or neighborhood group, Microsoft Word 2002 is the program for you. Word contains all the tools and features you need to produce snazzy documents that say exactly what you mean and that have the look to match.

Microsoft Word is designed especially for working with text, so it's a snap to create and edit letters, reports, mailing lists, tables, or any other word-based communication. What makes Word perfect for your documents is its editing capabilities combined with its variety of views. For example, you can jot down your ideas in Outline view. Then switch to Normal view to expand your thoughts into complete sentences and revise them without retyping the entire page. Tools such as the Spelling and Grammar Checker and Thesaurus help you present your thoughts accurately, clearly, and effectively. Finally, in Print Layout view you can quickly add formatting elements such as bold type and special fonts to make your documents look professional.

Viewing the Word Window

Word processing program

A type of software you can use to create a letter, memo, or report.

Document

The file you create that contains text and graphics.

Before you can begin using Word, a **word processing program**, you need to start the program. The easiest way is to use the Start button on the taskbar. When Word opens, the program window displays a blank document—ready for you to begin working. The files you create and save in Word are called **documents**.

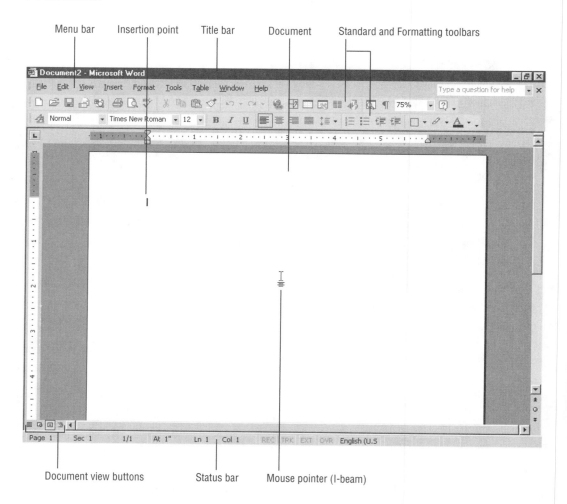

Menu bar   Insertion point   Title bar   Document   Standard and Formatting toolbars

Document view buttons   Status bar   Mouse pointer (I-beam)

Creating a New Document

When you open a new Word document, it's blank, ready for you to enter text. You can open and work on as many new documents as you'd like. There are several ways of creating new documents: using the New command on the File menu, the New Blank Document button on the Formatting toolbar, and using the New Document task pane. **Task panes** are groupings of related commands that Word displays to the right of the main document window.

The insertion point (blinking bar) appears in the document where text will appear when you type. You can move the insertion point anywhere within the document so that you can insert new text and edit (or insert, revise, or delete) existing text. As you type, text moves, or wraps, to a new line when the previous one is full. You can enter or edit text in any view.

Create a New Document

1. Choose **File** ➢ **New**. The New Document task pane opens.

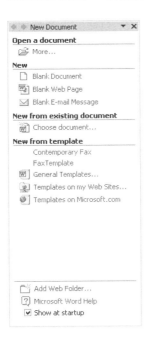

Task pane
An expanded display area to the right of the main document window that displays groups of related commands and wizards.

TIP   To open the New Document task pane, choose View ➢ Task Pane, click the drop-down arrow on the title bar of the task pane, and then click New Document.

---

2. In the task pane, click **Blank Document**. Word opens a blank document.

3. Click where you want to insert text, if necessary.

4. Begin typing, and then press the Enter key when you want to begin a new paragraph or insert a blank line.

 TIP To create a new document quickly, click the New Blank Document button on the Standard toolbar.

Changing Document Views

Word displays each new document in Normal view by default, the equivalent of a single, long piece of "paper," divided into pages by perforation marks. This view is fine for composition, but inadequate for editing or previewing your work prior to printing or other publication.

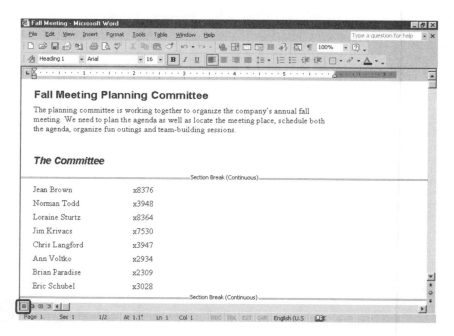

Web Layout view displays the document as it will appear on the Web. You can save documents as HTML code to make Web content creation easy.

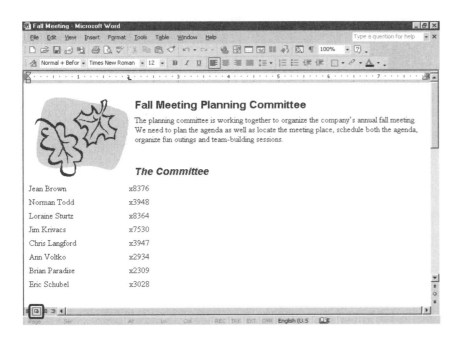

Print Layout view places a gray gap between each page to clearly delineate where each actual page break occurs. This view is best for previewing your work before printing, and it works well with the Zoom feature to display multiple pages of the same document simultaneously onscreen. To move between pages in this view, click the page to move the insertion point. Zoom in again to actually perform your edits.

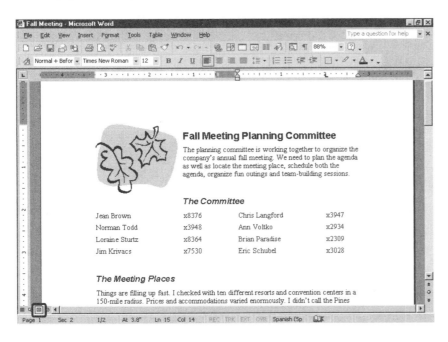

Outline view is used to make it easier to manage editing for long documents. When you shift to Outline view, Word automatically tags each of the headings of your document and displays them in outline form.

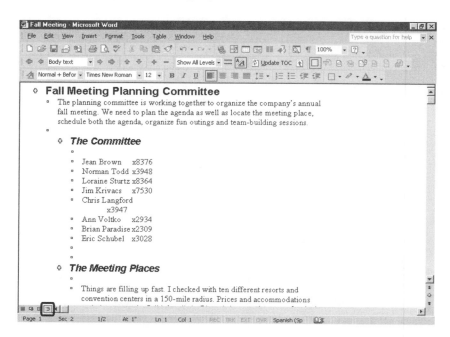

Each heading in Outline view has a clickable plus sign next to it. Double-click the plus sign to collapse all of the text under a given heading. Double-click the plus sign again to expand the text. Neither operation changes the contents of the document under the heading. You can drag a plus sign to move the heading and all of its associated text (whether expanded or collapsed) as a block to another location in the document.

1. Click a Document view button, or choose **View** ➢ the view name you want to use.

Moving Around in a Document

As your document gets longer, some of your work shifts out of sight. You can easily move any part of a document back into view. Scrolling moves the document line by line. Paging moves the document page by page. Browsing moves through your document by the item you specify, such as to the next word, comment, picture, table, or heading. The tools described here move you around a document no matter which document view you are in.

Scroll, Page, and Browse Through a Document

◇ To scroll through a document one line at a time, click the up or down scroll arrow on the vertical scroll bar.

◇ To scroll quickly through a document, click and hold the up or down scroll arrow on the vertical scroll bar.

◇ To scroll to a specific page or heading in a document, drag the scroll box on the vertical scroll bar until the page number or heading you want appears in the yellow box.

◇ To page through the document one screen at a time, press the Page Up or Page Down on the keyboard, or click above or below the scroll box on the vertical scroll bar.

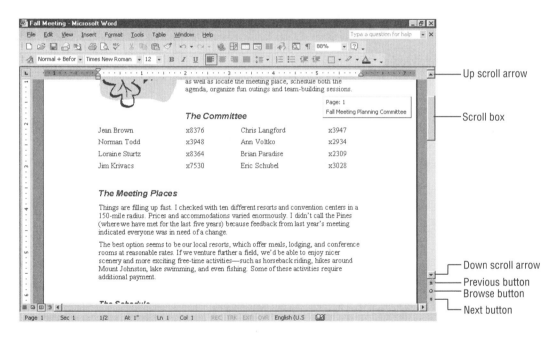

◇ To browse a document by page, edits, headings, or other items, click the **Browse** button, and then click that item. If a dialog box opens, enter the name or number of the item you want to find, and then click the **Previous** or **Next** button to move from one item to the next.

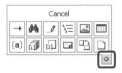

> **TIP**
> To change view options, choose Tools ➢ Options, click the View tab, select the show, view, and format options you want, and then click the OK button.

Working with Multiple Documents

When Word opens, the window displays a blank document, ready for you to begin working. By default, this document is titled Document1. Word numbers new documents consecutively. For example, if you open a new document without closing the first, it will appear in a separate Word window and be titled Document2.

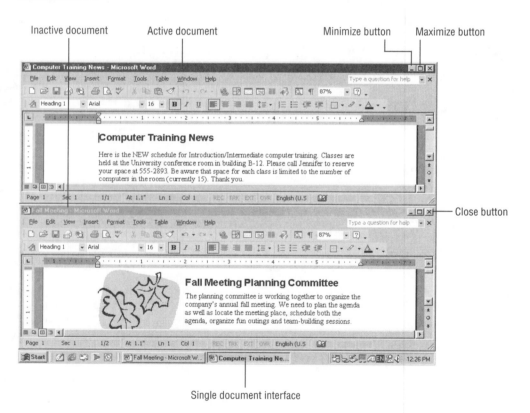

Single document interface

Single document interface

The default file management setting that opens a new window for each document and displays an icon for the window on the taskbar.

When you create a new document, Word opens a separate instance of the document in a new window and displays an icon for that window on the taskbar. When Word creates new windows for each open document is a function of the **single document interface**. This feature was first introduced in Word 2000 so that users could easily navigate from Word to documents open in other programs. If you primarily work with several Word documents at the same time, you can turn off the single document interface and employ a **multiple document interface**. This enables you to shift between multiple documents in a single instance of Word using the Window menu. Each open document displays its own button on the Windows taskbar.

> **TIP** To change to a multiple document interface, choose Tools ➤ Options, click the View tab, and then click the Windows in Taskbar check box to clear it.

You can change the size and position of a document window or the Word window using buttons in the upper-right corner of each window. Each set of resizing tools appears the same, but with one following exception. When you maximize a document, the document resizing tools are not surrounded by a box (unlike the Word resizing tools), and the document resizing tools now reside in the gray area beneath the blue title bar. These differences help you to easily distinguish the two sets of tools.

Minimize a window   To reduce a window to an icon on the taskbar, click the **Minimize** button ▬.

Maximize a window   To maximize a window to fit the screen, click the **Maximize** button ▢. Note that the button changes to the **Restore** button ▣. This button toggles between these two settings.

Restore a window   To revert from the full screen maximized view to a normal window, click the **Restore** button ▣. Notice that the button changes to the **Maximize** button ▢. This button toggles between these two settings.

Close a window   To close a window, click the **Close** button ✕.

> **TIP** To resize a window, position the mouse pointer over any edge of the window, and then click and drag the sizing handle, which appears as a double-ended arrow, to the size you want.

> **TIP** To change a window's location on your screen, drag the title bar of the document window to a different location.

Multiple document interface

An optional file management setting that allows the user to shift between multiple documents in a single Word window.

When you display multiple documents together on the same screen using the default scheme, the title bar of the active document will be blue and all other title bars will be gray. To switch between documents, click anywhere on the title bar or in the document window.

Switch between Windows

1. Choose **Window** ➢ document name to which you want to switch. The Window menu displays a list of open documents.

Setting Up the Page

Every document you produce and print might need a different page setup. Word simplifies and standardizes many page setup considerations so that you can control these processes from one dialog box. The quality of print you achieve will only be limited by the quality of your printer or other output device, not limitations of the program itself. The Page Setup dialog box, which is accessible from the File menu, contains three tabs that organize its subordinate functions by category: Margins, Paper, and Layout.

Adjust Margins

Margins adjust the space around the edge of a page. The Margins tab in the Page Setup dialog box contains settings for the left, right, top, and bottom margins. If you need additional margin space for binding pages into a book or binder, you can adjust the left or right gutter settings. **Gutters** allow for additional margin space so that all of the document text remains visible after binding. Unless this is your purpose, leave the default settings in place.

You can also select the page orientation (portrait or landscape) that best fits the entire document or any section. Portrait orients the page vertically (taller than it is wide) and landscape orients the page horizontally (wider than it is tall). When you shift between the two, the margin settings automatically change.

1. Choose **File** ➢ **Page Setup**. The Page Setup dialog box opens.

2. Click the **Margins** tab.

If you are using the default single document interface setting, you can switch between the open files by clicking the icons on the taskbar or by holding down the Alt+Tab keys on the keyboard.

Margins

Margins are the blank space between the edge of a page and the text.

Gutter

Additional blank space inserted into the margins of alternating left and right pages to allow for binding those pages without concealing any of the body text of the document.

3. Type new margin measurements (in inches) in the **Top**, **Bottom**, **Left**, or **Right** boxes.

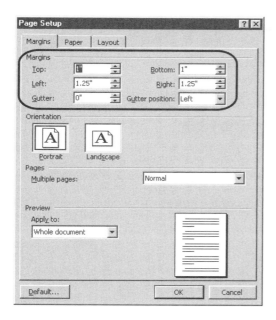

4. Click the **Apply To** drop-down arrow , and then click **Selected Text**, **This Point Forward**, or **Whole Document**.

5. To make the new margin settings the default for all new Word documents, click the **Default** button, and then click the **Yes** button.

6. Click the **OK** button.

TIP   To automatically set the gutters for normal binding, display the Margins tab in the Page Setup dialog box, click the Multiple pages drop-down arrow, and then click Book fold.

Adjust Paper Settings

Before printing your document, make sure you specify the proper size of the paper you are using. The default setting is 8.5 x 11 inches, the most common letter and copy size. All other standard sizes from index cards to legal pads are available from the pull-down menu on the Paper tab of the Page Setup dialog box, or you can input custom settings for special print jobs on odd-sized paper.

1. Choose **File ➢ Page Setup**. The Page Setup dialog opens.

2. Click the **Paper** tab.

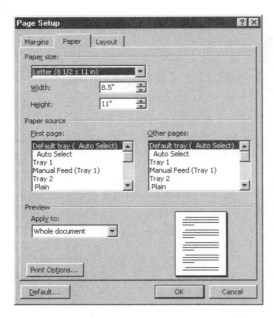

3. Specify your paper sizes and the paper source (because some printers have more than one tray that is used for storing paper).

4. If you want, click the **Print Options** button to view additional options, change the print options you want, and then click the **OK** button.

5. Click the **OK** button.

Change Your Layout

The third tab on the Page Setup dialog box is the Layout tab. Many of the functions of the Layout tab impact Word features that will be described in greater detail later in this chapter. This section contains an abbreviated overview that can be referred to again when these concepts are presented subsequently.

The Vertical alignment drop-down box is most useful when creating one-page documents. Experiment with the various settings to see how your text best fits on the page. The Line Numbers setting is most applicable to lengthy legal documents, where the capability to refer to a specific line of text quickly and easily is important.

1. Choose **File** ➢ **Page Setup**. The Page Setup dialog opens.

2. Click the **Layout** tab.

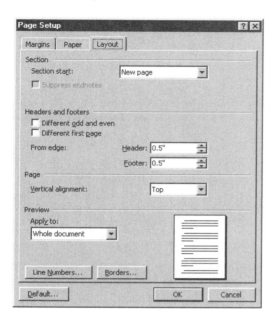

3. Change the layout options you want.

4. Click the **OK** button.

Selecting Text

The first step in working with text is to highlight, or select, the text you want. Once you've selected it, you can copy, move, format, and delete words, sentences, and paragraphs. When you finish with or decide not to use a selection, you can click anywhere in the document to deselect the text.

Select Text

1. Position the pointer in the word, paragraph, line, or part of the document you want to select.

2. Choose the method that accomplishes the task you want to complete in the easiest way.

To select	Do this
A single word	Double-click the word.
A single paragraph	Triple-click a word within the paragraph.
A single line	Click in the left margin next to the line.
Any part of a document	Click at the beginning of the text you want to select, and then drag to the end of the section you want to select.
A large section	Click at the beginning of the text you want to select, and then press and hold the Shift key while you click at the end of the text you want to select.
The entire document	Triple-click in the left margin.

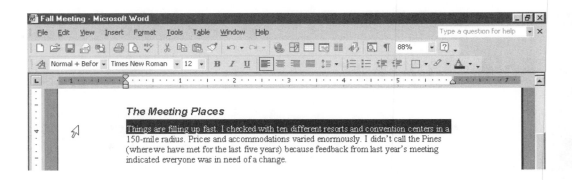

Finding and Replacing Formatting

In addition to finding and replacing text, you can also use the Find and Replace feature to locate formatting in a document and instantly substitute new formatting. For example, you can replace bold text in a document with italic text. You can find and replace any combination of formatting in a document.

Find or Replace Formatting

1. Choose **Edit** ➢ **Find** or **Replace**. The Find and Replace dialog box opens, displaying the **Find** or the **Replace** tab.

2. In the **Find what** box, enter the word or words you want to find.

3. Click the **More** button. This opens additional options to that you can fine tune your search.

4. Click the **No Formatting** button to erase any previous formatting settings.

5. Click the **Format** button, and then click a formatting item, specify formatting you want to locate, and then click the **OK** button.

6. To replace text, enter the word or words you want to replace in the **Replace with** box, click the **Format** button, and then click a formatting item, specify formatting you want to locate, and then click the **OK** button.

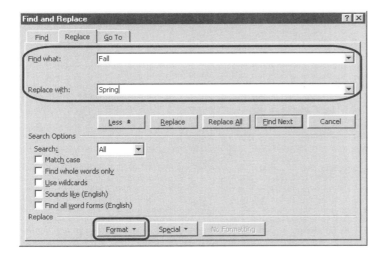

7. Click the **Find Next** button to select the next instance of the formatted text or click the **Replace** button or the **Replace All** button to substitute formatting.

8. Click the **OK** button to confirm Word finished the search, and then click the **Cancel** button.

TIP   The Go To tab quickly moves you to a place or item in your document.

Finding the Right Words

Synonyms
Words with similar meanings.

Antonyms
Words with opposite meanings.

Repeating the same word in a document can reduce a message's effectiveness. Instead, replace some words with **synonyms** or find **antonyms**. If you need help finding exactly the right words, use the shortcut menu to look up synonyms quickly or search Word's Thesaurus for more options. This feature can save you time and improve the quality and readability of your document. You can also install a thesaurus for another language.

> **TIP** To find a synonym quickly, right-click the word for which you want a synonym, point to Synonyms, and then click the synonym you want to substitute.

Use the Thesaurus

1. Select or type a word you want to look up.

2. Choose **Tools** ➣ **Language** ➣ **Thesaurus**. The Thesaurus dialog box opens.

3. Click a word to display its synonyms and antonyms.

4. Click the word you want to use.

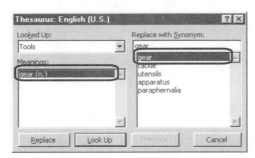

5. Click the **Replace** button to replace the original word with the one you want to use, click the **Previous** button to check out the previous word, or click the **Look Up** button to look up a new word.

Translating Words

Word offers basic translation capabilities with the Translate task pane. With the right bilingual dictionary installed on your computer, you can translate specific words or short phrases, selected text, or an entire document. If you need more extensive translation capabilities, you can connect to translation services on the World Wide Web directly from the Translate task pane.

Translate a Word

1. Select or type a word you want to translate.

2. Choose **Tools** ➢ **Language** ➢ **Translate**. The Translate task pane opens.

3. Select a translate option button.

- ❖ To translate a specific word or short phrase, click the **Text** option button, and then type it in the **Text** box.

- ❖ To translate text that is selected in your document, click the **Current selection** option button. If no text is selected, you can select it now.

- ❖ To translate the entire document, click the **Entire document** option button.

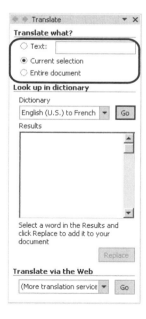

4. Click the **Dictionary** drop-down arrow, and then click the languages you want to translate from and to.

5. Click the **Go** button. The results appear in the Results box.

6. If you want to replace selected text with the translated text, select the translated text in the **Results** box, and then click the **Replace** button.

> The languages that appear in the Dictionary box depend on the language dictionaries that are installed on your computer.

Checking Spelling and Grammar

As you type, a red wavy line appears under words not listed in Word's dictionary (such as misspellings or names) or duplicated words (such as *the the*). A green wavy underline appears under words or phrases with grammatical errors. You can correct these errors as they arise or after you finish the entire document. Before you print your final document, use the Spelling and Grammar Checker to ensure that your document is error-free.

> Word uses wavy blue underlines to indicate possible instances of inconsistent formatting.

Correct Spelling and Grammar as You Type

1. Right-click a word with a red or green wavy underline.

2. Click a substitution, or click **Ignore All** (or **Ignore Grammar**) to skip any other instances of the word.

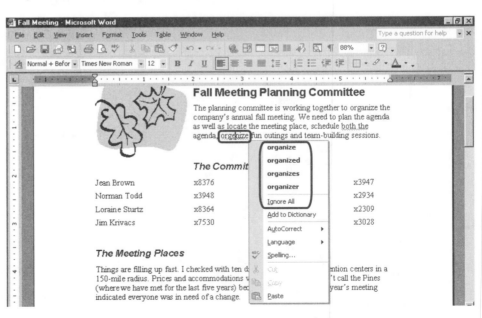

TIP To change spelling and grammar as you type options, choose Tools ➤ Options, click the Spelling & Grammar tab, click the Check spelling as you type and Check grammar as you type check boxes to select or clear them.

Correct Spelling and Grammar

1. Place the insertion point at the location in the document where you want to begin the spelling and grammar check.

2. Click the **Spelling and Grammar** button ![ABC checkmark] on the Standard toolbar. The spelling and grammar checkers scan the document, generating the Spelling and Grammar dialog box every time they encounter what is believed to be a spelling or grammatical error. The dialog box also suggests a corrected version.

3. Choose an option button.

- ◆ Click a suggestion, and then click the **Change** button to make a substitution.

- ◆ Click the **Ignore** button to skip the word or rule, or click the **Ignore All** button or the **Ignore Rule** button to skip every instance of the word or rule.

- ◆ If no suggestion is appropriate, click in the document and edit the text yourself. Click the **Resume** button to continue.

4. Click the **OK** button to return to the document.

> **TIP** To add a word (such as a person's name) to your dictionary, right-click the wavy line under the word in question, and then click Add to Dictionary.

Change Grammar and Spelling Options

1. Choose **Tools** ➢ **Options**. The Options dialog box opens.

2. Click the **Spelling & Grammar** tab.

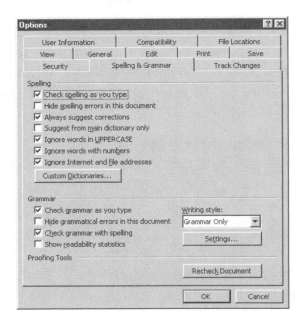

3. Click the spelling or grammar option check boxes you want to select or clear them.

4. Click the **Settings** button to change advanced grammar options, and then click the **OK** button.

5. Click the **OK** button.

Previewing and Printing a Document

When you are satisfied with the changes you have made to your document, use **Print Preview** to review your work. You can print a copy of your document using the current settings by clicking the Print button on the Standard toolbar

---

To learn the function of any of the Spelling and Grammar options displayed in the dialog box, right click the entry to display "What's This." Click the command to learn more about the option.

Print Preview
A miniature view of the entire document that shows you how your document will look when it is printed.

or on the Print Preview toolbar. You can also open the Print dialog box to choose what printer to use (assuming multiple printers are available), select the range of pages from the document that you want to print, and specify the number of copies to print.

Preview a Document

1. Choose **File** ➢ **Print Preview**. The Print Preview window opens.

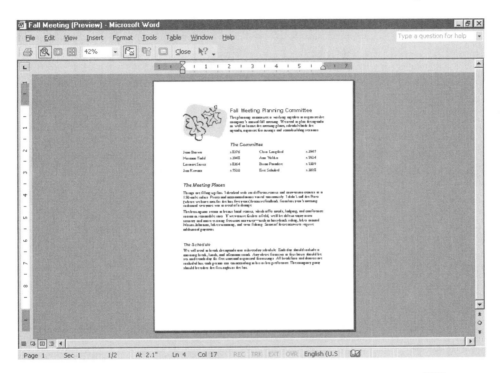

- ◆ To enlarge an area of the page, click the **Magnify** button on the Print Preview toolbar, position the Zoom pointer in the preview area, then and click the page.

- ◆ To print the document, click the **Print** button on the Print Preview toolbar.

2. When you're done, click the **Close Preview** button to return to the document.

Print a Document

You can click the Print button on the Standard toolbar to quickly print the selected document with the current Print dialog box settings. If you want to change the current Print dialog box settings, you can use the Print command on the File menu to open the Print dialog box.

1. Choose **File ➢ Print**. The Print dialog box opens.

2. Click the **Name** drop-down arrow ▾, and then select the printer you want to use from the list.

3. Click the **Print what** drop-down arrow ▾, and then select the area you want to print.

4. Click the **All**, the **Current page**, or the **Pages** option button. If you select the Pages option button, type the page range you want.

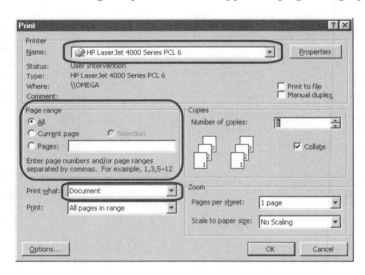

5. Click the **OK** button.

> **TIP** To change printer properties, choose File ➢ Print, and then click the Properties button to change general printer properties for paper size and orientation, graphics, and fonts.

> **TIP** To print more than one copy of the print range, click the Number of copies up or down arrow to specify the number of copies you want printed.

When you select the Collate check box, Word prints multiple copies of a document by complete sets. For two copies of a two-page document, the Collate option prints pages 1 and 2, and then prints pages 1 and 2 again.

5 Formatting a Document with Word

• •

The text of your document is perfect, but now how do you get others to notice your resume, read your newsletter, or think your document is fun, professional, interesting, dynamic, or extraordinary? Try Microsoft Word's extensive formatting features to lay out the information in your documents and create the exact look and mood you want.

Word documents are based on templates, which are predesigned and preformatted files that serve as the document's foundation. Each template is made up of styles that have common design elements, such as coordinated fonts and sizes, colors, and page layout designs. Start with a Word template for memos, reports, fax cover pages, Web pages, and so on. Apply the existing styles for headings, titles, body text, and so forth. Then modify the template's styles or create your own to better suit your needs. Make sure you get the look you want by adding emphasis with italics, boldface, and underline; changing text alignment; adjusting line and paragraph spacing; setting tabs and indents; and creating bulleted and numbered lists.

Formatting Text for Emphasis

You'll often want to format, or change the style of certain words or phrases to add emphasis to parts of a document. **Boldface**, *italics*, <u>underlines</u>, highlights, and other text effects are **toggle switches**. For special emphasis you can combine formats, such as bold and italics.

Format Existing Text Quickly

1. Select the text you want to apply emphasis.

2. Click the **Bold** button **B**, **Italic** button *I*, **Underline** button <u>U</u>, **Highlight** button, or other style buttons on the Formatting toolbar.

3. Click anywhere in the document to deselect the formatted text.

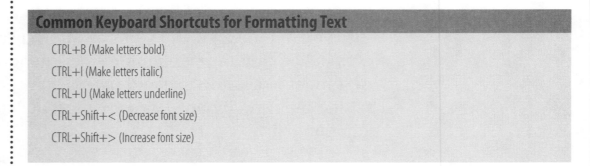

Common Keyboard Shortcuts for Formatting Text

CTRL+B (Make letters bold)

CTRL+I (Make letters italic)

CTRL+U (Make letters underline)

CTRL+Shift+< (Decrease font size)

CTRL+Shift+> (Increase font size)

Change the Font and Size of Existing Text Quickly

Using one **font** for headings and another for main text adds a professional look to your document. Although it is usually not considered good style to use numerous fonts in a document, and certainly not within paragraphs or other usually homogenous blocks of text, some designs incorporate multiple fonts.

The most commonly used text sizes for letters and memos (not headers or other layout elements) are 10 and 12 point type (typically abbreviated 10 pt., 12 pt.). Again, nothing limits you from breaking with convention, and you will also want to manipulate point sizes to keep your headers from wrapping to two lines or make other aesthetic changes from time to time.

1. Select the text you want to change.

2. Click the **Font** down arrow [▼] on the Formatting toolbar, and then click the font you want to use.

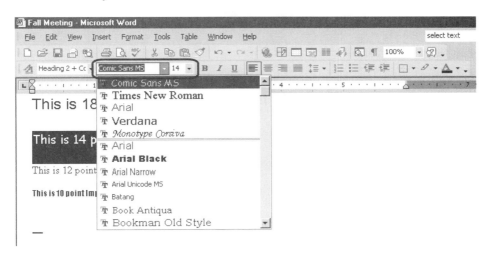

3. Click the **Font Size** down arrow [▼] on the Formatting toolbar, and then click the font size you want to use.

Apply Formatting Effects to Text

1. Select the text you want to apply emphasis.

2. Choose **Format ➤ Font**. The Font dialog box opens.

Font

A collection of characters, numbers, and symbols in the same letter design.

3. Click the **Font** tab.

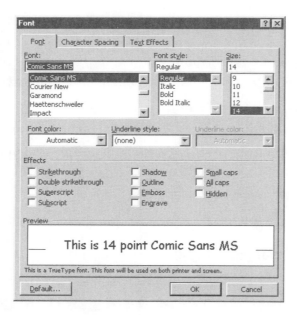

4. Click the types of emphasis you want to add, set the font color and make other Font dialog box choices.

5. To add some flashy effects to your text, click the **Text Effects** tab and click an animation.

6. To change character spacing settings, click the **Character Spacing** tab and change the settings.

7. Click the **OK** button.

Select or Clear Text Formatting

If you want to change formatting for all instances of formatted text, you can use the Styles and Formatting task pane to select all instances. If you have created formatted or stylized paragraphs and subsequently want to return to the default text settings, you can remove the existing formatting.

1. Select the text whose formatting you want to select or clear away.

2. Choose **Format ➢ Reveal Formatting**. The Reveal Formatting task pane opens.

3. Point to the **Selected text** box, click the down arrow, and then click **Select All Text With Similar Formatting** or **Clear Formatting**.

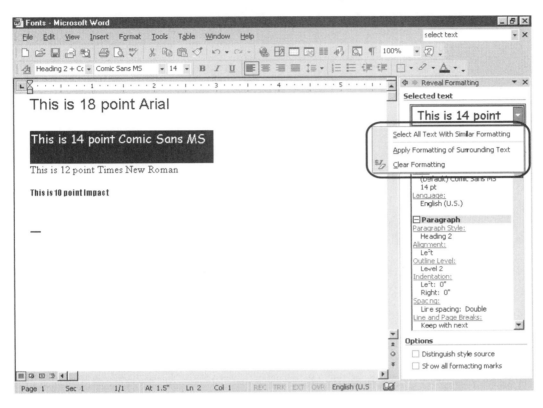

TIP You can also press Ctrl+Spacebar to remove paragraph or character formatting.

Copy Formatting with the Format Painter

The Format Painter copies and pastes formatting from one batch of selected text to another without copying the text.

1. Select the text with the formatting you want to copy.

2. Click the **Format Painter** button on the Standard toolbar.

3. Select the text you want to format with the Format Painter pointer.

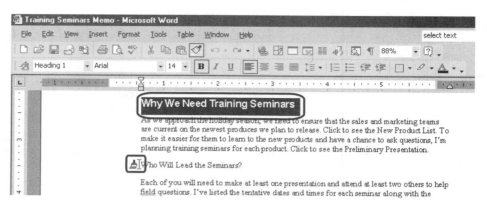

Changing Paragraph Alignment

Text starts out positioned evenly along the left margin, and uneven, or ragged, at the right margin. Left-aligned text works well for body paragraphs in most cases, but other alignments vary the look of a document and help lead the reader through the text. Right-aligned text, which is even along the right margin and ragged at the left margin, is good for adding a date to a letter. Justified text spreads text evenly between the margins, creating a clean, professional look, often used in newspapers and magazines. Centered text is best for titles and headings.

Align New Text with Click-And-Type

1. Place the I-beam at the left, right, or center of the line where you want to insert new text. When the I-beam shows the appropriate alignment, double-click to place the insertion point, and then type your text.

Pointer	Purpose
I ≡	Left-aligns text
≡ I	Right-aligns text
I	Centers text
I ≡	Creates a new line in the same paragraph

When you double-click the text alignment pointer, Word adds extra lines and tabs, and sets the alignment and text wrapping as needed. Use Click-And-Type to quickly center titles or set different text alignment on the same line.

Align Existing Text

1. Place the I-beam or select at least one line in each paragraph to align.

2. Click the appropriate button on the Formatting toolbar.

   ◇ **Align Left** button

   ◇ **Center** button

   ◇ **Align Right** button

   ◇ **Justify** button

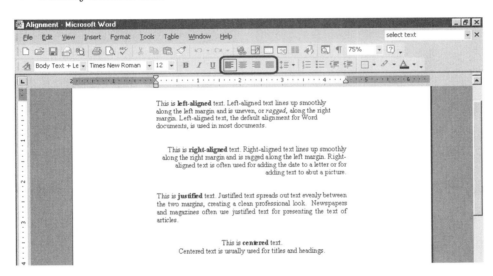

Changing Line Spacing

Certain documents, particularly academic papers and draft documents, are prepared with space and a half or even double spacing between lines to allow room for the reviewer of the document to hand write comments, corrections, or critique. The lines in all Word documents are single-spaced by default, which is appropriate for letters and most documents. But you can easily change your document line spacing to double or 1.5 lines to allow extra space between every line. This is useful when you want to make notes on a printed document. Sometimes, you'll want to add space above and below certain paragraphs, such as for headlines or indented quotations to help set off the text.

Change Line Spacing

1. Select the text you want to change.

NOTE   If you have not yet written your document, but want to do so at the proper spacing from the outset, skip step one.

2. On the Formatting toolbar, click the **Line Spacing** button drop-down arrow , and then click a spacing option:

✓   1.0
1.5
2.0
2.5
3.0
More…

- ❖ To apply a new setting, click the arrow, then select the number that you want (1.0 is single line space, 1.5 represents line-and-a-half, 2.0 signifies double spacing, etc.).

- ❖ To apply the setting you last used, click the **Line Spacing** button.

- ❖ Click **More**. This opens the Paragraph dialog box so that you can enter precise parameters.

TIP   You can quickly change line spacing for selected text or new paragraphs by pressing Ctrl+1 for single-space, Ctrl+5 for 1.5 space, or Ctrl+2 for double-space.

Change Paragraph Spacing

1. Choose the paragraph(s) whose spacing you want to change, and select that text.

2. Choose **Format ➢ Paragraph**. The Paragraph dialog box opens.

3. Click the **Indents and Spacing** tab.

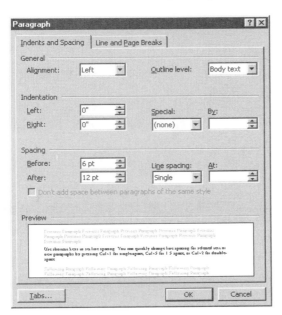

4. Under the **Spacing** header, enter the custom spacing parameters you want both before and after the paragraph(s), and then click the **OK** button to apply them.

NOTE The Before and After spacing boxes are measured in points (pt), a common typesetting term. One point equates to $1/72^{nd}$ of an inch. 72 points equate to one inch of space.

Displaying Rulers

Word rulers do more than measure. The horizontal ruler above the document shows the length of the typing line, and lets you quickly adjust left and right margins and indents, set tabs, and change column widths. The vertical ruler along the left edge of the document lets you adjust top and bottom margins and change table row heights. Hide the rulers to get more room for your document.

Show and Hide the Rulers

1. If a horizontal ruler isn't on the screen, choose **View ➢ Ruler**. The ruler appears.

- ◇ To view the horizontal ruler, click the **Normal View** button or the **Web Layout View** button.

- ◇ To view the horizontal and vertical rulers, click the **Print Layout View** button.

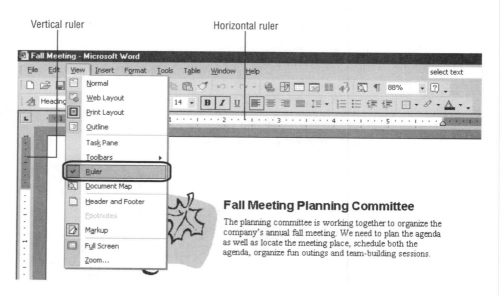

TIP   You can change the ruler to show inches, centimeters, millimeters, points, or picas. Choose Tools ➢ Options, click the General tab, click the Measurement Units drop-down arrow, and then select the measurement you want.

Setting Paragraph Tabs

Tab
A location in a paragraph to align text.

Tab stop
A predefined stopping point along the document's typing line.

In your document, **tabs** set how text or numerical data aligns in relation to the document margins. Default **tab stops** are set every half-inch, but you can set multiple tabs per paragraph at any location. Choose from four text tab stops: left, right, center, and decimal (for numerical data). The bar tab inserts a vertical bar at the tab stop. After tab stops are set, you can invoke them by pressing the Tab key.

Set Paragraph Tabs

1. Select one or more paragraphs in which you want to place a tab stop.

2. Click the **Tab** icon on the horizontal ruler until it shows the type of tab stop you want.

Icon	Purpose
⌊	Aligns text to the left of the tab stop
⌋	Aligns text to the right of the tab stop
⊥	Centers text on the tab stop
⊥.	Aligns numbers on the decimal point
		Inserts a vertical bar at the tab stop

3. Click the ruler where you want to set the tab stop.

4. If necessary, drag the tab stop to position it where you want.

5. To clear a tab stop, drag it off the ruler.

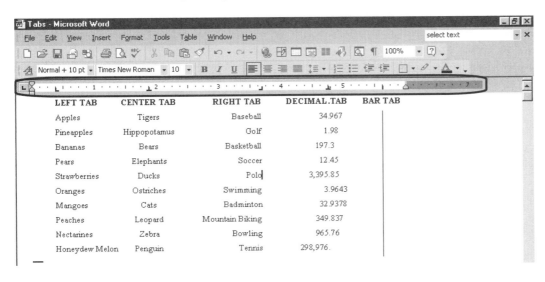

Setting Paragraph Indents

The default setting for paragraph indentation is $\frac{1}{2}$ inch (0.5"). You can quickly indent lines of text to precise locations from the left or right margin with the horizontal ruler. You can use the ruler to indent the first line of a paragraph (called a first-line indent) as books do to distinguish paragraphs, indent the second and subsequent lines of a paragraph from the left margin (called a hanging indent) to create a properly formatted bibliography, or indent the entire paragraph any amount from the left and right margin (called left indents and right indents) to separate quoted passages.

Set Indents with the Ruler

1. Select the paragraph you want to indent or just click to place your cursor within the confines of the paragraph.

2. If a horizontal ruler isn't on the screen, choose **View ➢ Ruler**. The ruler appears.

3. Use the markers on the ruler to set indents.

   ◈ To change the left indent of the first line, drag the **First Line Indent** marker ▽.

   ◈ To change the indent of the second and subsequent lines, drag the **Hanging Indent** marker △.

   ◈ To change the left indent for all lines, drag the **Left Indent** marker ▢.

   ◈ To change the right indent for all lines, drag the **Right Indent** marker △.

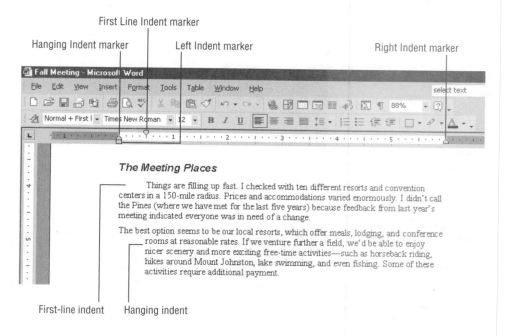

TIP You can change the indention in one half inch increments. Click the paragraph or select multiple paragraphs to indent. Click the Increase Indent button or the Decrease Indent button on the Formatting toolbar.

Set Indentation with the Tab key

1. Choose **Tools** ➢ **AutoCorrect Options**. The AutoCorrect Options dialog box opens.

2. Click the **AutoFormat As You Type** tab.

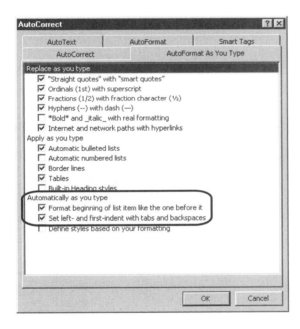

3. Click the **Set left- and first-indent with tabs and backspaces** check box to select it.

4. Click the **OK** button.

TIP You can indent the first line of a paragraph by clicking the beginning of the paragraph and pressing Tab. You can indent the entire paragraph by selecting it and pressing Tab.

Applying a Style

Style
A collection of formatting settings saved with a name.

When you want to apply multiple groupings of formatting, save each as a style. A **style** is formatting settings saved with a name in a document or template that you can apply to text at any time. If you modify a style, you make the change once, but all text tagged with that style changes to reflect the new format.

Apply a Style

1. Select any word, list, table, or other type of text block you want to see presented in another style.

2. Click the **Styles and Formatting** button on the Formatting toolbar. The Styles and Formatting task pane opens.

3. In the task pane, click the style you want to apply. When you select another style in the template, or make changes to the parameters for that style, they will be applied to the selected text automatically.

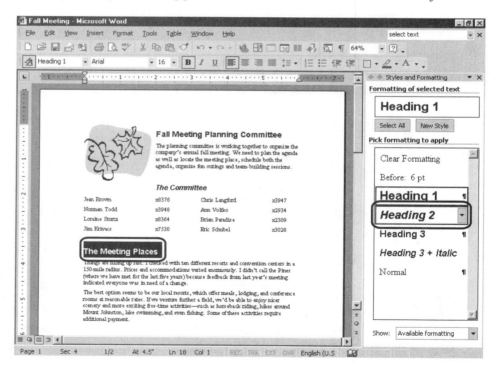

You can access additional styles by clicking the Show drop-down arrow, and then click All Styles.

Creating and Modifying Styles

There are two types of styles that can be created: character and paragraph. **Character styles** apply format settings only to text that has been selected by the user, not all of the text within a paragraph. **Paragraph styles** affect all of the characters within a paragraph whenever they are applied, so less selectivity is possible when using these types of styles.

NOTE The style list on the Formatting toolbar marks character styles with an underlined lowercase letter a, and paragraph styles with the ¶ symbol.

Create or Modify a Style

1. Select the text whose formatting you want to save as a style.

2. Click the **Styles and Formatting** button on the Formatting toolbar. The Styles and Formatting task pane opens.

3. To modify a style, click a style down arrow, and then click **Modify Style**. The Modify Style dialog box appears.

Character Styles
A group of format settings, font, size, effect (bold, italic etc.) that can be selectively applied to any block of text at the user's discretion.

Paragraph Styles
A group of format settings, font, size, indent, spacing and so forth, that can only be applied to all of the text within a paragraph (even if it is a one-line paragraph).

4. To create a new style, click the **New Style** button. The New Style dialog box appears.

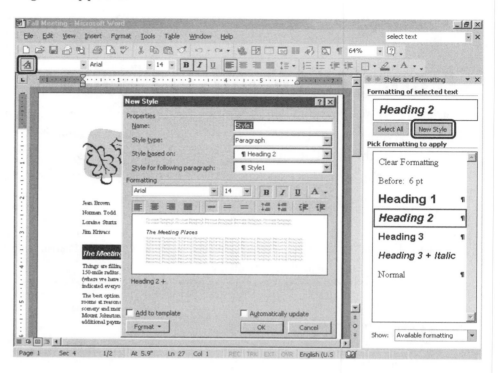

5. In the **Name** box, type a descriptive name.

6. Click the **Style Type** drop-down arrow ⬛, and then click **Paragraph** or **Character**.

7. Click the **Style For Following Paragraph** drop-down arrow ⬛, and then click the name of the style you want to be applied.

8. Use the Formatting toolbar to apply character or paragraph formatting.

9. Select the formatting options that suit your new style, or click the **Format** button to see more options including the option to assign a shortcut key to the style you are creating.

10. Click the **Automatically update** check box to select it if you want all instances of the style to be updated in the existing document.

11. Click the **Add to template** check box to select it to make the style part of the existing template set.

12. Click the **OK** button to close the New Style dialog box.

Creating Bulleted and Numbered Lists

The best way to draw attention to a list is to format the items with bullets or numbers. You can even create multilevel lists. For different emphasis, change any bullet or number style to one of Word's many predefined formats. For example, switch round bullets to check boxes or Roman numerals to lowercase letters. You can also customize the list style or insert a picture as a bullet. If you move, insert, or delete items in a numbered list, Word sequentially renumbers the list for you.

Create a Bulleted or Numbered List

1. Click where you want to create a bulleted or numbered list.

2. Click the **Bullets** button or **Numbering** button on the Formatting toolbar.

3. Type the first item in your list, and then press the Enter key to insert a new bullet or the next number.

4. Type the next item, press the Enter key, and then press the Enter key again to end the list.

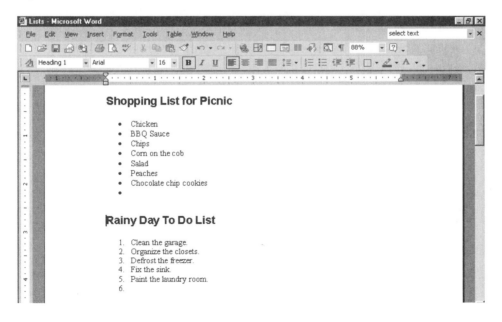

> **TIP** To create a multilevel bulleted or numbered list, press the Tab key to indent to the next level, type the item, and then press the Enter key. Press Shift+Tab to return to the previous level.

Change a Bulleted or Numbered List

1. Select the list you want to change.

2. Choose **Format ➢ Bullets and Numbering**. The Bullets and Numbering dialog box opens.

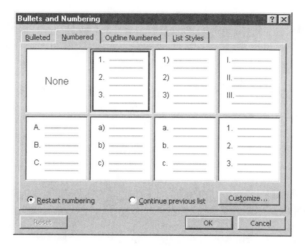

3. Click the **Bulleted** tab or the **Numbered** tab.

4. Click a predefined format.

5. To add a graphic bullet, click the **Customize** button, click the **Picture** button, and then select the picture you want.

6. Click the **OK** button.

Inserting New Pages and Sections

When you fill a page, Word inserts a **page break** and starts a new page. As you add or delete text, this soft page break moves. To start a new page before the current one is filled, insert a hard page break that doesn't shift as you edit text. A section is a mini-document within a document that stores margin settings,

Page break

A command that stops flowing text on the current page and proceeds to the top of a new page.

page orientation, page numbering, and so on. A **section break** appears at the start and end of a section.

Insert a Page Break

1. Click the document to position the insertion point where you want the page break to occur.

2. Choose **Insert** ➢ **Break**. The Break dialog box opens.

3. Click the **Page Break** option button to select it, if necessary.

NOTE   Column breaks are used in two-column layouts to move the text after the insertion point to the top of the following column. Text wrapping breaks are inserted when flowing text around pictures in desktop publishing to move the text after the insertion point to the beginning of the first full line after the picture.

4. Click the **OK** button.

TIP   You can also quickly insert a page break by pressing Ctrl+Enter.

TIP   To delete a page or section break, choose View ➢ Normal, click the page break to select it, and then press the Delete key.

Section break
A document within a document that uses a different layout for the text that follows the break.

Start a new line but not a new paragraph. Insert a text wrapping break to force text to the next line in the same paragraph—the perfect tool to make a phrase fall on one line. Press Shift+Enter where you want to insert a text wrapping break.

Insert a Section Break

Even and odd section breaks are usually used when you want each new section to begin on the left or right page in a bound document.

1. Click the document to position the insertion point where you want the page break to occur.

2. Choose **Insert ➢ Break**. The Break dialog box opens.

3. Under the **Section** break types subhead, choose one of the following four options:

- ◆ **Next Page** inserts both a section and page break at the insertion point and moves the insertion point to the top of the next page.

- ◆ **Continuous** inserts only a section break at the insertion point. The insertion point remains on the same page to begin inputting the new section.

- ◆ **Even page** begins a new section on the next even page, skipping a page if necessary to do so.

- ◆ **Odd page** begins a new section on the next odd page, skipping a page if necessary to do so.

4. Click the **OK** button.

NOTE　To move a page or section break, choose View ➢ Normal to switch to Normal view, select the break you want to move, and then drag the break to its new location and release the mouse button.

Addressing Envelopes and Labels

A formatted document needs a matching envelope or mailing label. Addresses can contain text, graphics, and bar codes. The POSTNET bar code is a machine-readable depiction of a U.S. zip code and delivery address; the FIM-A code identifies the front of a courtesy reply envelope. You can print a single-label or multiple labels.

Address and Print Envelopes

1. Choose **Tools** ➢ **Letters and Mailings** ➢ **Envelopes and Labels**, and then click the **Envelopes** tab.

2. In the **Delivery address** box, type the recipient's name and address, or click the **Insert Address** button to search for it.

3. In the **Return address** box, type your name and address.

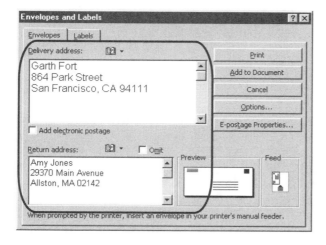

4. Click the **Options** button, select a size, placement, bar code, and font, and then click the **OK** button.

5. Insert an envelope in your printer, and then click the **Print** button.

Address and Print Mailing Labels

1. Choose **Tools** ➤ **Letters and Mailings** ➤ **Envelopes and Labels**, and then click the **Labels** tab.

2. In the **Address** box, type the recipient's name and address.

3. In the Print area, click an option button to select which labels to print.

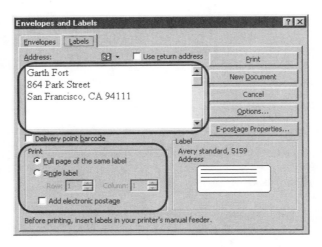

4. Click the **Options** button, select a type or size, and then click the **OK** button.

5. Insert labels in your printer, and then click the **Print** button.

Working with Templates

A template is a special document that stores text, styles, formatting, macros, and page information for use in other documents. You can start a new document with a predefined Word template or use one you created from a document. If you are working with an existing document, you can quickly try a new look by attaching a different template to your current document. The attached template's styles replace the styles in your document.

NOTE By default, all Word documents use the Normal template, which formats text in 12-point Times New Roman and offers three different heading styles.

Save a Document as a Template

1. Open a new or existing document and make the changes you want to appear in all documents based on this template.

2. Choose **File ➢ Save As**. The Save As dialog box opens.

3. Click the **Save as Type** drop-down arrow 🔽, and then click **Document Template**.

4. Make sure the Templates folder (usually located in the Microsoft Office folder in the Programs folder) or one of its subfolders appears in the Save In box.

5. In the **File name** box, type a name for the new template.

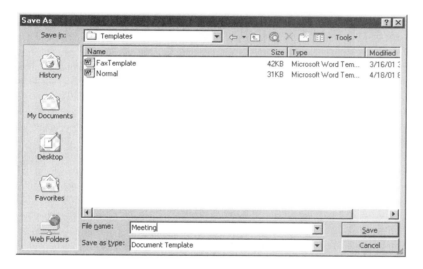

6. Click the **Save** button.

Attach a Template to an Existing Document

1. Open the document to which you want to attach a template.

2. Choose **Tools** ➢ **Templates and Add-Ins**. The Templates and Add-Ins dialog box opens.

3. Click the **Attach** button. The Attach Template dialog box opens.

4. Select the template you want to attach, and then click the **Open** button.

5. Click the **OK** button.

TIP To preview and attach a template to an existing document, open the document to which you want to apply a new template, choose Format ➢ Theme, click the Style Gallery button, click a template, and then click the OK button.

6 Enhancing a Document with Word

Once you've mastered the basics, Microsoft Word 2002 has plenty of advanced features to enhance your documents. Whether it's a single-page flyer or a twenty-page report, you can arrange the text and add enhancements that make your document appealing and easy to read.

After you create your basic document, consider how you can improve its appearance and communicate its message more effectively. For example, if your document is a brochure or newsletter, arrange the text in columns and add an enlarged capital letter to the first word to convey expertise and quality. Or organize information in a table to draw attention to important data or clarify the details of a complicated paragraph. Another way to impress clients, business associates, social groups, or even family members is to create personalized form letters for any occasion—an upcoming meeting, a holiday greeting, or a family announcement. Create a formatted document and enter the text that doesn't change. Any data that changes from person to person (such as names) goes into another file, which you merge with the form letter. In a snap, you've got personalized letters that show you care.

Adding Headers and Footers

Most books, including this one, use headers and footers to help you keep track of where you are. A **header** is text printed in the top margin of every page. **Footer** text is printed in the bottom margin. Commonly headers and footers contain your name, the document title, the filename, the print date, and page numbers. If you divide your document into sections, you can create different headers and footers for each section.

Headers
Formatted blocks of text or text and art that appear at the top of pages within a document.

Footers
Formatted blocks of text or text and art that appear at the bottom of pages within a document.

What are odd and even pages? As in books, odd pages appear on the right and even pages appear on the left.

Create and Edit Headers and Footers

1. Choose **View ➢ Header and Footer**. The Header and Footer toolbar opens.

2. Click the header or footer box, and then type or edit the text you want.

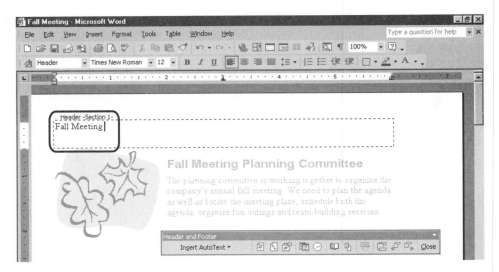

TIP Use default tab stops to align header and footer text. Headers and footers have two default tab stops. The first, in the middle, centers text. The second, on the far right, aligns text on the right margin. To left align text, don't press Tab. You can add and move the tab stops as needed.

3. Use the buttons on the Header and Footer toolbar to navigate between headers and footers.

❖ To toggle display of the document text on and off, click the **Show/Hide Document Text** button.

◆ To switch the display between the header and footer, click the **Switch Between Header and Footer** button ▣.

◆ To apply the header and footer style from the previous section to the current section, click **The Same as Previous** button ▣.

◆ To go to the previous header or footer, click the **Show Previous** button ▣.

◆ To go to the next header or footer, click the **Show Next** button ▣.

4. Use the buttons on the Header and Footer toolbar to insert commonly used items in headers and footers.

◆ To insert any of the most commonly common phrases, such as the Author, Page number and Date, or Filename, click the **Insert AutoText** button `Insert AutoText ▾`.

◆ To number each page according to the existing pagination Click the **Insert Page Number** button ▣.

◆ To track the current page number of the document versus the total number of pages, click the **Insert Number of Pages** button ▣.

◆ To change the format of page numbering, click the **Format Page Number** button ▣.

◆ To place the current date on the document, click the **Insert Date** button ▣.

◆ To place the current time on the document, click the **Insert Time** button ▣.

◆ To specify a different header or footer for odd and even pages in a document, such as one might do when binding or printing double sided, click the **Page Setup** button ▣.

5. When you're done, click the **Close Header and Footer** button `Close` on the Header and Footer toolbar.

TIP To add a graphic to either a header or footer, such as a company logo, click the header or footer to position the insertion point, choose Insert ➢ Picture ➢ click the type of file and the location of the file on the submenus that follow.

Inserting Page Numbers and the Date and Time

Adding page numbers and the date to your document can help you keep track of your work. Page numbering usually isn't required for shorter documents, but is almost essential for longer documents. You can number the entire document consecutively or each section independently and pick a numbering scheme, such as roman numerals or letters. The date and time field ensures you know which printout is the latest. Word uses your computer's internal calendar and clock as its source. You can insert the date and time for any installed language.

Insert Page Numbers

1. Choose **Insert ➢ Page Numbers**. The Page Numbers dialog box opens.

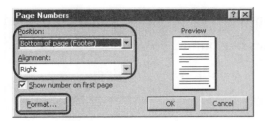

2. Click the **Position** drop-down arrow , and then click **Top of page (Header)** or **Bottom of page (Footer)**.

3. Click the **Alignment** drop-down arrow, and then click **Left**, **Right**, **Center**, **Inside**, or **Outside**.

4. Click the **Format** button. The Page Number Format dialog box opens.

5. Click the **Number format** drop-down arrow, and then select the format you want to use.

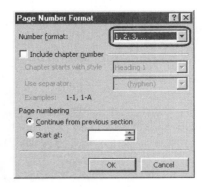

6. By default, chapter numbering is not included. If you want to include the chapter number in your page numbering (Example 11-1, 11-2 etc.), then click the **Include chapter number** option button.

7. Click the option button to specify whether numbering will be continuous from section to section or begin again at a point or points that you specify within the document.

8. Click the **OK** button twice to apply your selections.

Insert the Date and Time

1. Choose **Insert ➢ Date and Time**. The Date and Time dialog box opens.

2. If you want, click the **Language** drop-down arrow 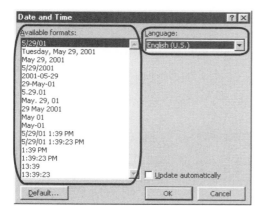, and then select a language.

3. In the **Available formats** box, click the date or time format you want.

4. Click the **Update Automatically** check box to select it.

5. Click the **OK** button to apply your selections.

TIP   To set the current date and time as the default, click the Default button in the Date and Time dialog box, and then click the Yes button.

Inserting Symbols and AutoText

Word comes with a host of symbols and special characters for every need. Insert just the right one to keep from compromising a document's professional appearance with a hand- drawn arrow (⟨⟨) or missing mathematical symbol (å). AutoText stores text and graphics you want to reuse, such as a company logo, boilerplate text, or formatted table. Use the AutoText entries that come with Word, or create your own.

Insert Symbols and Special Characters

1. Click the document where you want to insert a symbol or special character.

2. Choose **Insert** ➤ **Symbol**. The Symbol dialog box opens.

3. Click the **Symbols** tab or the **Special Characters** tab.

4. To see other symbols, click the **Font** drop-down arrow ▾, and then click a new font.

5. To see a subset of the symbols, click the **Subset** drop-down arrow ▾, and then select the subset type you want.

6. Click a symbol or character.

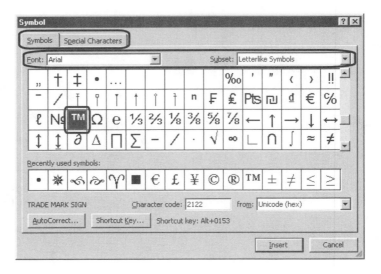

7. Click the **Insert** button.

TIP Assign a shortcut key to insert a symbol. In the Symbol dialog box, select a symbol, click the Shortcut Key button, and then enter the shortcut key information requested.

Insert AutoText

1. Click the document where you want to insert AutoText.

2. Choose **Insert** ➢ **AutoText**.

3. Point to an AutoText category.

4. Click the AutoText entry you want.

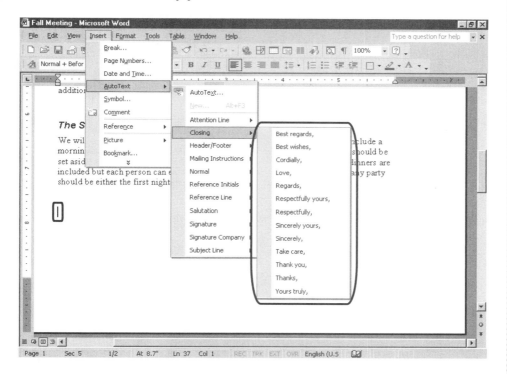

TIP Create your own AutoText. Select the text or object for your AutoText entry, choose Insert ➢ AutoText ➢ New, enter a name for the entry, and then click the OK button.

Adding Desktop Publishing Effects

A few simple elements—drop caps, borders, and shading—make your newsletters and brochures look like a design whiz produced them. A *drop cap* is the enlarged first letter of a paragraph. *Borders* are lines or graphics that appear around a page, paragraph, selected text, or table cells. *Shading* is a color that fills the background of selected text, paragraphs, or table cells. For more attractive pages, add clips or columns.

Add a Dropped Capital Letter

1. Click the **Print Layout View** button ▣.

2. Click the paragraph where you want the drop cap.

3. Choose **Format** ➢ **Drop Cap**. The Drop Cap dialog box opens.

4. Click a drop cap position.

5. Click the **Font** drop-down arrow ▾, and then select a drop cap font.

6. Change the drop cap height and distance between the drop cap and paragraph.

7. Click the **OK** button.

Add a Page Border

1. Choose **Format** ➢ **Borders and Shading**. The Borders and Shading dialog box opens.

2. Click the **Page Border** tab.

3. In the **Setting** area, click a box setting, and then a style in the **Style** area.

4. Click the **Art** drop-down arrow , and then select a line or art style.

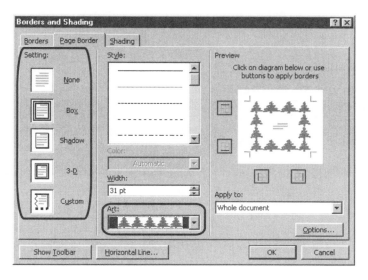

5. In the **Width** box, type a border width.

6. Click the **Apply to** drop-down arrow , and then select the pages you want to have borders.

7. Click the **OK** button to close the dialog box and apply the border.

Add Paragraph Borders and Shading

1. Select the text you want to border or shade.

2. Click the **Tables and Borders** button on the Standard toolbar. The Tables and Borders toolbar opens.

3. If necessary, click the **Draw Table** button on the Tables and Borders toolbar to deselect it.

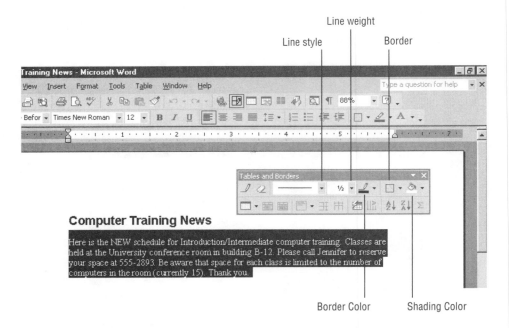

4. Use the Tables and Borders toolbar to add borders and shading.

- Click the **Line Style** drop-down arrow, and then select a line pattern.

- Click the **Line Weight** drop-down arrow, and then select a border thickness.

- Click the **Border Color** drop-down arrow, and then select the border you want.

- Click the **Border** drop-down arrow, and then select the border you want to add.

- Click the **Shading Color** drop-down arrow, and then select the background shading you want.

5. When you're done, click the **Close** button on the Tables and Borders toolbar.

TIP   You can also use the Borders and Shading dialog box to add paragraph borders and shading. Select the text you want to add a border or shading, choose Format ➤ Borders and Shading, click the Borders tab or the Shading tab, make changes, and then click the OK button.

Arranging Text in Columns

Newspaper-style columns can give newsletters and brochures a more polished look. You can format an entire document, selected text, or individual sections into columns. If necessary, Word inserts a section break, and then balances the columns. To view the columns side-by-side, switch to print layout view.

Create Columns

1. Click the **Print Layout View** button ▣.

2. Select the text you want to arrange in columns.

3. Click the **Columns** button ▦ on the Standard toolbar.

4. Drag to select the number of columns you want, and then click the option.

Modify Columns

1. Click the **Print Layout View** button ▣, and then click in the columns you want to modify.

2. Choose **Format** ➤ **Columns**. The Columns dialog box opens.

3. In the **Presets** area, click a column format

4. In the **Number of columns** box, type the number of columns you want, if necessary.

5. Enter the width and spacing you want for each column.

6. Click the **OK** button.

Inserting a Table of Contents

Table of contents

An outline of the main topics and page location in a document.

Leader

A line in the table of contents that connects an entry to its page number.

A **table of contents** provides an outline of main topics and page locations. Word builds a table of contents based on the styles in a document that you choose. By default, Heading 1 is the first-level entry, Heading 2 the second level, and so on. In a printed table of contents, a **leader**, a line whose style you select, connects an entry to its page number. In Web documents, entries become hyperlinks. Hide nonprinting characters before creating a table of contents so text doesn't shift to other pages as you print.

Insert a Table of Contents

1. Choose **Insert** ➤ **Reference** ➤ **Index and Tables**. The Index and Tables dialog box opens.

2. Click the **Table of Contents** tab.

3. Click the **Show Page Numbers** and the **Right Align Page Numbers** check boxes to select them.

4. Click the **Tab leader** drop-down arrow 🔽, and then select a leader style.

5. Click the **Formats** drop-down arrow 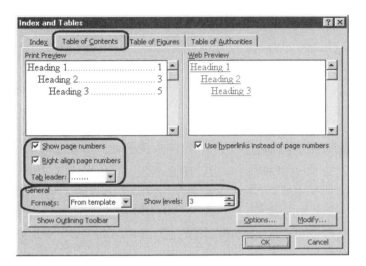, and then select a table of contents style.

6. In the **Show levels** box, enter the number of heading levels you want.

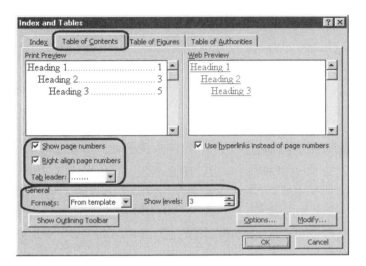

7. Click the **OK** button.

You can also use the Index and Tables dialog box to create an index, table of figures, or table of authorities, which tracks legal notations.

Creating a Table

When you need to present a group of related information, either numerical or contextual, one of the common methods of doing so is to display it in table form. A **table** organizes information neatly into rows and columns. The intersection of a row and column is called a **cell**. You can create a table from existing text separated by paragraphs, tabs, or commas, or you can draw a custom table with various sized cells and then enter text. If you decide not to use a table, you can convert it to text.

Table
A structure that organizes information into rows and columns.

Cell
The intersection of a row and column in a table or spreadsheet.

127

Create a Table

1. Place the insertion point at the location where you want to create a table.

2. Choose **Table** ➢ **Insert** ➢ **Table**. The Insert Table dialog box opens.

3. In the **Table Size** area, enter the number of columns (vertical) and rows (horizontal) you want.

4. In the **AutoFit Behavior** area, select an option button to adjust the table size.

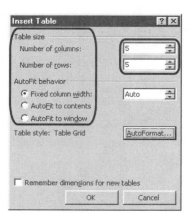

5. Click the **OK** button.

> **TIP** To quickly create a table from existing text, select the text for the table, and then choose Table ➢ Insert ➢ Table. If you want to specify options, choose Table ➢ Convert ➢ Text to Table.

> **TIP** You can also draw a table. Click the Tables and Borders button on the Standard toolbar, click the Draw Table button on the Tables and Borders toolbar, and then draw a table. Press and hold the Shift key, and then click lines to erase them.

Enter Text in a Table

1. Place the insertion point in the table cell where you want to enter text.

2. After you type text in a cell, press the Enter key to start a new paragraph within that cell, the Tab key to move to the next cell to the right, or the arrow keys or click in a cell to move to a new location.

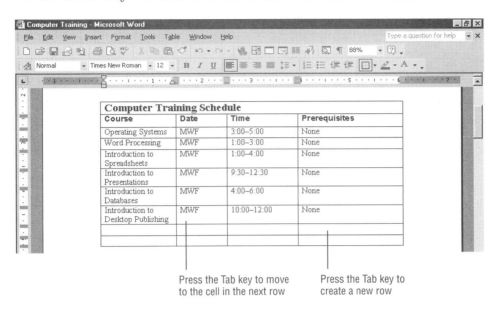

Press the Tab key to move to the cell in the next row

Press the Tab key to create a new row

TIP You can calculate the sum of a table column. Click the Tables and Borders button on the Standard toolbar, click in the blank cell in the bottom of the column you want to total, and then click the AutoSum button on the Tables And Borders toolbar.

NOTE Row height expands as you type. As you type in a cell, text wraps to the next line and the height of a row expands as you enter text that extends beyond the column width.

Modifying a Table

As you begin to work on a table, you might need to modify its structure by adding more rows, columns, or cells to accommodate new text, graphics, or other tables. The table realigns as needed to accommodate the new structure. When you insert rows, columns, or cells, the existing rows shift down, the existing columns shift right, and you choose in what direction the existing cells shift. Similarly, when you delete unneeded rows, columns, or cells from a table, the table realigns itself. Moreover, you can modify the width of any column and height of any row to better present your data.

Often there is more to modifying a table than adding or deleting rows or columns; you need to make cells just the right size to accommodate the text you are entering in the table. For example, a title in the first row of a table might be longer than the first cell in that row. To spread the title across the top of the table, you can *merge* (combine) the cells to form one long cell. Sometimes to indicate a division in a topic, you need to *split* (or divide) a cell into two.

Insert Additional Rows and Columns

1. Select the row or column next to where you want the new row or column to appear.

2. Drag to select the number of rows or columns you want to insert.

3. Choose **Table** ➢ **Insert** ➢ **Rows Above**, **Rows Below**, **Columns to the Left**, or **Columns to the Right**.

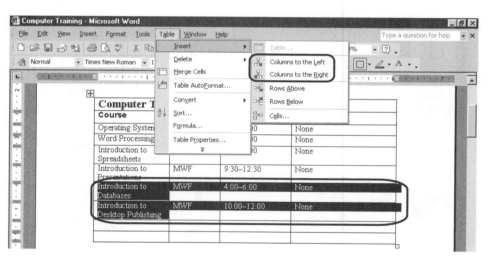

TIP To insert additional cells, select the cells where you want the new cells to appear, choose Table ➢ Insert ➢ Cells. In the Insert Cells dialog box, select the direction in which you want the existing cells to shift, and then click the OK button.

Delete Rows, Columns, or Cells

1. Select the rows, columns, or cells you want to delete.

2. Choose **Table** ➢ **Delete** ➢ **Rows**, **Columns**, or **Cells**.

3. For the Cells command, select the direction in which you want the remaining cells to shift to fill the space, and then click the **OK** button.

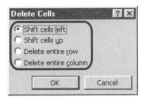

NOTE You can quickly select elements in a table using the mouse. To select a table, point anywhere in the table, and then click the Select Table button in the upper-left corner of the table. To select a row or column, click in the left margin next to the row or above the column you want to select. To select one or more cells, drag the cells.

Adjust Row Heights and Columns Widths

1. Select the rows or columns to change.

2. Choose **Table ➢ Table Properties**. The Table Properties dialog box.

3. Click the **Row** tab or the **Column** tab.

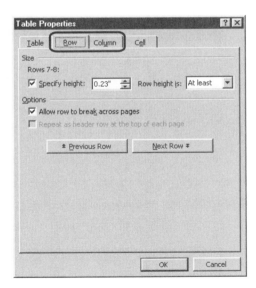

4. In the **Specify height** box, type a row height measurement, or in the **Preferred width** box, type a column width measurement.

5. Click the **OK** button.

> **TIP** To quickly adjust a row height or column width, position the pointer over the boundary of the row or column you want to adjust until it changes to the resize pointer, and then drag to resize the row or column.

> **TIP** To align a table in a document, click in the table, choose Table ➢ Table Properties, click the Table tab, click the Left, Center, or Right box, click the Around box to wrap text to table sides if needed, and then click the OK button.

Merge and Split Table Cells

◆ To merge two or more cells into a single cell, select the cells you want to merge, and then choose **Table ➢ Merge Cells**.

◆ To split a cell into multiple cells, click the cell you want to split, and then choose **Table ➢ Split Cells**. The Split Cells dialog box opens. Enter the number of rows or columns (or both) you want to split the selected cell into, click the **Merge Cells Before Split** check box to clear it, and then click the **OK** button.

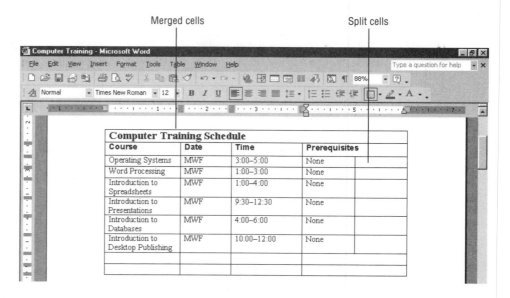

Merged cells   Split cells

> **TIP** To quickly merge two tables into one, delete the paragraph between them.

Formatting a Table

Tables distinguish text from paragraphs. In turn, formatting, alignment, and text direction distinguish text in table cells. Start by applying one of Word's predesigned table formats. Then customize your table by realigning the cells' contents both horizontally and vertically in the cells, changing the direction of text within selected cells, such as the column headings, and resizing the entire table. You can also add borders and shading to make printed tables easier to read and more attractive.

Format a Table Quickly

1. Select the table you want to format.

2. Choose **Table ➤ Table AutoFormat**. The Table AutoFormat dialog box opens.

3. Click a table style.

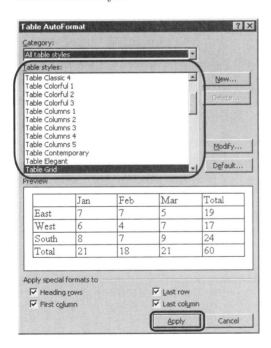

4. Click the **Apply** button.

> **TIP** You can also choose Format ➢ Border and Shading, and click the Borders tab or the Shading tab to format individual parts of a table.

> **TIP** To resize the entire table proportionally, click the place the insertion point in the table, and then drag the resize handle in the lower-right corner until the table is the size you want.

Align Text Within Cells

1. Click the **Tables and Borders** button 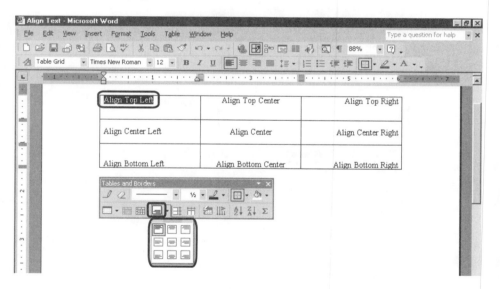 on the Standard toolbar. The Tables and Borders toolbar opens.

2. Select the cells, rows, or columns you want to align.

3. Click the **Align** button drop-down arrow on the Tables and Borders toolbar.

4. Click one of the alignment buttons on the menu.

Change Text Direction Within Cells

1. Click the **Tables and Borders** button 🔲 on the Standard toolbar. The Tables and Borders toolbar opens.

2. Select the cells you want to change.

3. Click the **Change Text Direction** button 🔲 on the Tables and Borders toolbar until the text is the direction you want.

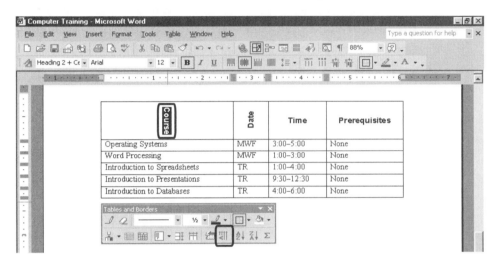

Creating a Form Letter

Did you ever send the same letter to several people and spend a lot of time changing personal information, such as names and addresses? If so, form letters will save you time. **Mail merge** is the process of combining names and addresses stored in a data file with a main document (usually a form letter) to produce customized documents. There are six main steps to merging. First, select the document type you want to use. Second, select a starting document. Third, create a data file with the variable information. Fourth, create the main document with the boilerplate (unchanging information) and merge fields. Fifth, merge the two and preview the results. Finally, personalize and print the individual letters. You can use the Mail Merge Wizard to merge a data source and a main document step by step. The Mail Merge Wizard can also be used to personalize large groups of e-mails, create mailing labels, address envelopes, and create **directories**.

Mail Merge
A process that combines a main document, such as a form letter, with a list, database, or other data document to create a new custom document.

Directory
Any document that contains recurring fields that are suitable for a merge, such as an inventory list, parts list, or catalog.

Create a Form Letter

1. Choose **Tools** ➢ **Letters and Mailings** ➢ **Mail Merge Wizard**. The Mail Merge task pane opens. Step 1 of 6 appears in the task pane.

2. Click a document type option button (such as **Letters**), and then click **Next** at the bottom of the task pane. Step 2 of 6 appears in the task pane.

3. Click a starting document option button (such as **Use the current document**), and then click **Next** at the bottom of the task pane. Step 3 of 6 appears in the task pane.

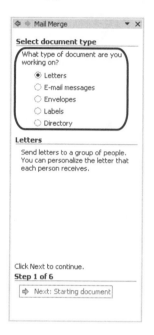 

4. Click a recipient option button (such as **Use an existing list**), click **Browse**, double-click a data document, click the **OK** button to select the mail recipients, and then click **Next** at the bottom of the task pane. Step 4 of 6 appears in the task pane.

5. Type your letter, click a location in the document, and then click one of the field items in the task pane (such as **Address block** or **Greeting line**), select the options you want, click the **OK** button, and then click **Next** at the bottom of the task pane. Step 5 of 6 appears in the task pane.

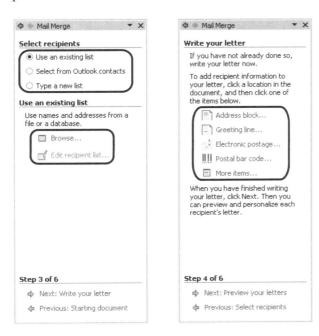

6. Preview the data in the letter and make any changes, and then click **Next** at the bottom of the task pane. Step 6 of 6 appears in the task pane.

7. Click **Print** in the task pane, select a print option, click the **OK** button, and then click the **OK** button to print the new document.

8. Click the **Close** button on the title bar in the Mail Merge task pane.

Creating a Worksheet with Excel

Are you spending too much time number-crunching, rewriting financial reports, drawing charts, or searching for your calculator? Throw away your pencil, graph paper, and calculator, and start using Microsoft Excel 2002.

Excel is a **spreadsheet program**, designed to help you record, analyze, and present quantitative information. With Excel you can track and analyze sales, organize finances, create budgets, and accomplish a variety of business tasks in a fraction of the time it would take using pen and paper. With Excel, you can create a variety of documents for analysis and record keeping, such as monthly sales and expense reports, charts displaying annual sales data, an inventory of products, or a payment schedule for an equipment purchase.

Excel offers several tools that make your worksheets look more attractive and professional. Without formatting, a worksheet can look like a sea of meaningless data. To highlight important information, you can change the appearance of selected numbers and text by adding dollar signs, commas, and other numerical formats, or by applying attributes such as boldface and italics.

Viewing the Excel Window

Spreadsheet program

A type of software you can use to enter, evaluate, manipulate, and communicate quantitative information.

Workbook

The file you create that contains one or more worksheets.

Worksheet

A page from a workbook that contains lines and grids.

Before you can begin using Excel, a **spreadsheet program**, you need to start the program. The easiest way to start Excel is to use the Start menu, which you open by clicking the Start button on the taskbar. When Excel starts, it displays a new **workbook**, which contains a collection of **worksheets.** Worksheets look similar to an accountant's ledger sheets, but can perform calculations and other tasks automatically.

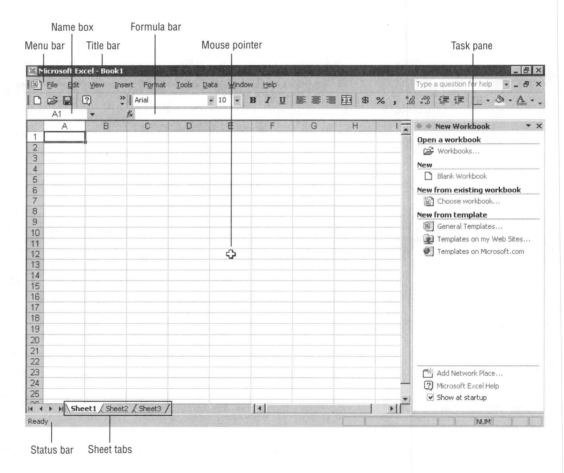

You can open more than one workbook window at a time. That means that if you are working with one workbook and need to check or work with data in another, you don't need to close the current file. You can view open windows one at a time, or arrange all of them on the screen at the same time, and then click the window in which you want to work. You can also move and resize each window to suit your viewing needs and work habits.

You can move around a worksheet or workbook using your mouse or the keyboard. You might find that using your mouse is most convenient when moving from cell to cell, while using various keyboard combinations is easier for covering large areas of a worksheet quickly. However, there is no one right way; whichever method feels the most comfortable is the one you should use. You can also use the Tab and arrow keys on the keyboard, but bear in mind if you are moving across several cells, arrow keys are less effective and can cause eyestrain.

Making Label Entries

Excel has three types of cell entries: labels, values, and formulas. Excel uses values and formulas to perform its calculations. A **label** is text in a cell that identifies the data on the worksheet so readers can interpret the information, such as titles or column headings. A **value** is a number you enter in a cell. To enter values easily and quickly, you can format a cell, a range of cells, or an entire column with a specific number-related format.

To perform a calculation in a worksheet, you enter a formula in a cell. A **formula** performs an operation on one or more cells. Excel calculates the formula based on cell references, values, and arithmetic operators. The result of a formula appears in the worksheet cell where you entered the formula. When you enter a formula in a cell, the contents appear on the formula bar. Entering cell references rather than actual values in a formula has distinct advantages. When you change the data in the worksheet (for example, changing the contents of cell C4 from .45 to .55) or copy the formula to other cells (copying a formula to the cell below), Excel automatically adjusts the cell references in the formula and returns the correct results.

When you press the Enter key on the keyboard, Excel's default is to move the active cell down one cell. To change the default direction, choose Tools ➤ Options, click the Edit tab, click the Direction drop-down arrow, select a direction, and then click the OK button.

Label
Cell text used in titles and column or row headings, and not included in calculations.

Value
The number you enter in a cell that is in calculations.

Formula
A series of values, cell references, and mathematical operators that results in a calculation.

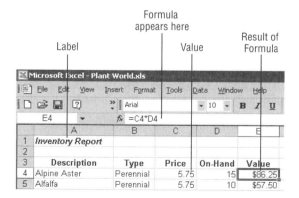

Label

Formula appears here

Value

Result of Formula

Select a Contiguous Range

In order to work with a cell—to enter data in it, edit or move it, or perform an action—you **select** the cell so it becomes the active cell. When you want to work with more than one cell at a time—to move or copy them, use them in a formula, or perform any group action—you must first select the cells as a **range**. A range can be **contiguous** (where selected cells are adjacent to each other) or **noncontiguous** (where the cells may be in different parts of the worksheet and are not adjacent to each other). As you select a range, you can see the range reference in the Name box. A **range reference** contains the cell address of the top-left cell in the range, a colon (:), and the cell address of the bottom-right cell in the range.

> **TIP** To deselect a range, click anywhere in the worksheet.

1. Click the first cell you want to include in the range.

2. Drag the mouse to the last cell you want to include in the range. When you select a range, the cell pointer surrounds the top-left cell, and Excel highlights the additional cells in color.

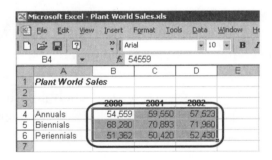

Select a Noncontiguous Range

1. Click the first cell you want to include in the range.

2. Drag the mouse to the last contiguous cell, and then release the mouse button.

3. Hold down the Ctrl key on the keyboard, and then click the next cell, or drag the mouse pointer over the next group of cells you want in the range.

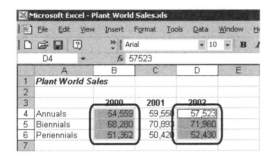

4. Repeat steps 3 and 4 until you select the cells you want.

Enter a Text Label

Labels turn a worksheet full of numbers into a meaningful report by identifying the different types of information it contains. You use labels to describe or identify the data in worksheet cells, columns, and rows. You can enter a number as a label (for example, the year 2002), so that Excel does not use the number in its calculations. To help keep your labels consistent, you can use Excel's **AutoComplete** feature, which automatically completes your entries based on the format of previously entered labels.

1. Click the cell where you want to enter a label.

2. Type a label. A label can include uppercase and lowercase letters, spaces, punctuation, and numbers.

3. Press the Enter key on the keyboard, or click the **Enter** button ☑ on the formula bar.

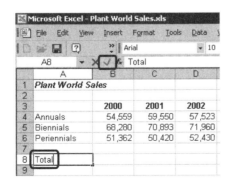

AutoComplete
A feature that finishes entering your text entries based on the entries you previously entered in a column. AutoComplete does not work with numbers, dates, or times.

You can accept an entry in different ways. After you've entered a value, you can click the Enter button on the formula bar to leave the insertion point in the active cell, or you can press the Enter key on the keyboard to move the insertion point down one cell on the worksheet.

Enter a Number as a Label

1. Click the cell where you want to enter a number as a label.

2. Type ′ (an apostrophe). The apostrophe is a label prefix and does not appear on the worksheet—it instructs Excel to treat the contents as text, not as a value.

3. Type a number. Examples of numbers that you might use as labels include a year, a tax form number, or a part number.

4. Press the Enter key on the keyboard, or click the **Enter** button ☑ on the formula bar.

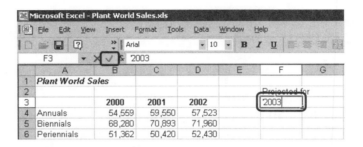

NOTE When you enter a label that is wider than the cell it occupies, the excess text appears to spill into the next cell to the right—unless there is data in the adjacent cell. If that cell contains data, the label will appear truncated—you'll only see the portion of the label that fits in the cell's current width. Click the cell to see its entire contents displayed on the formula bar.

Enter a Label Using AutoComplete

1. Type the first few characters of a label. If Excel recognizes the entry, AutoComplete completes it.

2. To accept the suggested entry, press the Enter key on the keyboard or click the **Enter** button 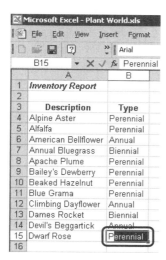 on the formula bar.

3. To reject the suggested completion, simply continue typing.

If you receive an error that Excel does not recognize the entry, verify that the AutoComplete option is turned on. To turn on the feature, click Tools ➢ Options ➢ Edit tab, click the Enable AutoComplete For Cell Values check box to select it, and then click the OK button.

Entering Values

You can enter values as whole numbers, decimals, percentages, or dates. You can enter values using the numbers on the top row of your keyboard, or the numeric keypad on the right side of your keyboard. When you enter a date or the time of day, Excel automatically recognizes these entries (if entered in an acceptable format) as numeric values and changes the cell's format to a default date, currency, or time format.

You can use the numeric keypad like a calculator to enter numbers on your worksheet. Before using the numeric keypad, make sure NUM appears in the lower-right corner of the status bar. If NUM is not displayed, you can turn on this feature by pressing the Num Lock key on the numeric keypad.

Enter a Value

1. Click the cell where you want to enter a value.

2. Type a value. To simplify your data entry, type the values without commas and dollar signs. You can apply a numeric format to them later.

3. Press the Enter key on the keyboard, or click the **Enter** button ☑ on the formula bar.

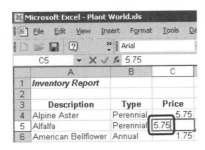

Enter Repeating Data Using AutoFill

AutoFill

A feature that fills in data based on entries in adjacent cells.

Fill handle

A tool that copies cell data or fills in a series of cells. When you select a cell, the fill handle is a small black box. When you point to the fill handle, it changes to a black plus sign.

To select additional AutoFill commands from the Edit menu, click Fill to select additional fill commands such as Up, Down, Left, Right, Series, or Justify

The **AutoFill** feature automatically fills in data based on the data in adjacent cells. Using the **fill handle**, you can enter data in a series, or you can copy values or formulas to adjacent cells. The entry in a cell can create an AutoFill that repeats a value or label, or the results can be a more complex extended series, such as days of the week, months of the year, or consecutive numbering.

1. Select the first cell in the range you want to fill.

2. Enter the starting value that you want to repeat.

3. Position the mouse pointer on the lower-right corner of the selected cell. The fill handle (a small black box) changes to the fill handle pointer (a black plus sign).

4. Drag the fill handle pointer over the range where you want to repeat the value.

Fill handle
pointer

7	Annual Bluegrass	Biennial	4.50
8	Apache Plume	Perennial	5.75
9	Bailey's Dewberry		5.75
10	Beaked Hazelnut		5.75
11	Blue Grama		5.75
12	Climbing Dayflower	Annual	1.75
13	Dames Rocket	Biennial	4.50
14	Devil's Beggartick	Annual	1.75

Perennial

Create a Complex Series Using AutoFill

1. Select the first cell in the range you want to fill.

2. Enter the starting value for the series, and then click the **Enter** button ✓ on the formula bar.

3. Position the mouse pointer on the lower-right corner of the selected cell, and then hold down the Ctrl key on the keyboard. The pointer changes to the fill handle pointer (a black plus sign with a smaller plus sign)

4. Drag the fill handle pointer over the range where you want the value extended. The destination value appears in a small box by the fill handle pointer.

On-Hand	Value	Item #
15	$86.25	101
10	$57.50	
6	$10.50	
12	$54.00	
24	$138.00	
15	$86.25	

104

Editing Cell Contents

No matter how much you plan, you always can count on having to make changes to a worksheet. Sometimes it's because you want to correct an error or see how your worksheet results would be affected by different conditions, such as higher sales, producing fewer units, or other variables. You can edit data just as easily as you entered it: using the formula bar or directly editing the active cell.

TIP To edit cell contents using the formula bar, click the cell you want to edit, click on the formula bar, and then edit the cell contents.

NOTE To change editing options, choose Tools ➤ Options ➤ Edit tab, change the editing options you want, and then click the OK button.

Edit Cell Contents

1. Double-click the cell you want to edit. The insertion point appears in the cell. (The status bar now displays Edit instead of Ready.)

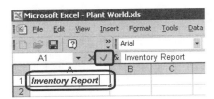

2. If necessary, use the Home, End, and arrow keys on the keyboard to position the insertion point in the cell contents.

3. Use any combination of the Backspace and Delete keys on the keyboard to erase unwanted characters, and then type new characters as needed.

4. Click the **Enter** button ✓ on the formula bar or press the Enter key on the keyboard to accept the edit, or click the **Cancel** button to cancel it.

Clear Cell Contents, Formatting, and Comments

You can clear a cell to remove its contents. Clearing a cell does not remove the cell from the worksheet; it just removes contents from the cell. When clearing a cell, you must specify whether to remove one, two, or all three of these elements from the selected cell or range.

1. Select the cell or range you want to clear.

2. Choose **Edit** ➢ **Clear**.

3. Click **All**, **Formats**, **Contents**, or **Comments**.

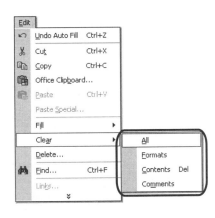

You can search for a value or data in a cell and then replace it with different content. Click the cell or cells containing content you want to replace. Choose Edit ➢ Find ➢ Replace tab for additional options.

Inserting and Deleting Cells

You can insert new, blank cells anywhere on the worksheet in order to enter new data or insert data that you forgot to enter earlier. Inserting cells moves the remaining cells in the column or row in the direction of your choice, and Excel adjusts any formulas so they refer to the correct cells. You can also delete cells if you find you don't need them; deleting cells shifts the remaining cells to the left or up—just the opposite of inserting cells. When you delete a cell, Excel removes the actual cell from the worksheet, not just the data it contains.

Deleting a cell removes the cell from the worksheet. When you choose Delete from the Edit menu or from the shortcut menu, you can choose to shift the remaining cells left or up, or to remove the entire row or column.

Insert a Cell

1. Select the cell or cells where you want to insert the new cell(s). For example, to insert two blank cells at the position of C10 and C11, select cells C10 and C11.

2. Choose **Insert ➤ Cells**. The Insert dialog box opens.

3. Click the option you want.

❖ If you want the contents of cells C10 and C11 to move to cells D10 and D11, click the **Shift Cells Right** option button.

❖ If you want the contents of cells C10 and C11 to move to cells C12 and C13, click the **Shift Cells Down** option button.

By using either method, you will replace two blank cells with the data that was in cells C10 and C11.

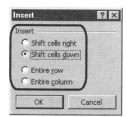

4. Click the **OK** button.

TIP Deleting a cell is different from clearing a cell: deleting removes the cells from the worksheet; clearing removes only the cell content.

Delete a Cell

1. Select the cell or range you want to delete.

2. Choose **Edit ➢ Delete**. The Delete dialog box opens.

3. Click the option you want.

   ❖ If you want the remaining cells to move left, click the **Shift Cells Left** option button.

   ❖ If you want the remaining cells to move up, click the **Shift Cells Up** option button.

4. Click the **OK** button.

Selecting and Naming a Worksheet

Active sheet

The sheet on which you are currently working.

By default, each new workbook you open contains three worksheets, although you can add additional sheets. You can easily switch among the sheets to enter or modify related information, such as budget data for separate months. Whichever sheet you are working on is the **active sheet**. Excel names each sheet consecutively—Sheet1, Sheet2, Sheet3, and so on. When you can rename a sheet to give it a more meaningful name; the size of the sheet tab adjusts to accommodate the name's length, up to 30 characters.

NOTE   Although the size of a sheet tab can expand to display a long tab name, a shorter tab name ensures that more sheet tabs to be visible. Being able to see all the sheet tabs is especially important if your workbook contains several worksheets.

Select a Worksheet

1. Move the mouse pointer over the sheet tab of the worksheet you want to make active.

2. Click the sheet tab of the worksheet you want to make active.

Name a Worksheet

1. Double-click the sheet tab of the worksheet you want to name.

2. Type a new name. Excel automatically replaces the current name, which is selected when you begin typing.

3. Press the Enter key on the keyboard.

Insert a Worksheet

You can add or delete sheets in a workbook. If, for example, you are working on a project that requires more than three worksheets, you can insert additional sheets in one workbook rather than open multiple workbooks. If, on the other hand, you are using only one or two sheets in a workbook, you can delete the unused sheets to save disk space.

1. Click the sheet tab of the worksheet to the right of where you want to insert the new sheet.

2. Choose **Insert** ➢ **Worksheet**. Excel inserts a new worksheet to the left of the selected worksheet.

Delete a Worksheet

1. Click the sheet tab of the worksheet you want to delete, or click any cell on the sheet.

2. Choose **Edit** ➢ **Delete Sheet**.

3. Click the **Delete** button to confirm the deletion.

Move a Worksheet Within a Workbook

After adding several sheets to a workbook, you might want to reorganize them. You can arrange sheets in chronological order or in order of their importance. You can easily move or copy a sheet within a workbook or to a different open workbook. Copying a worksheet is easier and often more convenient than reentering similar information on a new sheet.

1. Click the sheet tab of the worksheet you want to move, and then hold down the mouse button.

2. When the mouse pointer changes to a sheet of paper, drag it to the right of the sheet tab where you want to move the worksheet.

3. Release the mouse button.

Copy a Worksheet

1. Click the sheet tab of the worksheet you want to copy.

2. Choose **Edit** ➢ **Move or Copy Sheet**. The Move or Copy dialog box opens.

3. If you want to copy the sheet to another open workbook, click the **To Book** drop-down arrow 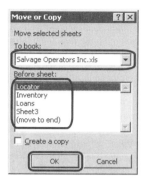, and then select the name of that workbook. The sheets of the selected workbook appear in the Before Sheet list.

4. Click a sheet name in the **Before Sheet** list. Excel inserts the copy to the left of this sheet.

5. Click the **Create a copy** check box to select it.

6. Click the **OK** button.

Working with Columns or Rows

You can select one or more columns or rows in a worksheet in order to apply formatting attributes, insert or delete columns or rows, or perform other group actions. The **header buttons** above each column and to the left of each row indicate the letter or number of the column or row. You can select multiple columns or rows even if they are non-contiguous.

Select a Column or Row

1. Click the column or row header button of the column or row you want to select.

	A	B	C	D
1	**Salvage Operators**			
2				
3	Automobile	Part	Purchase	Sales
4			Price	Price
5	1975 Chrysler Newport	Distributor	5.00	$9.50
6	964 Dodge Pickup	Driver's door	15.00	$25.50
7	1982 Chevy Cavalier	Hood	20.00	$32.50
8	1989 Pontiac Grand Am	Tail light lens	5.00	$7.00
9	1987 Toyota Camry LE	Seat belt glide	4.50	$7.95
10	1979 Volkswagon Rabbit	Hatch door	25.00	$42.75
11				

Row header button

Header buttons
Buttons at the top of each column and to the left of each row that you can click to select an entire column or row.

> **TIP** To select contiguous multiple columns or rows, drag the mouse over the header buttons of any contiguous columns or rows you want to select. To select non-contiguous columns or rows, hold down the Ctrl key on the keyboard while clicking each additional column or row header button.

Insert a Column or Row

You can insert blank columns and rows between columns and rows on a worksheet without disturbing any existing data. Excel repositions existing cells to accommodate the new columns and rows and adjusts any existing formulas so that they refer to the correct cells. When you insert one or more columns, Excel inserts them to the left of the selected column. When you add one or more rows, Excel inserts them above the selected row.

1. To insert a column, click anywhere in the column to the right of the location of the new column you want to insert. To insert a row, click anywhere in the row immediately below the location of the row you want to insert.

2. Choose **Insert** ➤ **Columns** (or **Rows**).

Excel inserts a new column to the left of the selected column; Excel inserts a new row above the selected row.

> **TIP** To insert multiple columns, drag the column or row header buttons for the number of columns or rows you want to insert. Choose Insert ➤ Columns (or Rows).

Delete a Column or Row

At some time, you may want to remove an entire column or row from a worksheet, rather than deleting or editing individual cells. You can delete columns and rows just as easily as you insert them. You can choose whether the remaining columns and rows move to the left or move up to join the other remaining cells.

1. Click the column or row header button of the column(s) or row(s) you want to delete.

2. Choose **Edit** ➢ **Delete**.

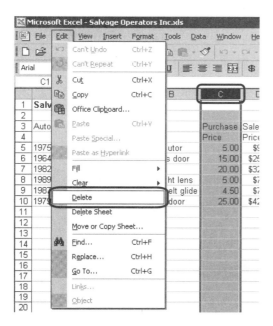

Change Column Width Using AutoFit

As you build your worksheet, you'll want to change the default width of some columns or the default height of some rows to accommodate long strings of data or larger font sizes. Changing the width of a column or the height of a row will enhance the readability of your worksheet. You can manually change column widths or row heights, or you can use the **AutoFit** feature. Excel automatically adjusts column or row size to fit data you have entered.

AutoFit
A feature that automatically resizes a column or row to the width/height of its largest entry.

1. Position the mouse pointer on the right edge of the header button of the column you want to adjust. The pointer changes to a double-headed arrow.

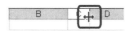

2. Double-click the mouse button. The column width automatically adjusts to fit the longest cell entry in the column.

TIP The Narrow Column ToolTip shows you the value in a column that is too narrow to display its contents. If a value does not fit in the column, the value displays as ##### in the cell.

Change Row Height Using AutoFit

1. Position the mouse pointer on the bottom edge of the header button of the row you want to adjust. The pointer changes to a double-headed arrow.

2. Double-click the mouse button. The row height automatically adjusts to fit the largest font size.

Adjust Column Width or Row Height Using the Mouse

1. Position the mouse pointer on the right edge of the column header button or the bottom edge of the row header button for the column or row you want to change.

2. When the mouse pointer changes to a double-headed arrow, drag the pointer to a new width or height.

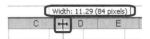

Formatting Text and Numbers

You can change the appearance of the data in the cells of a worksheet without changing the actual value in the cell. You can **format** text and numbers with font **attributes**, such as bolding, italics, or underlining, in order to catch the reader's attention. You can also apply **numeric formats** to numbers to accurately reflect the type of information they represent—dollar amounts, dates, decimals, and so on. For example, you can format a number to display up to 15 decimal places, or none at all.

By default, each column in each worksheet is 8.43 points wide, and each row is 12.75 points high. A point is a unit of measurement used to size text and space on a worksheet. One inch equals 72 points.

Format
Cosmetically enhance the appearance of label and values in a worksheet.

Attributes
Effects that change the appearance of characters.

Numeric formats
Displaying values in different formats, such as changing the number of decimal places or whether currency symbols appear.

To freeze column or row headings so they are always visible on the screen, select the column to the right or the row below the one you want to freeze, and then choose Window ➢ Freeze Panes. To unfreeze headings, select the column or row, and then choose Window Unfreeze ➢ Pane.

Change the Appearance of a Number Quickly

1. Select a cell or range that contains the number(s) that you want format.

2. Click the **Toolbar Options** drop-down arrow ➤ to display numeric formatting buttons, if necessary.

3. Click a formatting button to apply the numeric attribute that you want the selected range. You can continue to apply attributes as long as you select the range.

Button	Name	Example
B	Bold	**Excel**
I	Italic	*Excel*
U	Underline	<u>Excel</u>
$	Currency Style	$5,432.10
%	Percent Style	54.32%
,	Comma Style	5,432.10
.00	Increase Decimal	5,432.10 becomes 5,432.100
.00	Decrease Decimal	5,432.10 becomes 5,432.1

Format a Number Using the Format Cells Dialog Box

1. Select a cell or range that contains the number(s) format.

2. Choose **Format** ➢ **Cells**, and then click the **Number** tab. The Format Cells dialog box opens.

3. Click a category in the list. The options available for each category appear on the right side of the Format Cells dialog box.

4. Select the options that you want apply. You can preview your selections in the Sample box.

5. Click the **OK** button.

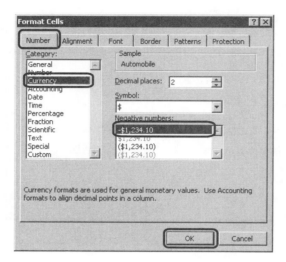

TIP   To quickly open the Format Cells dialog box, right-click a selected cell or range, and then click Format Cells on the shortcut menu.

Changing Data Alignment

When you enter data in a cell, Excel aligns labels on the left edge of the cell and aligns values and formulas on the right edge of the cell. **Horizontal alignment** is the way in which Excel aligns the contents of a cell relative to the left or right edge of the cell; **vertical alignment** is the way in which Excel aligns cell contents relative to the top and bottom of the cell. Excel also provides an option for changing the character flow and rotation of text in a cell. You can select the **orientation** of the text in a cell to be vertical or horizontal. You can tilt, or rotate text in horizontal orientation up or down. The default orientation is 0 degrees—the text is level in a cell.

Horizontal alignment
Aligning cell contents relative to the left and right edge of the cell.

Vertical alignment
Aligning cell contents relative to the top and bottom edge of the cell.

Orientation
The appearance of cell text, which can be level or tilted or rotated horizontally up or down.

158

> **NOTE** You can use the Format Cells dialog box to select other alignment options, but for centering text across columns and simple left, right, and center alignment, it's easier to use the Formatting toolbar buttons.

Change Alignment Using the Formatting Toolbar

1. Select a cell or range containing the data to be realigned.

2. Click the **Align Left**, **Center**, **Align Right**, or **Merge And Center** button on the Formatting toolbar.

Changing Data Color

You can change the color of the numbers and text on a worksheet. The strategic use of font color can be an effective way of visually uniting similar values. For example, on a sales worksheet you might want to display sales in blue and returns in red.

The Font Color button on the Formatting toolbar displays the last font color you used. To apply this color to another selection, simply click the button.

Change Font Color Using the Formatting Toolbar

1. Select a cell or range that contains the text you want change.

2. Click the **Font Color** button drop-down arrow on the Formatting toolbar.

3. Click a color.

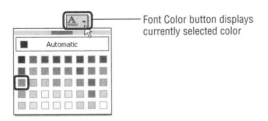
Font Color button displays currently selected color

Adding Color and Patterns to Cells

You can fill the background of a cell with a color or a pattern so that the data stands out. Fill colors and patterns can also lend consistency to related information on a worksheet. For example, on a sales worksheet, you can format the second-quarter sales figures with a blue background and the fourth-quarter sales with a yellow background so that each group is easily identifiable. You can use fill colors and patterns in conjunction with text attributes, fonts, and font colors to further enhance the appearance of your worksheet.

 When you paint a format using the Format Painter button on the Standard toolbar, Excel also copies the fill colors and patterns to the selected cell or range.

Choose a Fill Color Using the Formatting Toolbar

1. Select a cell or range.

2. Click the **Fill Color** button drop-down arrow on the Formatting toolbar.

3. Click a color.

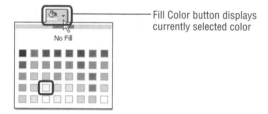

Fill Color button displays currently selected color

Adding Borders to Cells

You've probably noticed the light gray grid that displays on the worksheet screen and discovered that it helps your eyes track from cell to cell. By default, Excel does not include this grid on printouts, but you can choose to print gridlines or alter on the grid pattern by adding different types of borders to a worksheet. You can add borders of varying line widths and colors to some or all sides of a single cell or cell range.

NOTE
You can use the Format Cells command to format a border. To apply a border color other than the default (black), select the range to which you want to apply a border. Right-click the range, then choose Format Cells ➢ Border tab. Select the color you want for the border from the color palette, and then click the OK button.

TIP
To place a border around the entire worksheet, click the Select All button at the top left of your worksheet, and then apply the border.

Apply a Border Using the Formatting Toolbar

1. Select a cell or range to which you want to apply a border.

2. Click the **Borders** button drop-down arrow ⊞ ▾ on the Formatting toolbar to select a border. The most recently selected style displays on the Borders button.

3. Select a border from the border palette.

Formatting Data with AutoFormat

Formatting worksheet data can be a lot of fun but also very time-consuming. To make formatting data more efficient, Excel includes 18 AutoFormats. An **AutoFormat** includes a combination of fill colors and patterns, numeric formats, font attributes, borders, and font colors that are professionally designed to enhance your worksheets. If you don't select any cells before choosing the AutoFormat command, Excel will "guess" which data should be formatted.

AutoFormat
Pre-designed format that you can apply to data ranges, and include numeric formats and font attributes.

> **TIP**
> AutoFormat overrides previous formatting. When you apply an AutoFormat, it erases any existing formatting

Apply an AutoFormat

1. Select a cell or range to which you want to apply an AutoFormat, or skip this step if you want Excel to "guess" which cells to format.

2. Choose **Format ➤ AutoFormat**. Samples of each AutoFormat style appear in the AutoFormat dialog box.

3. Click an AutoFormat in the list. Refer to each sample to see the type of formatting that will apply.

4. Click the **Options** button. Additional options appear at the bottom of the dialog box.

5. Click one or more **Formats To Apply** check boxes to turn a feature on or off.

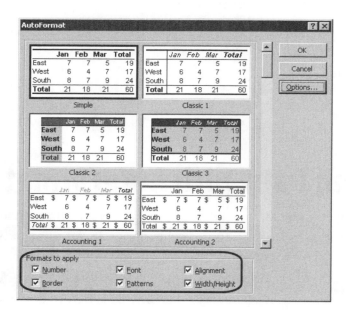

6. Click the **OK** button.

8 Designing a Worksheet with Excel

Once you enter the data on a worksheet, you'll want to add formulas to calculate values. You can create your own formulas or insert built-in formulas, called **functions**, for more complex computations.

In addition to using a worksheet to calculate values, you can also use it to manage a list of information, called a **list** or **database**. You can use an Excel worksheet to keep an inventory list, a school grade book, or a customer database. You can enter information directly on a worksheet, or use a **Data Form**, which lets you quickly enter information by filling in blank text boxes, similar to a paper form. Excel provides a variety of tools that make it easy to keep lists up-to-date and analyze them to get the information you want quickly. Excel's data analysis tools include alphabetical organizing (called **sorting**), and collecting information that meets specific criteria (called **filtering**).

When you're ready to share data with others, a worksheet might not be the most effective way to present the information. Excel makes it easy to create and modify a **chart**, also called a **graph**, which is a visual representation of selected data in your worksheet. When you're ready to print your workbook, you can choose to print all or part of the worksheets, and add headers and footers to create a professional look.

Creating a Simple Formula

Formula

A series of values, cell references, and mathematical operators that results in a calculation.

A **formula** calculates values to return a result. In an Excel worksheet, you create a formula using values (such as *147* or *$10.00*), arithmetic operators (shown in the table below), and cell references (such as *B3:F20*). An Excel formula always begins with the equal sign (=). By default, Excel displays the results of the formula in a cell, but you can change your view of the worksheet to display formulas instead of results.

> **NOTE** When you build a formula that uses cell references, you can click a cell in your spreadsheet to add it to your formula, rather than typing its address. Clicking the precise cell ensures that you reference the correct cell.

Enter a Formula

1. Click the cell where you want to enter a formula.

2. Type =(an equal sign). If you do not begin a formula with an equal sign, Excel will display the information you type as text, instead of using the data in a calculation.

Argument

The cell references or values in a formula that contribute to the result. Each function uses function-specific arguments, which may include numeric values, text values, cell references, ranges of cells, and so on.

3. Enter the first **argument**. An argument can be a number or a cell reference. If it is a cell reference, you can type the reference or click the cell on the worksheet.

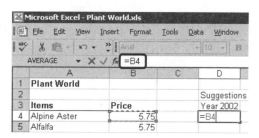

4. Enter an arithmetic operator (such as * [an asterisk] for multiplication).

5. Enter the next argument.

6. Repeat steps 4 and 5 as needed to complete the formula.

7. Click the **Enter** button ☑ on the formula bar, or press the Enter key on the keyboard. Notice that the result of the formula appears in the cell. If you select the cell, the formula appears on the formula bar.

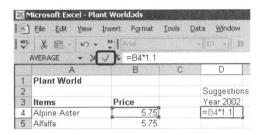

NOTE   You can use the order of precedence to create correct formulas. Excel calculates formulas that contain more than one operator according to the order of precedence: exponentiation, multiplication and division, and finally, addition and subtraction. Therefore, in the formula *(5+2) * 3*, Excel performs multiplication first and addition next for a result of 11. Excel calculates operations within parentheses first. Thus, the result of the formula *(5+2) * 3* is 21.

Editing a Formula

You can edit formulas just as you do other cell contents: use the formula bar or work in the cell. You can select, cut, copy, paste, delete, and format cells that contain formulas, just as you do cells that contain labels or values. Using AutoFill, you can quickly copy formulas to adjacent cells. If you need to copy formulas to different parts of a worksheet, use the Windows Clipboard or Office Clipboard.

Edit a Formula Using the Formula Bar

1. Select the cell that contains the formula you want to edit.

2. Press the F2 key on the keyboard to change to **Edit mode**.

3. If necessary, use the Home, End, and arrow keys on the keyboard to position the cursor within the cell contents.

4. Use any combination of the Backspace and Delete keys on the keyboard to erase unwanted characters, and then type new characters as needed.

Edit mode
Status bar state indicating that you can edit the contents of a cell.

5. Click the **Enter** button ☑ on the formula bar, or press the Enter key on the keyboard.

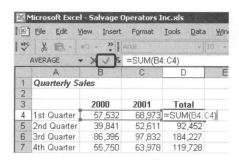

Copy a Formula Using AutoFill

1. Select the cell that contains the formula you want to copy.

2. Position the fill handle pointer on the lower-right corner of the selected cell.

3. Drag the mouse down until you select the adjacent cells where you want to paste the formula, and then release the mouse button.

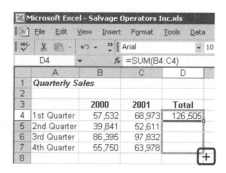

NOTE   You can use the Paste Special command to copy formulas only. Select the cells that contain the formulas you want to copy, click where you want to paste the data, choose Edit ➢ Paste Special, click the Formulas option button, and then click the OK button.

Performing Calculations Using Functions

Functions are pre-designed formulas that save you the time and trouble of creating commonly used or complex equations. Excel includes hundreds of functions that you can use alone or in combination with other formulas or functions. Functions perform a variety of calculations, from adding, averaging, and counting to more complicated tasks, such as calculating the monthly payment amount of a loan. You can enter a function manually if you know its name and all the required arguments, or you can easily insert a function using the Paste Function feature.

Functions
Built-in formulas that make it easy to create complex calculations that involve one or more values, performing an operation, and returning one or more values.

Enter a Function

1. Click the cell where you want to enter the function.

2. Type = (an equal sign), type the name of the function, and then type ((an open parenthesis). For example, to insert the SUM function, type *=SUM(*.

3. Type the argument or select the cell or range you want to insert in the function.

4. Click the **Enter** button ✓ on the formula bar, or press the Enter key on the keyboard. Excel automatically completes the function by adding a close parenthesis.

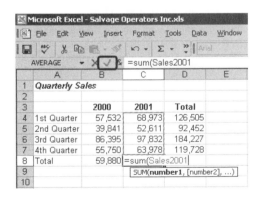

Function	Description	Sample
SUM	Displays the sum of the argument	=SUM(*argument*)
AVERAGE	Displays the average value in the argument	=AVERAGE(*argument*)
COUNT	Calculates the number of values in the argument	=COUNT(*argument*)
MAX	Determines the largest value in the argument	=MAX(*argument*)
MIN	Determines the smallest value in the argument	=MIN(*argument*)
PMT	Determines the payment of a loan	=PMT(*argument*)

Enter a Function Using the Insert Function

Insert Function

Feature that organizes Excel's functions and makes it easy to create a complex calculation.

Trying to write a formula that calculates various pieces of data, such as calculating payments for an investment over a period of time at a certain rate, can be difficult and time-consuming. The **Insert Function** feature organizes Excel's functions into categories so they are easy to find and to use. A function defines all the necessary components (also called arguments) you need to produce a specific result; all you have to do is supply the values, cell references, and other variables. You can even combine one or more functions if necessary.

1. Click the cell where you want to enter the function.

2. Click the **Insert Function** button ƒx on the formula bar. The Insert Function dialog box opens.

3. Click a function you want to use. A description of the selected function appears at the bottom of the Insert Function dialog box.

4. Click the **OK** button.

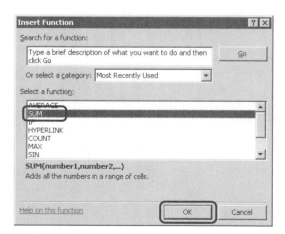

5. Enter the cell addresses in the text boxes. Type them or click the **Collapse Dialog** button to the right of the text box, select the cell or range using your mouse, and then click the **Expand Dialog** button. In many cases, the Insert Function might try to "guess" which cells you want to include in the function.

Collapse
Dialog button

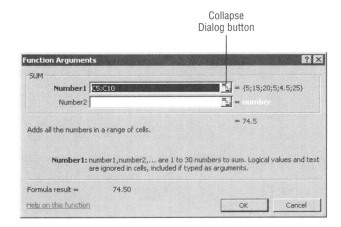

6. Click the **OK** button.

Creating a Chart

You have to make many decisions when you create a chart, from selecting the chart type, to adding and formatting objects. Excel simplifies the process with a feature called the Chart Wizard. The **Chart Wizard** is a series of dialog boxes that lead you through all the steps necessary to create an effective, eye-catching chart. In Excel 2002, the Chart Wizard includes additional 3-D combination charts and options to format data, multi-level axes, and time-scale labels. After you create your chart, you can always make changes to it.

Chart Wizard
A series of dialog boxes that require your input in order to create a chart.

TIP To move backward or forward in the Chart Wizard, click the Back button or the Forward button. You can click the Finish button at any time.

Create a Chart Using the Chart Wizard

1. Select the data range you want to chart. Include the column and row labels in the data range. Excel will automatically add the labels to the chart.

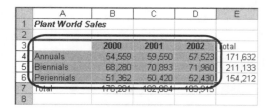

2. Click the **Chart Wizard** button 📊 on the Standard toolbar.

3. Click a chart type, and then click a chart sub-type.

4. If you want, click the **Press And Hold To View Sample** button to preview your chart as you build it.

5. Click the **Next** button to continue.

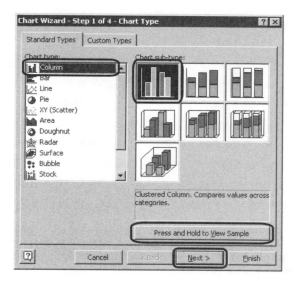

NOTE Before you choose a chart type, try to imagine how your audience will view the chart. Pretend that you're seeing the chart for the first time. Can you easily grasp the pertinent information? If not, how can you improve it?

TIP When you choose to place the chart on an existing sheet, rather than on a new sheet, the chart is called an embedded object. You can then resize or move it just as you would any graphic object.

6. Make sure you've selected the correct data range. If the data range is incorrect, click the **Collapse Dialog** button to the right of the text box and select the data range.

7. Select the appropriate option button to plot the data series in rows or in columns.

8. Click the **Next** button to continue.

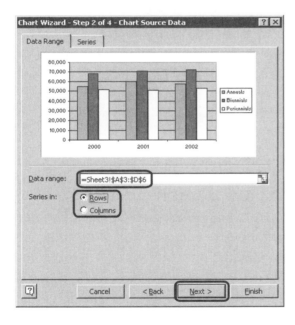

9. Type titles in the appropriate text boxes to identify each category of data. If you want, click other tabs to change additional chart options.

10. Click the **Next** button to continue.

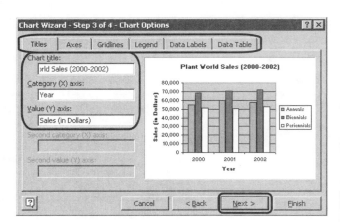

11. Click an option to choose whether to place the chart on a new work-sheet or embed it on an existing worksheet.

12. Click the **Finish** button.

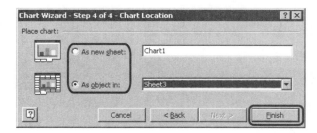

Editing a Chart

When you edit a chart, you alter its features, which can include selecting data or formatting elements. For example, you might want to use different colors or patterns in a data series. To change the type of chart or any element in it, you must first select the chart or element. When you select a chart, **handles** display around the window's perimeter, and the Chart toolbar displays on screen (docked or floating). When you select a chart, all of buttons on this toolbar become active. You can use the ScreenTip feature to display the data value and the name of any object or area on a chart. When you select an object in a chart, the name of the object appears in the Chart Objects list box on the Chart tool-bar, which indicates that you can now edit the object.

Editing a chart does not affect the data used to create it. You don't need to worry about updating a chart if you change data in the worksheet, because

Excel automatically updates the chart. You can change the data range at any time. If you want to plot more or less data in a range, you can select the data series on the worksheet, and then drag the range to the chart.

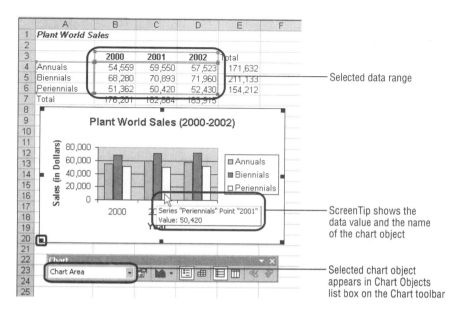

Selected data range

ScreenTip shows the data value and the name of the chart object

Selected chart object appears in Chart Objects list box on the Chart toolbar

Select and Deselect a Chart Object

1. Select a chart. The Chart toolbar appears when you select a chart.

2. Position the mouse pointer over a chart object, click the object to select it, or click the **Chart Objects** drop-down arrow on the Chart toolbar, and then click the name of the object you want to select.

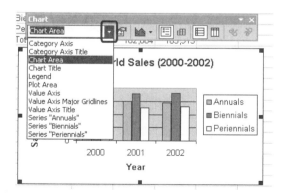

3. Click another area of the chart, or press the Esc key on the keyboard to deselect a chart object.

Changing a Chart Type

Excel's default chart type is the column chart, although there are many other types from which to choose. A column chart might adequately display your data, but you should experiment with a variety of chart types to find the one that shows your data in the most effective way.

TIP To quickly apply another chart type, click the chart to select it, click the Chart Wizard button on the Standard toolbar, and then choose a different chart type. You can also right-click the chart, and then click Chart Type.

Change a Chart Type Quickly

1. Select a chart whose chart type you want to change.

2. Click the **Chart Type** button drop-down arrow 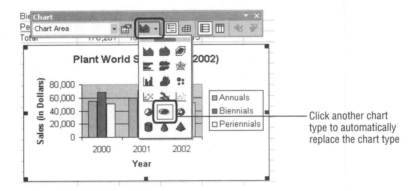 on the Chart toolbar.

3. Select a chart type. Excel automatically changes the chart type when you release the mouse button.

Click another chart type to automatically replace the chart type

Adding and Deleting a Data Series

Data Series
A group of related data points in a datasheet or worksheet.

Data Point
A single value in a data series.

Many components make up a chart. Each range of data that comprises a bar, column, or pie slice is called a **data series**; each value in a data series is called a **data point**. The data series is defined when you select a range on a worksheet and then open the Chart Wizard. However, what if you want to add a data series once a chart is complete? You can add a data series by using the mouse, the Chart menu, or the Chart Wizard. As you create and modify additional charts using the same data, you might find it helpful to delete or change the order of one or more data series. You can delete a data series without re-creating the chart.

Add a Data Series to a Chart Quickly

1. Select the range that contains the data series that you want to add to your chart.

2. Drag the range into the existing chart.

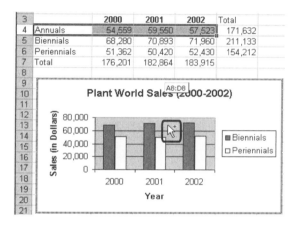

3. Release the mouse button.

TIP To delete a data series, select the chart, click any data point in the data series, and then press the Delete key.

Enhancing a Data Series

When you initially use the Chart Wizard, Excel automatically selects the colors that it will use to represent each data series. You can change one or all of the default colors. You may want more dynamic colors—adding patterns and texture to further enhance a data series. Or, perhaps you'll be printing your charts in black and white and you want to ensure the readability of each data series. You can also insert a picture in a chart so that its image occupies a bar or column.

TIP   To format a chart object quickly, double-click an object to open a corresponding Format dialog box, which you can use to change the object's attributes. Depending on which objects are selected, your formatting options will vary.

Change a Data Series Color or Pattern

1. Click any data point in a data series to select it.

2. Double-click a data point in the selected data series.

3. Click the **Patterns** tab.

4. Click a color in the Area palette. The selected color displays in the Sample box.

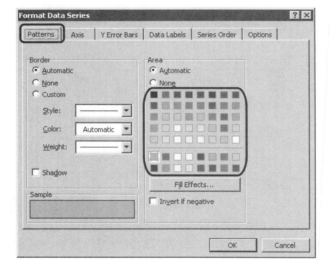

5. If you want to add effects, such as textures, patterns, gradients, or pictures, click the **Fill Effects** button. The Fill Effects dialog box opens.

6. Click the **Gradient**, **Texture**, or **Pattern** tab to change the qualities of the data series color.

7. When you're done, click the **OK** button.

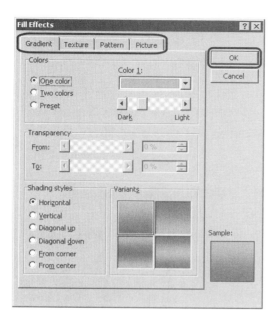

8. Click the **OK** button if you're satisfied with the results shown in the Sample box, or select different options.

Enhancing a Chart

Add chart options to enhance the appearance of the chart and increase its overall effectiveness. Chart options include **chart objects** such as titles, legends, text annotations, and gridlines. A **chart title** identifies the primary purpose of the chart; adding a title for each axis also clarifies the data that you're plotting. Titles can be any length and you can format them just like other worksheet text. A **legend** helps the reader connect the colors and patterns in a chart with the data they represent. **Gridlines** are horizontal and vertical lines that help the reader determine data point values in a chart. You can modify legends and gridlines at any time.

Add a Title

1. Select a chart to which you want to add one or more titles.

2. Choose **Chart** ➢ **Chart Options**, and then click the **Titles** tab.

3. In the **Chart title** box, type the text you want for the title of the chart.

Chart Objects
Individual items within a chart (such as a title or legend) that you can select and modify.

Chart Title
Text you can insert to clarify the purpose of the chart.

Legend
An identifier that matches colors or patterns in the chart with data.

Gridlines
Horizontal or vertical lines of a specified width and interval that aid in a chart's readability.

4. To add a title for the x-axis, press the Tab key on the keyboard, and then type the text in the **Category (x) axis** box.

5. To add a title for the y-axis, press the Tab key on the keyboard, and then type the text in the **Category (y) axis** box.

6. If you want a second line for the x-axis or y-axis, press the Tab key on the keyboard to move to the **Second category (x) axis** or **Second value (y) axis** box, and then type the title text (if available).

7. Click the **OK** button.

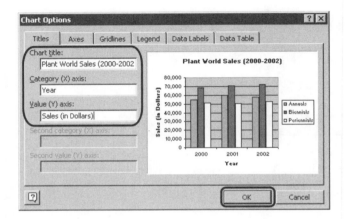

Add or Delete a Legend

1. Select the chart to which you want to add or delete a legend.

2. Click the **Legend** button ⊞ on the Chart toolbar. You can drag the legend to move it to a new location.

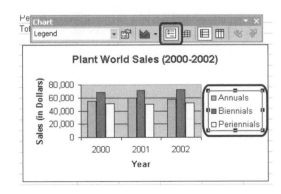

Legend text is derived from the data series plotted within a chart. You can rename an item within a legend by changing the text in the data series.

> **NOTE** Major gridlines occur at each value on an axis; minor gridlines occur between values on an axis. Use gridlines sparingly and only when adding them improves the readability of a chart.

Understanding List Terminology

A database is a collection of related records. Examples of databases are an address book, a customer list, product inventory, and a telephone directory. In Excel, a database is referred to as **list**, and consists of the following components.

List range. The block of cells that contains the list or part of the list you want to analyze. A list range can occupy no more than one worksheet.

Record. One set of related fields, such as all the fields pertaining to one customer or one product. On a worksheet, each row represents one record.

Field name. The title given to a field. In an Excel list, the first row contains the names of each field. The maximum length for a field name is 255 characters, including upper case and lower case letters and spaces.

Field. One piece of information, such as a customer's last name or an item's code number. On a worksheet, each column represents a field.

List
A collection of related records in an Excel worksheet.

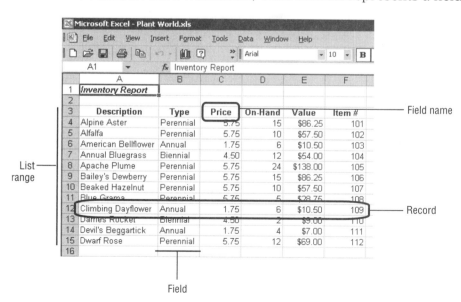

Creating a List

To create a list in Excel, you enter data in worksheet cells, just as you do when you create any worksheet. You can enter records in any order and sort them at any time. When you create a list, you need to follow a few rules:

- Enter field names as the top row in adjacent columns in a list.

- Enter each record in a single row, with each field in the column corresponding to the correct field name.

- Do not include any blank rows within the list range.

- Do not use more than one worksheet for a single list range.

Enter Data in a List

1. Open a blank worksheet, or use a worksheet that has a sufficient number of empty columns and rows for the list.

2. Enter a name for each field across the first row.

3. Enter the field information for each record in the row, directly beneath the field names. Adjust column width as necessary.

Sorting Data in a List

Sorting

Alphabetically or numerically organizing a list using one or more fields.

Once you enter records in a list, you can reorganize the information by **sorting** the records. You can sort a list alphabetically or numerically (in ascending or descending order) using one or more fields as the basis for the sort. You can quickly perform a simple sort (sorting a list on one field) using the Standard toolbar, or perform a complex sort (sorting on multiple fields) using the Data menu. A simple sort organizes alphabetically by last name a list that has last names, telephone numbers, and states. Sorting first by state and then by last name is an example of a complex sort. The list will be grouped alphabetically by state and then alphabetically by last name within each state.

Sort Data Quickly

1. Click a field name on which you want to sort.

2. Click the **Sort Ascending** button $\frac{A}{Z}\downarrow$ or the **Sort Descending** button $\frac{Z}{A}\downarrow$ on the Standard toolbar. In a list sorted in ascending order, records beginning with a number in the sort field are listed before records beginning with a letter (0-9, A-Z). In a list sorted in descending order, records beginning with a letter in the sort field are listed first (Z-A, 9-0).

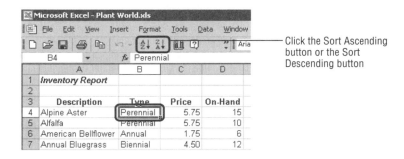

Click the Sort Ascending button or the Sort Descending button

Sort a List Using More Than One Field

1. Click anywhere within the list range.

2. Choose **Data** ➢ **Sort**. The Sort dialog box opens.

3. Click the **Sort By** drop-down arrow, and then select the field on which the sort will be based (the *primary sort field*).

4. Click the **Ascending** or **Descending** option button.

5. Click the first **Then By** drop-down arrow, and then click the **Ascending** or **Descending** option button.

6. If necessary, click the second **Then By** drop-down arrow, and then click the **Ascending** or **Descending** option button.

7. Click the **Header Row** option button to exclude the field names (in the first row) from the sort, or click the **No Header Row** option button to include the field names (in the first row) in the sort.

8. Click the **OK** button.

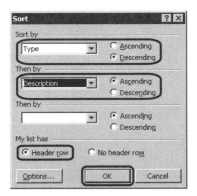

> **TIP** If you want to sort data in rows instead of in columns, chose Data ➢ Sort, click the Options button, and then click the Sort Left To Right option button in the Sort Options dialog box.

Entering Data in a List

Entering data in a list—whether you use the Data Form or the worksheet—can be tedious and repetitive. You can enter data using the Pick From List or List AutoFill feature to make the job easier. **Pick From List** is activated once you have entered at least one record in the list. Pick From List displays previous entries made in the current field in a list format. As you add data to a list, **List AutoFill** considers the preceding cells to determine what formatting and formulas should be extended to the current field.

Enter Data in a List Using Pick From List

1. Right-click the cell in which you want to use Pick From List, and then click **Pick From List** on the shortcut menu.

2. Click a selection in the list.

Pick From List

Feature that lists previous field entries for you to use to enter information in a field.

List AutoFill

Feature that automatically extends the list's formatting and formulas to adjacent cells.

182

3. Press the Enter key or the Tab keys on the keyboard to accept the entry, or press the Esc key to cancel the entry.

Copy Data Formats and Formulas in a List Using List AutoFill

1. Format the data in a list the way you want. For example, you might want to format the fields names in bold and center them.

2. Select the blank cell following the last field name.

3. Type a field name.

4. Click the **Enter** button  on the formula bar, or press the Enter key on the keyboard. Excel formats the new field name with the characteristics you had selected for the previous field names.

Inserting Page Breaks

If you want to print a worksheet that is larger than one page, Excel divides it into pages by inserting **automatic page breaks**. Excel breaks pages based on the paper size, margin settings, and scaling options you set. You can change the rows or columns that are printed on the page by inserting **horizontal** or **vertical page breaks**. In **page break preview**, you can view the page breaks and move them by dragging them to a different location on the worksheet.

Insert a Page Break

1. To insert a vertical page break, click the column header button to the right of the location where you want to insert a page break.

Automatic page breaks
A control that Excel automatically inserts to begin a new page.

Horizontal or vertical page breaks
Controls that let you determine where a new page will begin.

Page break preview
Feature that lets you move page breaks as you view your work.

New page break
Inserts a page break below and to the right of the selected cell.

Other page break options include a horizontal page break and a **new page break**.

◆ Horizontal page break: click the row header button below the location where you want to insert a page break.

◆ New page break: click the cell below and to the right of the location where you want a new page.

2. Choose **Insert ➢ Page Break**.

> **NOTE**   To remove a page break, select the column or row next to the page break, choose Insert ➢ Remove Page Break.

Preview and Move a Page Break

1. Choose **View ➢ Page Break Preview**.

2. To move a page break to a new location, place the mouse pointer over the page break, and then drag the line to a new location.

3. Choose **View ➢ Normal** to return to normal editing mode.

Setting Up the Page

Page orientation
Determines how the worksheet data is arranged on the page when you print it—vertically or horizontally.

Print scaling
Resizes text and graphics to fit a specific paper size.

You can set up the worksheet page to print just the way you want. With the Page Setup dialog box, you can choose the **page orientation**, which determines whether Excel prints the worksheet data vertically or horizontally. You can also adjust the **print scaling** (to reduce or enlarge the size of printed characters), change the **paper size** (to match the size of paper in your printer), and resize or realign the left, right, top, and bottom **margins** (the blank areas along each edge of the paper).

Paper size
The physical dimensions of the paper on which data is printed.

> **NOTE**   Changes made in the Page Setup dialog box are not reflected in the worksheet window. You can see them only when you preview or print the worksheet.

1. Choose **File ➢ Page Setup**, and then click the **Page** tab.

Margins
The blank area at the top, bottom, left, and right of the page.

2. Click the **Portrait** (8.5 x 11 inches) option button (the default) or click the **Landscape** (11 x 8.5 inches) option button to select page orientation.

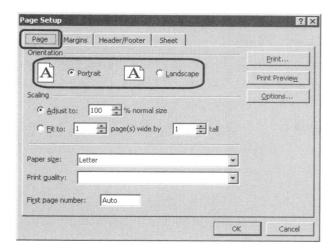

3. Click the **OK** button.

Change the Margin Settings

1. Choose **File ➢ Page Setup**, and then click the **Margins** tab.

◆ Click the **Top**, **Bottom**, **Left**, and **Right** up or down arrows to adjust the margins.

◆ Click the **Center on page** check boxes to automatically center data relative to the left and right margins (horizontally) or the top and bottom margins (vertically).

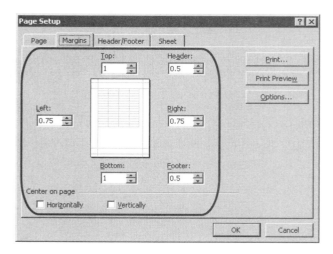

2. Click the **OK** button.

Change a Header or Footer

Adding a header or footer to a workbook is a convenient way to make your printout easier for readers to follow. Using the Page Setup command, you can add information such as page numbers, the worksheet title, or current date at the top and bottom of each page or section of a worksheet or workbook. Using the Custom Header and Custom Footer buttons, you can include information such as your computer's system date and time, the name of the workbook and sheet, a graphic, and other custom information.

> **TIP** To preview the header and footer, click the Print Preview button.

1. Choose **File ➢ Page Setup** and then click the **Header/Footer** tab.

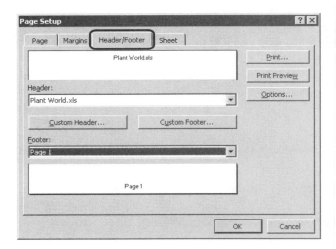

2. If the Header box doesn't contain the information you want, click the **Custom Header** button. The Header dialog box opens.

3. Type the information in the left, middle, or right section text boxes, or click a button to insert built-in header information. If you don't want a header to appear at all, delete the text and codes in the text boxes.

4. Select the text you want to format, and then click the **Font** button. Excel will use the default font, Arial, unless you change it.

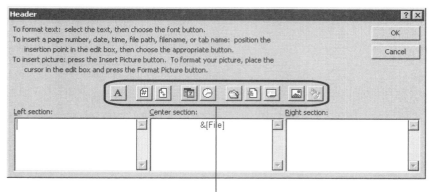

Type custom footer text in a section or press an icon to insert a built-in option

5. Click the **OK** button.

6. If the Footer box doesn't contain the information that you want, click the **Custom Footer** button. The Footer dialog box opens.

7. Type information in the left, middle, or right text boxes, or click a button to insert the built-in footer information.

8. Click the **OK** button twice.

TIP   To insert a picture in a header or footer, choose View ➤ Header and Footer, click the Custom Header button or the Custom Footer button, click the Insert Picture button, and then double-click the picture you want to insert.

Previewing and Printing a Worksheet

You should always preview your work before sending it to the printer. By using **print preview**, you can view all or part of your worksheet as it will appear when you print it. You can print a copy of your worksheet by clicking the Print button on the Standard toolbar or on the Print Preview toolbar. You can open the Print dialog box to specify several print options, such as choosing a new printer, selecting the number of pages in the worksheet you want printed, and specifying the number of copies.

Print Preview
A miniature display of the worksheet that shows how the worksheet will look when it is printed.

187

Preview a Worksheet

1. Click the **Print Preview** button on the Standard toolbar or choose **File ➢ Print Preview**.

2. Click the **Zoom** button on the Print Preview toolbar, or position the Zoom pointer anywhere on the worksheet and click it to enlarge a specific area of the page.

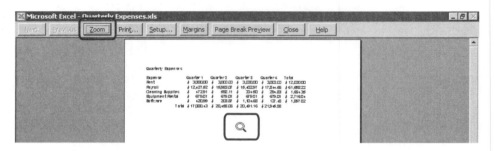

3. If you do not want to print from Print Preview, click the **Close** button to return to the worksheet.

4. If you want to print from Print Preview, click the **Print** button on the Print Preview toolbar to open the Print dialog box.

Print a Worksheet

1. Choose **File ➢ Print**. The Print dialog opens.

2. To choose another (installed) printer, click the **Name** drop-down arrow , and then select the printer you want to use from the list.

3. To print selected pages (rather than all pages), click the Page(s) option button, and then click the **From** and **To** up or down arrows to specify the page range you want.

4. To print more than one copy of the print range, click the **Number of copies** up or down arrow to specify the number of copies you want.

5. To change the worksheet print area, click one of the **Print What** option buttons that correctly identifies the area to be printed.

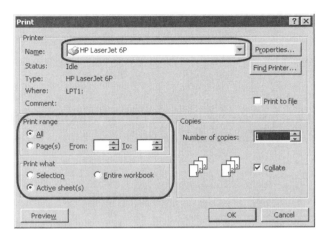

6. Click the OK button.

To print a worksheet quickly using current print settings, click the Print button on the Standard toolbar. Excel prints the selected worksheet with the current Print dialog box settings.

Print Part of a Worksheet

When you're ready to print your worksheet, you can choose several printing options. You can print all or part of any worksheet and control the appearance of many features, such as whether gridlines are displayed, whether column letters and row numbers are displayed, and whether to include **print titles**, which are the columns and rows that repeat on each page.

The section of your worksheet that Excel prints is known as the **print area**. You can set the print area when you customize worksheet printing or any time when you are working on a worksheet. For example, you might want to print a different range in a worksheet for different people. In order to use headers and footers, you must first establish, or **set**, the print area. You can design specific headers and footers for a specific print area. The print area can consist of a single cell or a contiguous or non-contiguous range.

Print titles
Columns and rows that Excel prints on each page.

Print area
The specific range you want to print.

Set
Establish a specific range you want to print.

TIP
If you have already set a print area, you do not need to select it. When you set a print area, it appears in the Print Area box on the Sheet tab of the Page Setup dialog box.

1. Choose **File ➢ Page Setup**, and click the **Sheet** tab. The Page Setup dialog box opens.

2. Click in the **Print area** box, and then type the range you want to print. You can also click the **Collapse Dialog** button, select the cells you want to print, and then click the **Expand Dialog** button to restore the dialog box.

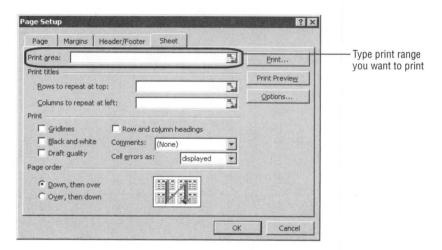

Type print range you want to print

3. Click the **OK** button.

TIP
You can also set and clear the Print area using menus. Choose File ➢ Print Area ➢ Set Print Area or Clear Print Area.

9 Creating a Presentation with PowerPoint

Whether you need to put together a quick presentation of sales figures for your management team, or create a polished slide show for your company's stockholders, Microsoft PowerPoint 2002 can present your information efficiently and professionally. PowerPoint is a **presentation graphics program**: software that creates a slide show presentation. A slide show presentation is made up of a series of slides that can contain charts, graphs, bulleted lists, eye-catching text, animated elements, multimedia video, sound clips, and more. PowerPoint makes it easy to generate and organize ideas, and it provides tools for creating the parts of an effective slide show presentation.

Creating a New Presentation

Wizard
A series of dialog boxes that guide you through a task.

Template
A file that defines the styles, fields, formatting, and layout of a document.

Design template
A template that includes visual elements, such as colors and graphics.

Content template
A template that includes visual elements and suggested text.

Masters
Slides designed for specific uses throughout a presentation.

Color scheme
Eight professionally coordinated colors that PowerPoint uses throughout a presentation.

When you start PowerPoint, you see a dialog box that lists your options for creating a presentation. You can use a **wizard** to guide you through the steps of creating a presentation. Using a wizard is the quickest way to create a presentation.

You can also select a **template**—a document with predefined formatting and placeholder text—that provides a structure for creating your presentation. If you want to start from scratch, you can instruct PowerPoint to provide a blank screen. PowerPoint offers two kinds of templates. **Design templates** include professionally designed colors, graphics, and other visual elements you can apply to your presentation. **Content templates** contain both design and content. **Masters**, which contain the formatting information for each slide in your presentation, are available for each part of your presentation—slides, handouts, and speaker notes. A presentation's **color scheme** is a set of eight balanced colors that coordinate your presentation's text, borders, fills, backgrounds, and so on.

Start a New Presentation

1. Start PowerPoint. The New Presentation task pane opens

2. Click the task pane option that you want to use to begin your presentation.

3. Follow the instructions, which vary depending on the presentation option you chose.

Start a New Presentation Within PowerPoint

1. Choose **File** ➢ **New**. The New Presentation task pane opens.

2. Click the task pane option that corresponds to the way you want to begin your presentation.

Creating a Presentation Using the AutoContent Wizard

Often, the most difficult part of creating a presentation is knowing where to start. PowerPoint solves this problem for you. You can use the AutoContent Wizard to develop presentation content on a variety of business and personal topics. An AutoContent presentation usually contains 5 to 10 logically organized slides, whose text you can edit as necessary. Many AutoContent presentations are available in Standard and Online formats.

TIP To use the AutoContent Wizard, choose File ➢ New, click General Templates, click the General tab, click the AutoContent Wizard icon, and then click the OK button.

Create a Presentation Using the AutoContent Wizard

1. Start PowerPoint or choose File ➢ New, and then click **From AutoContent Wizard** in the New Presentation task pane.

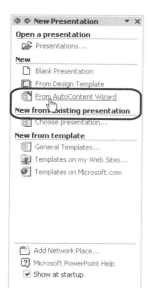

2. Read the first wizard dialog box. Click the **Next** button to continue.

3. Click the presentation type that you want to use. If you want to focus on one particular presentation, such as a brainstorming session, click the appropriate category button, and then click the presentation type you want.

4. Click the **Next** button to continue.

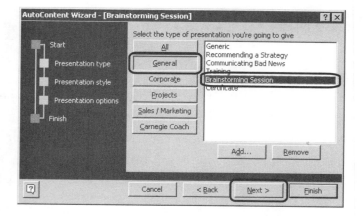

5. Click the presentation style you want to use. Click the **Next** button to continue.

6. Select options, including a presentation title and items you want to include on each slide. Click the **Next** button to continue.

7. Read the last wizard dialog box, and then click the **Finish** button.

Choosing a Template

PowerPoint provides a collection of professionally designed templates that you can use to create effective presentations. Each template contains its own format and color scheme, so you only need to add text. You can select a new template for your presentation at any time.

> **TIP** You can create a new presentation with a template at any time. Choose File ➢ New, click General Templates, click the Design Templates tab, click the template you want to use, and then click the OK button.

Choose a Template for a Presentation

1. Start PowerPoint and click **From Design Template** on the New Presentation task pane or click the **Slide Design** button on the Formatting toolbar.

2. Click a design in the **Available For Use** pane. PowerPoint applies the design to the new presentation.

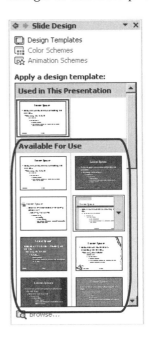

Viewing the PowerPoint Window

The PowerPoint workspace lets you manipulate every component of your presentation. The figure below identifies the elements that you can manage in a presentation.

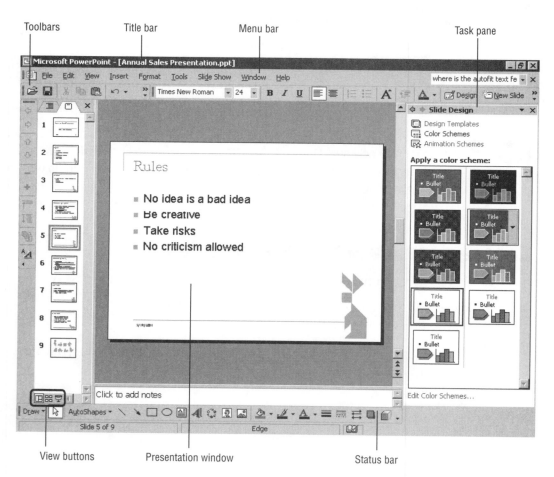

Toolbars   Title bar   Menu bar   Task pane

View buttons   Presentation window   Status bar

The PowerPoint Views

You can arrange the PowerPoint screen in three views: Normal, Slide Sorter, and Slide Show. You can switch from one view to another by clicking a view button located next to the horizontal scroll bar.

Normal View

Use the Normal view to work with the three underlying elements of a presentation—the outline, slide, and notes—each in their own **pane**. These panes provide an overview of your presentation; you can modify your presentation in each section. You can adjust the size of the panes by dragging the pane borders. You can use the outline pane to develop and organize your presentation's content—view a text outline of all the slides in your presentation, or view a **thumbnail** or miniature illustration of each slide. Use the slide pane to add text, graphics, movies, sounds, and hyperlinks to individual slides. Use the notes pane to add speaker notes or notes that you want to share with your audience.

You can preview each slide in Normal View. Click the number of the slide you want to view in the outline pane. You can also use the scroll bars or the Previous and Next Slide buttons to move from slide to slide. When you drag the scroll box up or down on the vertical scroll bar, a label appears that indicates which slide will be displayed when you release the mouse button.

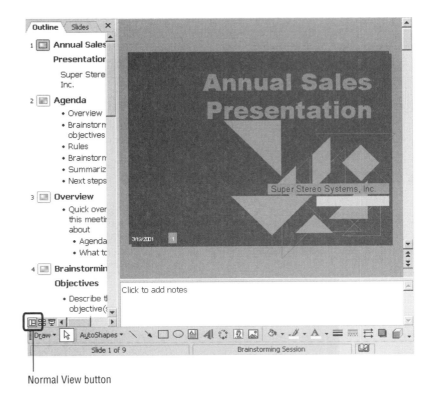

Normal View button

Pane
An individual window within the PowerPoint screen.

Thumbnail
A miniaturization of the current slide or image.

Slide Sorter View

Slide transitions
Effects applied to individual slides that determine how one slide advances to the next.

Use Slide Sorter view to organize your slides, add actions between slides—called **slide transitions**—and apply other effects to your slide show. The Slide Sorter toolbar adds slide transitions and helps control the timing of your presentation. When you add a slide transition, PowerPoint inserts an icon that indicates an action will take place as one slide replaces another during the show. If you hide a slide, an icon appears indicating that the slide will not display during the presentation.

Slide Show View

Slide Show view presents your slides one at a time. Use this view when you're ready to preview, rehearse, or give your presentation. To move through the slides, right-click the navigation button on the screen to access navigation controls, or press the Enter key or Spacebar on the keyboard to move through the show. To quit Slide Show view, press the Esc key on the keyboard.

Slide Show view button

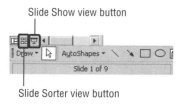

Slide Sorter view button

Creating Consistent Slides

AutoLayout
A feature that makes it easy to arrange objects consistently on your slides.

You need to arrange the objects on your slides in a visually meaningful way so that others can understand your presentation. PowerPoint's **AutoLayout** feature helps you arrange objects on your slide in a consistent manner. Choose from 27 AutoLayout designs that accommodate most common slide arrangements. When you create a new slide, you apply an AutoLayout to it. You see design elements and placeholders for text and other objects. You can also apply an AutoLayout to an existing slide at any time. When you change a slide's AutoLayout, you keep existing information. PowerPoint applies the new AutoLayout, and you can arrange the placeholders the way you want them.

Insert a New Slide

1. Click the slide where you want to place the new slide.

2. Click the **New Slide** button 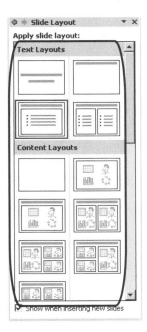 on the Formatting toolbar. PowerPoint inserts a new slide following the slide you selected.

3. Click the AutoLayout you want to use.

Apply an AutoLayout to an Existing Slide

1. In Normal view, display the slide you want to change.

2. Choose **Format** ➤ **Slide Layout**. The Slide Layout task pane opens.

3. Click the AutoLayout you want to use.

Enter Information in a Placeholder

When you apply an **AutoLayout** to a slide, an arranged group of placeholders appears—one placeholder for each object on the slide. The placeholders include instructions for entering object contents.

◇ For text placeholders, click the placeholder, and then type the text.

◇ For other objects, double-click the placeholder, and then use the tools for the accessory that PowerPoint starts.

Entering Text

Text placeholder

An empty text box used to simulate where actual text would appear.

AutoFit Text

A feature that adjusts the size of characters or the spacing between lines to make text fit within a text box.

Insertion point

The blinking cursor that indicates where PowerPoint will place the text that you enter.

In Normal or Slide view, you type text directly into the text placeholders. A **text placeholder** is an empty text box. If you type more text than can fit in the placeholder, PowerPoint automatically resizes the text to fit in the textbox. The **AutoFit Text** feature changes the line spacing—or *paragraph spacing*—between lines of text and then changes the font size to ensure that the text fits. You can also manually increase or decrease the line spacing or font size of the text. The **insertion point** (the blinking vertical line) indicates where the text will appear when you type. To place the insertion point into your text, move the pointer arrow over the text. The pointer changes to an I-beam to indicate that you can click and then type.

Enter Text into a Placeholder

1. In Normal view, click the text placeholder (if it isn't already selected).

2. Type the text that you want to enter.

3. Click outside the text object to deselect the object.

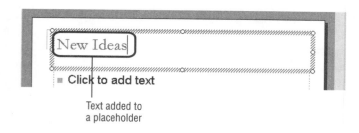

Text added to a placeholder

Placeholder	Description
Bulleted List	Displays a short list of related items
Clip Art	Inserts a picture
Chart	Inserts a chart
Organization Chart	Inserts an organizational chart
Table	Inserts a table from Microsoft Word
Media Clip	Inserts a music, sound, or video clip
Object	Inserts an object created in another program, such as an Excel spreadsheet or a WordArt object

Insert Text

1. Click to place the insertion point where you want to insert text.

2. Type the text. When you enter bulleted text, make sure that the insertion point is at the beginning of the line, and then press the Tab key on the keyboard to indent a level or hold down the Shift+Tab keys on the keyboard to move back out a level

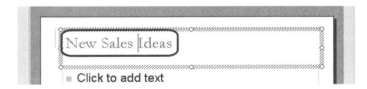

NOTE   You can enter symbols in your text, such as © and ®, or accented characters, such as ô, depending on the fonts installed on your computer. Choose Insert ➢ Symbol, click the Font drop-down arrow, click the font that contains the symbol you want, click the symbol, click the Insert button, and then click the Close button when you're done.

TIP   When you decrease paragraph spacing, make sure you leave enough space for the height of each entire letter, including extenders such as the bottom of "p" and the top of "b."

Enter Text in a Bulleted List

1. In Normal view, click the bulleted text placeholder.

2. Type the first bulleted item.

3. Press the Enter key on the keyboard.

4. Type the next bulleted item.

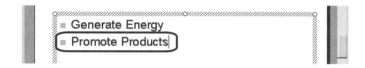

5. Repeat steps 3 and 4 until you complete the list.

Adjust Paragraph Line Spacing

1. Click anywhere in the paragraph you want to adjust.

2. Choose **Format ➢ Line Spacing**. The Line Spacing dialog box opens.

3. Set the spacing options that you want.

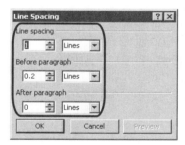

4. Click the **OK** button.

Developing an Outline

If you create your presentation using an AutoContent Wizard, PowerPoint generates an outline. If you prefer, you can develop your own outline from a blank presentation. As you develop an outline, you can add new slides and duplicate existing slides in your presentation. You can also insert an outline you created in another program, such as Microsoft Word. Make sure that the document that contains the outline is set up using outline heading styles. When you insert the outline in PowerPoint, it creates slide titles, subtitles, and bulleted lists based on those styles.

TIP If the Outlining toolbar is not visible, right-click a visible toolbar, and then click Outlining.

NOTE To change the display view size, click the Zoom drop-down arrow on the Standard toolbar, and then select a view size.

Enter Text in Outline View

1. In the Outline tab of Normal view, click to position the insertion point where you want the text to appear.

2. Type the text you want to enter, pressing the Enter key on the keyboard after each line. If you want show or hide formatting, click the **Show Formatting** button on the Outlining toolbar.

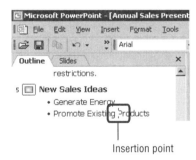

Insertion point

Add a Slide in Outline View

1. In the Outline tab of Normal view, click at the end of the slide text where you want to insert a new slide.

2. Click the **New Slide** button 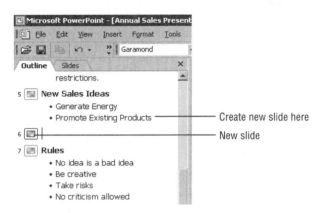 on the Formatting toolbar and then double-click a layout, or hold down the Ctrl+Enter keys on the keyboard to insert a slide using the existing slide layout.

Create new slide here

New slide

TIP   You can delete a slide in several ways. In the Outline tab or Slide Sorter view, select the slide you want to delete, and then press the Delete key on the keyboard. In Slide view, select the slide you want to delete, and then choose Edit ➢ Delete Slide.

NOTE   To open an outline from another program in PowerPoint, click the Open button on the Standard toolbar, click the Files Of Type drop-down arrow, click All Outlines, and then double-click the outline file you want to open.

Rearranging Slides

You can instantly rearrange slides in an outline or in Slide Sorter view. You can use the drag-and-drop method or the Cut and Paste buttons to move slides to a new location. In the Outline tab of Normal view, you can use the Move Up and Move Down buttons to move selected slides within the outline. You can also collapse the outline to its major points to easily see its structure.

NOTE To select an entire slide, click the slide icon in the Outline tab or the slide miniature in Slide Sorter view. To select more than one slide, hold down the Shift key on the keyboard while you click each slide.

Rearrange a Slide in Slide Sorter View

1. Click the **Slide Sorter View** button ⊞.

2. Click to select the slide that you want to move.

3. Drag the selected slide to a new location. A vertical bar appears next to the slide where the slides will be moved when you release the mouse button.

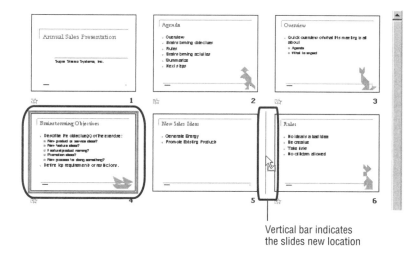

Vertical bar indicates
the slides new location

Rearrange a Slide in an Outline

1. Click the **Normal View** button ▣.

2. If necessary, choose **View** ➤ **Toolbars** ➤ **Outlining** to display the Outlining toolbar.

3. Click the slide icon of the slide you want to move.

205

4. Click the **Move Up** button  to move the slide up, or click the **Move Down** button to move the slide down. Repeat until the slide is where you want it.

> **NOTE** To change the indent level, in Normal view, Slide view, or Outline tab, click in the line of the body of text you want to indent, click the Demote button to move the line in one level, or click the Promote button to move the line out one level.

> **TIP** If you are in Slide Sorter view and you want to open a slide in Slide view, double-click the slide.

Collapse and Expand Slides in an Outline

1. In an outline, select the slide, and then click the button you want. You can expand or collapse your view of a slide—the content is unaffected. In the Outline tab of Normal view, double-click a collapsed slide to expand and show all bullets on that slide; or double-click an expanded slide to collapse the content and show only the title.

❖ To collapse the selected slides, click the **Collapse** button ⬜. A horizontal line appears below a collapsed slide in Outline view.

❖ To expand the selected slides, click the **Expand** button ⬜.

❖ To collapse all slides, click the **Collapse All** button.

❖ To expand all slides, click the **Expand All** button.

Move a Slide with Cut and Paste

1. In an outline or in Slide Sorter view, select the slides you want to move.

2. Click the **Cut** button on the Standard toolbar.

3. Click the new location.

4. Click the **Paste** button on the Standard toolbar.

Cut button   Paste button   Slide pasted into Office Clipboard

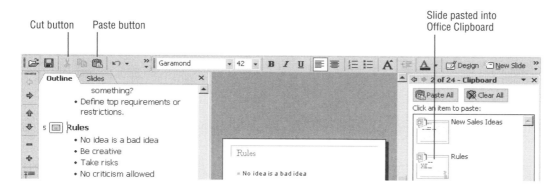

Controlling Slide Appearance with Masters

If you want an object, such as a company logo or clip art, to appear on every slide in your presentation (except the title slide), place it on the slide master. You can also select the slides in which you do not want the object to appear. You can also create unique slides that do not contain any formatting from the masters. If you change your mind, you can easily re-apply a master format to a slide that you altered. As you view the master, you can use the Slide Miniature window to view a sample miniature of the slide.

TIP   To view a master quickly, hold down the Shift key on the keyboard, point to a view button to determine the master, and then click a view button to go to a master view.

Include an Object on Every Slide

1. Choose **View** ➣ **Master** ➣ **Slide Master**. To display the Master toolbar while in master view, choose **View** ➣ **Toolbars** ➣ **Master**.

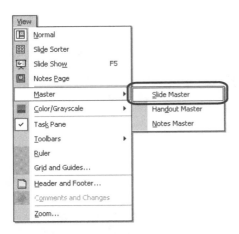

2. Add the object you want and modify its size and placement.

3. Click the **Close Master View** button on the Master toolbar.

> **TIP**   Click the vertical scroll arrows to switch between the slide master and the title master. An object that you place on the slide master does not appear on the title slide unless you also place it on the title master.

> **NOTE**   The Handout Master toolbar has buttons for displaying two, three, four, six, and nine slides per page, and for setting how the outline appears.

Working with Color Schemes

You can apply a color scheme to one slide or all of the slides in a presentation. You can choose from one or more standard color schemes in each template. You can also create and save your own color scheme that you can apply to other slides and other presentations.

To view a presentation in black and white, click the Color/Grayscale button on the Standard toolbar. Click the button again to view the presentation in color.

You can change the background color or fill effect. Display the slide you want to change, choose Format ➤ Background, click the Background Fill drop-down arrow, and then select a color; or click Fill Effects and the gradient, texture, pattern, or picture effect you want, and then click the Apply To All button or the Apply button.

Choose a Color Scheme

1. Click the **Slide Design** button ![Design] on the Formatting toolbar.

2. Click **Color Schemes** in the Slide Design task pane.

3. Click the color scheme you want.

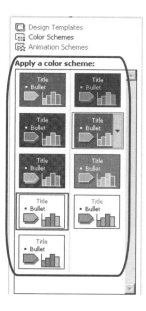

Delete a Color Scheme

1. Click the **Slide Design** button ![Design] on the Formatting toolbar.

2. Click **Edit Color Schemes** in the Slide Design task pane. The Edit Color Scheme dialog box opens.

3. Click the **Standard** tab to view the available color schemes.

4. Click the scheme that you want to delete.

5. Click the **Delete Scheme** button.

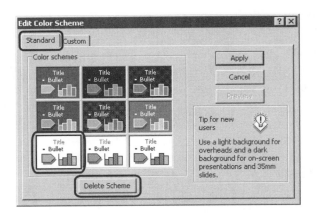

NOTE You can change a color in a standard color scheme. In Slide view, right-click a blank area of the slide whose color scheme you want to change, and then click Slide Color Scheme. Click the Custom tab, click the element you want to change in the Scheme Colors list, click Change Color, click a color on the Standard tab, click the OK button, and then click the Apply button or the Apply To All button.

TIP To save a changed color scheme, choose Format ➤ Slide Color Scheme, and then click the Custom tab. Alter the eight colors that comprise the color scheme as you wish, and then click the Add As Standard Scheme button.

Creating a Text Box

AutoShape
A collection of pre-designed shapes that you can easily insert in a slide.

Usually you use the title, subtitle, and bulleted list placeholders to place text on a slide. However, when you want to add text outside one of the standard placeholders, you can create a text box. Your text box doesn't have to be rectangular—you can also use one of PowerPoint's **AutoShapes**, a collection of shapes that range from rectangles and circles to arrows and stars. When you place text in an AutoShape, the text becomes part of the AutoShape.

TIP Text boxes appear in the slide pane of Normal view or in Slide view, but not in the Outline tab.

TIP You can orient text in text boxes, table cells, and AutoShapes vertically. Select the object with the text you want to change, choose Format ≻ Text Box, click the Rotate Text Within AutoShape By 90° check box to select it, and then click the OK button.

Create a Text Box

1. In Normal view, choose **View** ≻ **Toolbars** ≻ **Drawing** to display the toolbar, if necessary.

2. Click the **Text Box** button 🔲 on the Drawing toolbar.

3. To add text that wraps, drag to create a box and then start typing. To add text that doesn't wrap, click and then start typing.

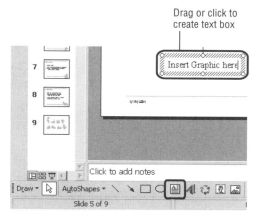

Drag or click to create text box

4. Click outside the text box to deselect it.

Add Text to an AutoShape

1. Click the **AutoShapes** button AutoShapes ▾ on the Drawing toolbar.

2. Point to the shape category you want to use.

3. Click the shape you want.

4. Drag to draw the shape on the slide.

Slide 5 of 9

5. Type the text.

Inserting Slides from Other Presentations

Slide Finder

Feature that makes it easy to find a specific slide by letting you view miniature versions of each slide.

To insert slides from other presentations in a slide show, you can open the presentation and then copy and paste the slides you want, or you can use the **Slide Finder** feature. With Slide Finder, you don't have to open the presentation first; instead, you view a miniature of each of the slides, and then insert only the ones you select. With Slide Finder, you can also create a list of favorite presentations that you can use for future slide shows.

> **TIP** You can add or remove a slide presentation from your list of favorites. Choose Insert ➤ Slides From Files, locate the presentation you want to add, and then click the Add To Favorites button. To remove a presentation, click the List Of Favorites tab, select a presentation, and then click the Remove button.

Insert Slides Using the Slide Finder

1. Choose **Insert** ➤ **Slides From Files**. The Slide Finder dialog box opens.

2. Click the **Find Presentation** tab.

3. Click the **Browse** button, locate and select the file you want, and then click the **Open** button.

4. If necessary, click the **Display** button to display a miniature of each slide.

5. Select the slides you want to insert.

◇   To insert just one slide, click the slide and then click the **Insert** button.

◇   To insert multiple slides, click each slide you want to insert, and then click the **Insert** button.

◇   To insert all the slides in the presentation, click the **Insert All** button.

6. Click the **Close** button.

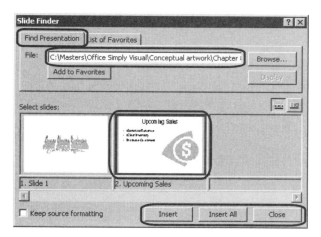

Adding a Header and Footer

You can add a header and a footer that will appear on each slide. Headers and footers often include information such as the presentation title, slide number, date, and name of the presenter. Use the masters to place header and footer information on your slides, handouts, or notes pages. Be sure to keep the text in your header and footer brief and uncomplicated so that they do not clutter your slide

> **TIP** To remove the header or footer from the title slide only, choose View ➢ Header And Footer, click the Slide tab, click the Don't Show On Title Slide check box to select it, and then click the Apply To All button.

Add a Header and Footer

1. Choose **View ➢ Header And Footer**. The Header and Footer dialog box opens.

2. Click the **Slide** or **Notes And Handouts** tab.

3. Enter or select the information you want to include on your slide or your notes and handouts.

4. Click the **Apply** button to apply your selections to the current slide, or click the **Apply To All** button to apply the selections to all slides.

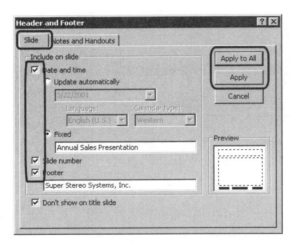

Change the Look of a Header or Footer

1. Choose **View ➢ Master**.

2. Click the master you want to change.

3. Make the necessary changes to the header and footer placeholders. You can move or resize them or change their text attributes.

4. Click the **Close Master View** button on the Master toolbar.

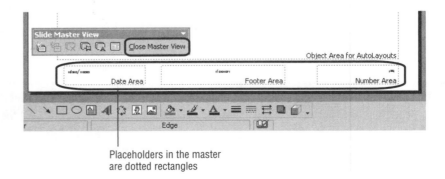

Placeholders in the master
are dotted rectangles

Preparing Speaker Notes and Handouts

You can add speaker notes to a slide in Normal view using the notes pane. Every slide has a corresponding **notes page** that displays a reduced image of the slide and a text placeholder where you can enter speaker notes. Once you have created speaker notes, you can reference them as you give your presentation, either from a printed copy or from your computer. You can enhance your notes by including objects on the notes master.

Notes page
A page that contains a miniature version of a slide and speaker notes.

TIP
To change the size of the notes pane in Normal view, point to the top border of the notes pane until the pointer changes to a double-headed arrow, and then drag the border until the pane is the size you want.

Enter Notes in Normal View

1. Switch to the slide in which you want to enter notes.

2. Click in the notes pane and type your notes.

Enter Notes in Notes Page View

1. Switch to the slide for which you want to enter notes.

2. Choose **View** ➤ **Notes Page**. Notes Page view appears.

3. If necessary, click the **Zoom** drop-down arrow , and then increase the zoom percentage to better see the text as you type it.

4. Click the text placeholder.

5. Type your notes.

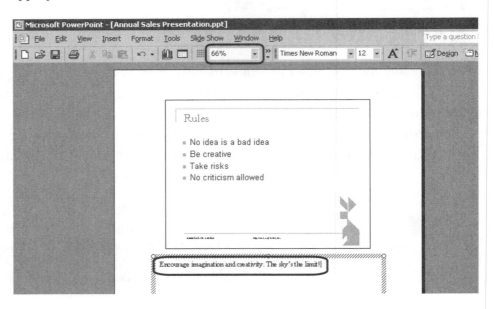

TIP Objects on the notes master don't appear in the notes pane in Normal view or when you save your presentation as a Web page. They will appear when you print the notes pages.

NOTE You can insert the date and time on the current slide. Click to place the insertion point where you want the date and time, choose Insert ➢ Date and Time, select the date and time format you want, and then click the OK button.

10 Creating a Slide Show with PowerPoint

Microsoft PowerPoint 2002 provides many tools to help make your slide show a complete multimedia production. Before you can deliver a slide show, you need to set up the type of show you want. Some presentations include slides that are appropriate for one audience but not for another. PowerPoint lets you create custom slide shows that include only a selection of slides, in whatever order you want, intended for a specific audience. A slide show can feature special visual, sound, and animation effects. For example, you can include special transitions, or actions, between slides, such as a new slide that begins with text flying in from the right. Using animations, effects that animate your slide elements, you can also control how the audience first sees each element of the slide. PowerPoint includes tools that let you time your presentation to make sure that it is neither too long nor too short. You can also make a PowerPoint presentation come alive with the proper use of narration and music.

Adding Action Buttons

When you create a self-running presentation to show at a conference kiosk, you might want a user to be able to move easily to specific slides or to view a different presentation altogether. You can insert **action buttons** to give this capability to your users. By clicking an action button, your users activate a **hyperlink**, a connection between two locations in the same document or in different documents.

> **TIP** To insert an action button using the Drawing toolbar, click the AutoShapes button, point to Action Buttons, and then click the action button you want to insert on your slide.

Insert an Action Button

1. Choose **Slide Show** ➢ **Action Buttons**.

2. Choose the action button you want to insert.

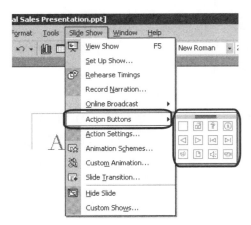

3. Drag the pointer to insert the action button, and then release the mouse button when the action button is the size you want. To create a square action button, hold down the Shift key on the keyboard as you drag. The Action Settings dialog box opens.

You can initiate an action button with a mouse click or mouse over in slide show. In the Action Settings dialog box, click the Mouse Click tab or the Mouse Over tab, and then select an action.

4. If necessary, fill out the Action Settings dialog box, and then click the **OK** button.

Test an Action Button

1. Click the **Slide Show View** button . Slide show starts.

2. Display the slide containing the action button.

3. Click the action button.

Annual Sales Presentation

Insert the Return action button to return to the slide you were previously viewing, regardless of its location in the presentation.

To edit a hyperlink, right-click the object with the hyperlink and then click Edit Hyperlink.

Create an Action Button to Go to a Specific Slide

1. Choose **Slide Show** ➢ **Action Buttons** ➢ **Custom** button.

2. Drag the pointer to insert the action button on the slide. The Action Settings dialog box opens.

3. Click the **Hyperlink To** option button, click the drop-down arrow 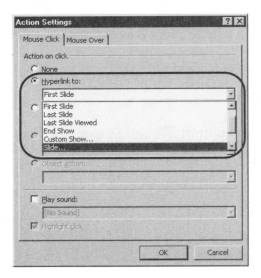, and then click **Slide** from the list of hyperlink destinations. The Hyperlink to Slide dialog box opens.

4. Select the slide to which you want the action button to jump.

5. Click the **OK** button.

6. Right-click the action button, and then click **Add Text**.

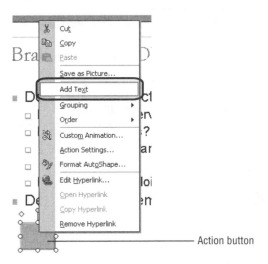

Action button

7. Type the name for the action button.

8. Click outside the action button to deselect it.

9. Run the slide show and test the action button.

Creating Slide Transitions

If you want to maintain your viewers' attention at all times in your presentation, you can add transitions between slides. For example, you can create a fade out effect so that one slide becomes lighter as it is replaced by a new slide, or you can have one slide appear to push another slide out of the way. You can also add sound effects to your transitions, although you need a sound card and speakers to play them.

TIP When you add a transition effect to a slide, the effect takes place between the previous slide and the selected slide.

Specify a Transition

1. Click the **Slide Sorter View** button .

2. Click the slide to which you want to add a transition effect.

3. Click the **Slide Transition** button `Transition` to display the Slide Transition task pane.

4. Click the transition effect you want.

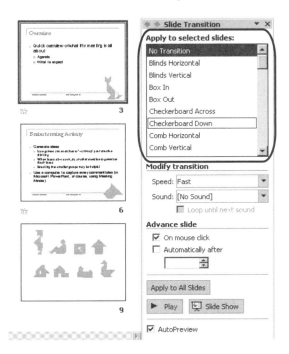

Apply a Transition to All Slides in a Presentation

1. Choose **Slide Show** ➢ **Slide Transition**. The Slide Transition task pane opens.

2. In the **Apply to selected slides** list, click the transition you want.

3. Click the **Apply To All Slides** button.

NOTE You can view a slide's transition by clicking the slide's transition icon in Slide Sorter view, or by playing the show in Slide Show view.

TIP In Slide Sorter view, click the Slide Transition button on the Slide Sorter toolbar to quickly open the Slide Transition dialog box.

Set Transition Effect Speeds

1. In Normal or Slide Sorter view, click or display the slide whose transition effect you want to edit.

2. Choose **Slide Show** ➢ **Slide Transition**. The Slide Transition task pane opens.

3. Click the Speed drop-down arrow 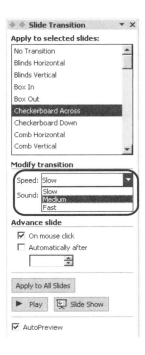, and then click the speed you want.

Add Sound to a Transition

1. In Normal or Slide Sorter view, click or display the slide to which you want to add a transition sound.

2. Choose **Slide Show** ➢ **Slide Transition**. The Slide Transition task pane opens.

3. Click the **Sound** drop-down arrow , and then click the sound you want.

Adding Animation

Animation schemes

Animated effects designed by PowerPoint and installed with the program.

Custom animations

Animated effects created by you or others.

You can use animation to introduce objects onto a slide one at a time or with special animation effects. For example, a bulleted list can appear one bulleted item at a time, or a picture or chart can fade gradually into the slide's foreground. You can use many kinds of animations with PowerPoint. Some are called **animation schemes**—effects that PowerPoint has designed for you. Many of the preset animations contain sounds. You can also design your own **customized animations**, including those with your own special effects and sound elements.

> **TIP** In Slide Sorter view, click a slide's animation icon to quickly view the animation.

Use Animation Schemes

1. Select the slide or object that you want to animate.

2. Choose **Slide Show** ➤ **Animation Schemes**. The Slide Design task pane opens.

3. In the **Apply to selected slides** list, click the animation you want.

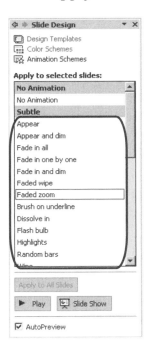

Preview an Animation

1. Click the **Normal View** 🖽 button or the **Slide Sorter View** button 🔠, and then display the slide containing the animation you want to preview. The Slide Design task pane opens.

2. Click the **Slide Design** button 📝 Design , and then click **Animation Schemes**. The Slide Design task pane opens.

3. Click the **Play** button.

TIP To remove an animation, view the slide in Normal view, click the Slide Design button, and then click Animation Schemes. Click the slide from which you want to remove the animation, and then click the No Animation option.

Apply a Customized Animation

1. In Normal view, right-click the object, and then click **Custom Animation**. The Custom Animation task pane opens.

2. Click the **Add Effect** button, point to an effect category, and then click the effect you want.

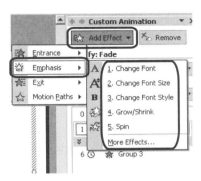

Using Specialized Animations

Using specialized animations, you can apply animations to particular objects. For example, for a text object, you can introduce the text on your slide all at once or by word or letter. Similarly, you can introduce bulleted lists one bullet item at a time and apply different effects to older items, such as graying out the existing items in a list as PowerPoint inserts new ones. You can animate charts by introducing chart series or chart categories one at a time.

NOTE Set times between animations. Display the slide in Normal view, click the Slide Show menu, click Custom Animation, and then click the list item you want to change. Choose one of the animations from the Animation Order list, and then click the Automatically option button. Enter the number of seconds between this animation and the previous event, and then click the OK button.

TIP Animate the attached shape with text. In the Custom Animation task pane, select the text object you want to animate, click the Add Effect button, hold down the Shift key on the keyboard, click the effects drop-down arrow, and then select an effects option.

Animate Text

1. In Normal view, right-click the selected text object, and then click **Custom Animation**. The Custom Animation task pane opens.

2. Click the **Add Effect** button, point to an effect category, and then click the effect you want.

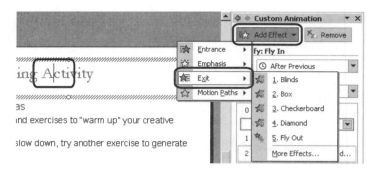

Animate Bulleted Lists

1. In Normal view, right-click the selected bulleted text object, and then click **Custom Animation**.

2. Click the **Add Effect** button, point to an effect category, and then click the effect you want to add..

3. Click the animation drop-down arrow for the bulleted text object, and then click **Effect Options**. The Box dialog box opens.

4. Click the **Text Animation** tab, if necessary, click the **Group Text** drop-down arrow ▼, and then click an option.

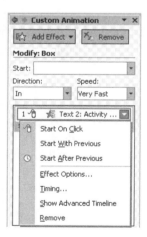

5. Click the **OK** button.

TIP

You can change the order of bullets from the last bulleted list item to the first. In the Custom Animation task pane, select the object with the text you want to reverse, click the Effects drop-down arrow, click the Text Animation tab in the Box dialog box, click the In Reverse Order check box to select it, and then click the OK button.

Fade Text After It Is Animated

1. In Normal view, right-click the text, and then click **Custom Animation**.

2. In the Custom Animation task pane, click the **Add Effect** button, and then click the effect you want to add.

3. Click the **Modify: Fade (Start)** drop-down arrow ▪, and then click when you want the fade to start.

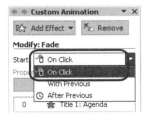

Modify the Animation Order

1. In Normal view, display the slide with the animation, and then choose **Slide Show ➤ Custom Animation**. The Custom Animation task pane opens.

2. Click the slide object whose animation order you want to change.

3. Click the **Re-Order Up** arrow button ⬆ or the **Re-Order Down** arrow button ⬇.

Timing a Presentation

Slide meter

Feature that helps you set the timing for each slide in a presentation.

If you have a time limit for presenting your slide show, you can use Power-Point's timing features to make sure that your presentation is not dragging on too long or going too fast. You can specify the amount of time allotted to each slide and test yourself during rehearsal using the **slide meter**, which ensures that your timings are workable. By rehearsing timings, you can vary the amount of time each slide appears on the screen. If you want the timings to take effect, make sure the show is set to use timings in the Set Up Show dialog box.

> **TIP** You can record a narration that accompanies your slides. Choose Slide Show ➤ Record Narration, set the microphone level and sound quality, click the OK button, click the Link Narrations In check box to select it, click the OK button, click Current Slide or First Slide, record your narration, and then click the Yes button to save the slide timings.

Set Timings Between All Slides

1. Choose **Slide Show** ➤ **Slide Transition**. The Slide Transition task pane opens.

2. Click the **Automatically After** check box to select it.

3. Enter the time (in seconds) before the presentation automatically advances to the next slide after displaying the entire slide.

4. Click the **Apply To All Slides** button.

Create Timings Through Rehearsal

1. Choose **Slide Show** ➤ **Rehearse Timings**. Slide show starts and the Rehearsal toolbar opens.

2. As the slide show runs, rehearse your presentation by pressing the Enter key or Spacebar on the keyboard to advance to the next slide, or by clicking the **Next** button.

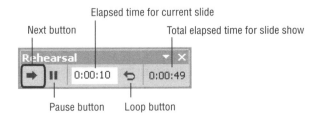

3. When you're finished, click the **Yes** button to accept the timings you just recorded.

4. Review the timings in Slide Sorter view.

Setting Up a Slide Show

PowerPoint offers several types of slide shows appropriate for a variety of presentation situations, from a traditional full-screen slide show, to a show that runs automatically on a computer screen at a conference kiosk. When you don't want to show all of the slides in a PowerPoint presentation to a particular audience, you can hide individual slides or specify the range of slides to show.

NOTE If you want a presentation file to open directly to a slide show rather than in a document window, choose File ➤ Save As, click the Save As Type drop-down arrow, and then click PowerPoint Show.

TIP To hide a slide, click the Slide Sorter View button, select the slides you want to hide, and then click the Hide Slide button on the Slide Sorter toolbar.

Set Up a Show

1. Choose **Slide Show** ➤ **Set Up Show**. The Set Up Show dialog box opens.

2. Choose the show type you want.

    ◆ Click the **Presented By A Speaker** option button to run a traditional full- screen slide show, where you can advance the slides manually or automatically.

    ◆ Click the **Browsed By An Individual** option button to run a slide show in a window and allow access to some PowerPoint commands.

❖ Click the **Browsed At A Kiosk** option button to create a self-running, unattended slide show for a booth or kiosk. The slides will advance automatically, or a user can advance the slides or activate hyperlinks.

3. Change additional show settings as appropriate.

❖ Loop continuously

❖ Show without narration

❖ Loop without animation

4. Click the **OK** button.

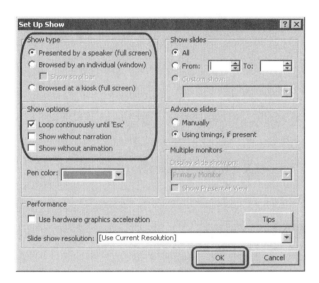

Creating a Custom Slide Show

If you plan to present a slide show to more than one audience, you don't have to create a separate slide show for each audience. Instead, you can create a **custom slide show** that allows you to specify which slides from the presentation you will use and the order in which they will appear.

Custom slide show
A presentation in which you have specified which slides will be used and their order of appearance.

> **NOTE** You can use the Set Up Show command to display a custom slide show. Choose Slide Show ➤ Set Up Show, click the Custom Show option button, click the Custom Show drop-down arrow, select the custom slide show, and then click the OK button.

> **TIP** To delete a custom slide show, choose Slide Show ➤ Custom Shows, click the show you want to delete, click the Remove button, and then click the Close button.

Create a Custom Slide Show

1. Choose **Slide Show** ➤ **Custom Shows**. The Custom Shows dialog box opens.

2. Click the **New** button.

3. Type a name for the show.

4. Double-click the slides you want to include in the show in the order you want to present them. You can change their order using the **Up** arrow button 🔼 and the **Down** arrow button 🔽.

5. Click the **OK** button.

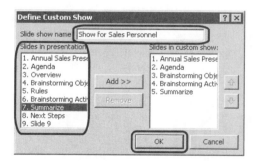

6. Click the **Close** button.

Show a Custom Slide Show

1. Choose **Slide Show** ➤ **Custom Shows**. The Custom Shows dialog box opens.

2. Click the custom slide show that you want to run.

3. Click the **Show** button.

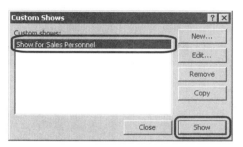

Starting a Slide Show

Once you have set up your slide show, you can start the show at any time. As you run your slide show, you can use the Slide Show view popup menu to access certain PowerPoint commands without leaving Slide Show view. If your show is running at a kiosk, you might want to disable this feature.

TIP To start a Slide Show quickly from the current slide, click the Slide Show button.

NOTE You can open the popup menu quickly in Slide Show view by right-clicking the screen.

Start a Slide Show and Display the Popup Menu

1. Choose **Slide Show** ➢ **View Show**. Slide show starts.

2. Move the mouse pointer to display the popup menu button.

3. Click the popup menu button in the lower-left corner of the slide to display the popup menu.

Click to display pop-up menu

Set Popup Menu Options

1. Choose **Tools** ➤ **Options**. The Options dialog box opens.

2. Click the **View** tab.

3. Click to select the popup menu options you want.

4. Click the **OK** button.

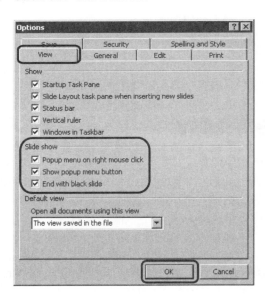

Navigating a Slide Show

In Slide Show view, you advance to the next slide by clicking the mouse button or by pressing the Enter key or spacebar on the keyboard. In addition to those basic navigational techniques, PowerPoint provides keyboard shortcuts that can take you to the beginning, end, or any particular slide in your presentation. You can also use the navigation commands on the shortcut menu to access slides in custom slide shows.

TIP After a period of inactivity during a normal full-screen slide show, PowerPoint automatically hides the pointer and the slide show icon. Move the mouse to display them again.

NOTE You can use a light pen during a slide show. In Slide Show view, press Ctrl+P to change the pointer to the shape of a pen. Simply drag to draw on the screen. Press the E key to erase the drawing. To change the pen color, right-click the screen in Slide Show view, point to Pointer Options, point to Pen Color, and then select a color.

Go to a Specific Slide

1. In Slide Show view, right-click a slide.

2. Point to **Go**, and then point to **By Title**.

3. Click the title of the slide to which you want to go.

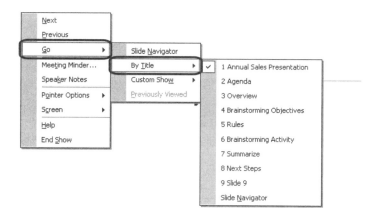

TIP You can quickly navigate in a slide show using keyboard shortcuts. Press the Left arrow or P key to go to the previous slide, press the Right arrow or N key to go to the next slide, or press the slide number and press the Enter key to go to a specific slide.

Printing a Presentation

You can print all the elements of your presentation—the slides, outline, notes, and handouts—in color or in black and white. The Print dialog box offers standard Windows features, giving you the option to print multiple copies, specify ranges, access printer properties, and print to a file.

When you print an outline, PowerPoint prints the presentation outline shown in the Outline tab.

TIP Use the Print button on the Standard toolbar only when you want to bypass the Print dialog box. If you need to select options in the Print dialog box, choose File ➤ Print.

Print a Presentation

1. Choose **File ➤ Print**. The Print dialog box opens.

2. Click the **Print What** drop-down arrow ▾, and then click what you want to print.

3. Change settings in the Print dialog box as necessary.

   ◆ Printer name

   ◆ Print range

   ◆ Number of copies

   ◆ Handouts

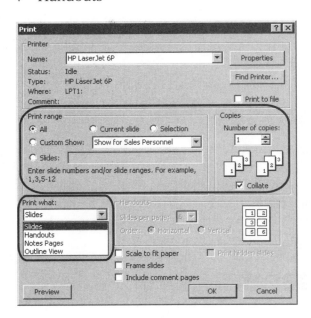

4. Click the **OK** button.

11

Creating a Database with Access

• •

Microsoft Access 2002 helps you get started working with databases right away by providing sample database applications that you can use to store your own personal or business data. Access also offers a set of database wizards that aid you in creating common business databases. You can study these samples to get ideas for database designs for other types of data that are not covered by the existing samples and wizards.

Starting out, you won't need to learn the complexities of database design in order to work with an existing database. You just need to know how to get around the database you are using. Some of the tasks you are likely to perform with an existing database include entering and viewing data or subsets of data, creating and printing reports, and working efficiently with all the windows in front of you.

Creating a Database

You can use a wizard to create a database, or you can create a custom database from scratch. The Access database wizards help you create databases suited to specific needs. Each wizard guides you through the process of selecting and creating fields, tables, queries, reports, and forms, which will make it easier to use the database. When you create a database, you need to assign a name and location to your database.

> **TIP** To open a sample database, click the Open button on the Database toolbar, click the Look in drop-down arrow, select the Samples folder located in Programs Files/Microsoft Office/Office, click the sample database you want to open, and then click the Open button.

Create and Save a New Database Using a Wizard

1. Click the **Start** button ⛁ Start on the taskbar, point to **Programs**, and then click **Microsoft Access**. A blank database page opens, and the New File task pane appears on the right side of the screen.

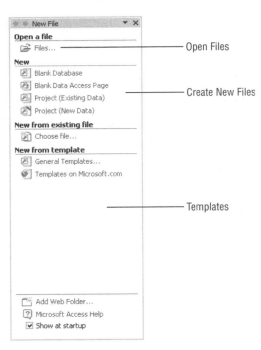

2. In the task pane, click **Blank Database**. The File New Database window opens.

3. Click the **Save In** drop-down arrow, and then select the location where you want to save the new database.

4. In the **File Name** box, type in a name for the database, and click the **Create** button. An Access database file format window opens.

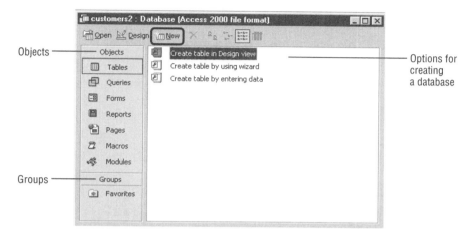

5. Click the **New** button on the toolbar in the Database window. A New Table dialog box appears.

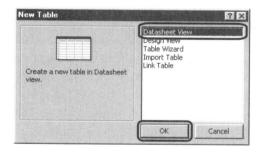

6. Click **Datasheet View**, and then click the **OK** button. A table appears in the access window. You can resize the fields by placing the cursor at the edge of a field and dragging the field to the desired size.

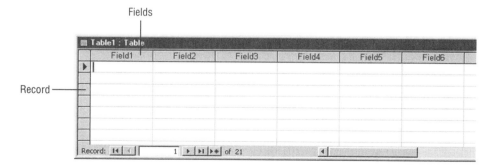

7. Enter information in the fields. Press the Tab key to move from one field to another.

8. When you are finished entering information for the fields, click the **Save** button 🖫 on the Database toolbar. The Save As dialog box opens.

9. In the **Table Name** box, type a name for the table, and then click the **OK** button. An alert box appears telling you that a primary key isn't necessary when creating a table but is recommended, and asks if you want to create a primary key now.

10. Select the option you want. Primary keys are discussed later in this chapter.

Stepping Through a Database Wizard

The choices that appear as you progress through a database wizard depend on the kind of information the database is designed to manage. All the wizards, however, share certain features, such as those in the following table.

Wizard Choice	Description
Field selection	The wizard presents a list of tables it will include in the database. Each table requires certain fields. You can click a table to see which fields it includes. Required fields are checked; optional fields appear in italics. To include an optional field in your database, click its check box.
Report style	You can choose from a set of report styles, such as Bold, Casual, or Corporate. Report styles give printed reports a professional look.
Screen style	Access offers a set of visual styles for on-screen database objects that use a variety of color, font, and background enhancements. Click the style you want to see a sample of it.
Name and picture	Access provides a default name for its wizard databases, but you can enter your own. You can also include a picture with your database.

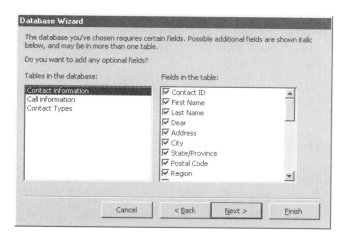

Viewing the Access Window

When you open a database, the Access program window opens and displays either the **Database window** or a **switchboard**. All sample databases that come with Access 2002 open with a switchboard. You can open the Database window by clicking the Window menu and then clicking the name of the database.

Database Window
A window that displays the database objects.

Switchboard
A window that gives easy access to the most common actions a database user might need to take.

Title bar   Menu bar   Database toolbar   Ask a Question box

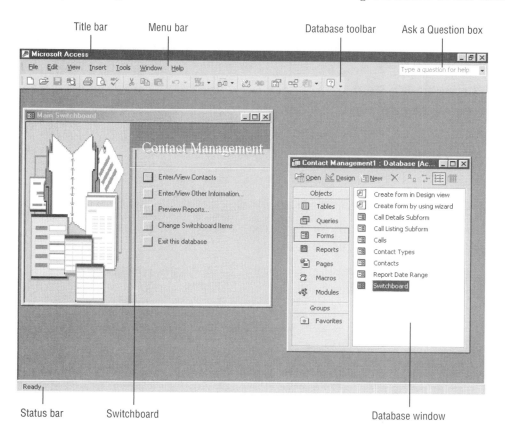

Status bar   Switchboard   Database window

NOTE You can easily customize the way Access starts up. Choose Tools ➢ Startup, set the startup options you want, and then click the OK button. The new options will take effect the next time you start Access.

Working with Database Objects

When you open an existing database, the first thing you usually see is the Database window. However, if the database was created with a switchboard, you must close the switchboard before you can view the Database window. The Database window is the container for all the objects in a database, including tables, forms, reports, queries, pages, macros, and modules. These database objects work together to help you store and manage your data. Objects are organized by object type on the Objects bar. You can open, group, rename, and delete database objects from the Database window. Below the Objects bar is the Group bar. The Groups bar allows you to group database objects the way you want them, creating shortcuts to objects of different types.

The following table identifies the database objects that you use when creating a database. For many of the tasks you do in Access, you will switch back and forth between Design and Datasheet view. In Design view, you format and set controls for queries, reports, forms, or tables that you are creating from scratch or modifying from an original wizard design. In Datasheet view, you observe the result of the modifications you have made in Design view.

Database Object	Description
Tables	Grids that store related information, such as a list of customer addresses
Queries	A question you ask a database to help locate specific information
Forms	A window that is designed to help you enter information easily and accurately
Reports	Summaries of information that are designed to be readable and accessible
Pages	Separate files outside the Access database in HTML format that can be placed on the Web to facilitate data sharing with the worldwide Internet community
Macros	Stored series of commands that carry out an action
Modules	Programs you can write using Microsoft Visual Basic

> **TIP** To switch between Design and Database views, click the View button on the toolbar, and then select the appropriate view.

Open and View a Database Object

1. Open the database whose objects you want to view. If necessary, choose **Window** ➢ database name to display the database.

2. Click the object type icon (**Tables**, **Queries**, **Forms**, **Reports**, **Pages**, **Macros**, or **Modules**) on the Objects bar.

3. In the Object list, click the object you want to open.

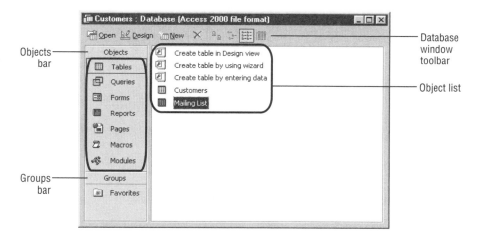

> **TIP** To create a new object, click the type of object you want to create on the Objects bar, and then click the New button on the Database window toolbar.

> **TIP** To delete an object, right-click it in the Object list and then click the Delete button.

> **TIP** To rename a database object, right-click the object in the Object list, click Rename, and then type a new name.

4. Click the **Open** button 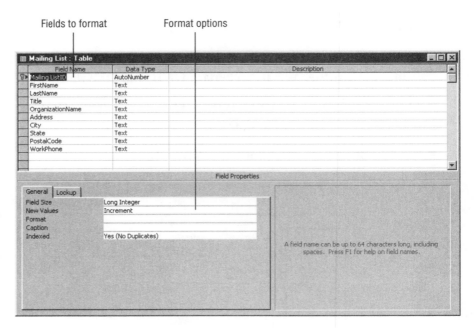 on the Database window toolbar to view the object's data, or click the **Design** button to work with the object's design.

Fields to format   Format options

Create a Group of Database Objects

1. In the Database window, click the **Groups** bar.

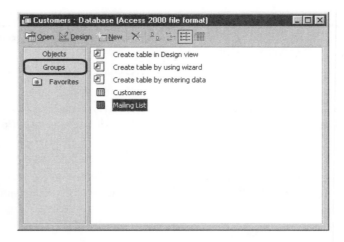

2. Right-click anywhere under the Groups bar, and then click **New Group** on the shortcut menu. The New Group dialog box opens.

3. In the **New Group Name** box, type a name for your group, and then click the **OK** button.

4. Drag an object from the Object list to the group.

> **TIP** To delete or rename a group, click the Groups bar in the Database window, right-click anywhere under the Groups bar, and click Delete Group or Rename Group. When you rename a group, type a new name, and then click the OK button.

Planning Tables

Although you can always make changes to your database when necessary, a little planning before you begin can save time later on. When you plan a database, consider how you will use the data. What kind of data are you collecting? What kind of data are you entering? How are data values related to one another? Can your data be organized into separate, smaller groups? What kinds of safeguards can you create to ensure that errors do not creep into your data? As you consider these questions, you should apply the answers as you structure your database.

Plan Tables

Tables are one of the fundamental building blocks of a database. Database planning begins with deciding how many and what kinds of tables your database will contain. Consider organizing your database information into several tables—each one containing fields related to a specific topic—rather than one large table containing fields for a large variety of topics. For example, you could create a Customers table that contains only customer information and an Orders table that contains only order information. By focusing each table on a single task, you greatly simplify the structure of those tables and make them easier to modify later on.

Choose Data Types

Data type

A format for fields that designates the types of data that can be entered in the field — text, number, date and time, currency, and so forth.

When you create a table, you must decide what fields to include and the appropriate format for those fields. Access allows you to assign a **data type** to a field, a format that defines the kind of data the field can accept. Access provides a wide variety of data types, ranging from text and number formats to object-based formats for images, sound, and video clips. Choosing the correct data type helps you manage your data and reduces the possibility of data-entry errors.

Specify a Primary Key

Primary key

Fields that have a unique value for each record in the table.

You should also identify which field or fields are the table's primary keys. **Primary keys** are those fields whose values uniquely identify each record in the table. A social security number field in a personnel table could be used as a primary key, since each employee has a unique social security number. A table with time-ordered data might have two primary keys—a date field and a time field (hours and minutes), which together uniquely identify an exact moment in time. Although primary keys are not required, using them is one way of removing the possibility of duplicate records existing within your tables.

Working with a Table

Field

An element for storing certain type of information.

Record

Data that is stored for a single entity, such as a customer's information or product information.

A database is made up of groups of fields organized into tables. A **field** is a specific category of information, such as a name or a product. Related fields are grouped in tables. All the fields dealing with customers might be grouped in a Customer table, while fields dealing with products might be grouped in a Products table. You usually enter data into fields one entity at a time (one customer at a time, one product at a time, and so on). Access stores all the data for a single entity in a **record**. You can view a table in Datasheet or Design view. Design view allows you to work with your table's fields. Datasheet view shows a grid of fields and records. The fields appear as columns and the records as rows.

> **TIP**   The first field in a table is often an AutoNumber field, which Access uses to assign a unique number to each record. You cannot select or change this value.

Open and View a Table

1. In the Database window, click **Tables** on the Objects bar.

2. In the Objects list, click the table.

3. Click the **Open** button ![Open]. The table opens in Datasheet view. To scroll through the fields in a table, drag the horizontal scroll box. To scroll through the records in a table, drag the vertical scroll box.

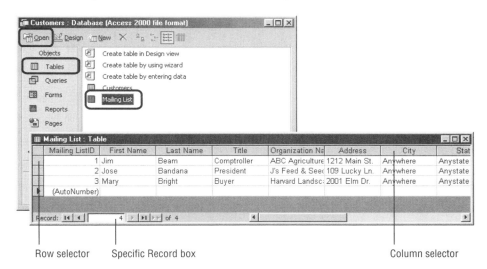

Row selector   Specific Record box   Column selector

NOTE   To select a column or row in a table, click the column or row selector.

NOTE   You can resize a column and change the height of rows. To resize a column, drag the border between two column selectors left or right. To change the height of all rows in the table, drag the border between two row selectors up or down.

Enter a New Record in a Table

1. Open the table from the Objects bar in the Database window.

2. Click the **New Record** button ![New Record]. The first field in a table is often an AutoNumber field, which Access uses to assign a unique number to each record. You can't select or change this value.

3. Press the Tab key on the keyboard to accept the AutoNumber entry.

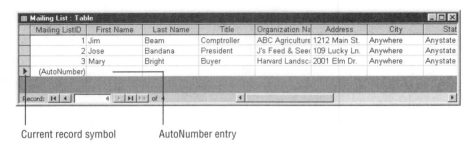

Current record symbol   AutoNumber entry

4. Enter the data for the first field. If you make a typing mistake, press the Backspace key on the keyboard.

5. Press the Tab key on the keyboard to move to the next field, or hold down the Shift+Tab keys on the keyboard to move to the previous field.

6. When you reach the end of the record, click one of the Record buttons (**First**, **Previous**, **Next**, and **Last**), or enter a record number in the Specific Record box and press the Enter key on the keyboard.

> **NOTE** To delete a record from a table, right-click the row selector with the record you want to delete, click Delete Record, and then click the Yes button to confirm the deletion. When you delete a record, such as a supplier, you might want to also delete the products the supplier supplies.

Creating a Table Using a Wizard

Table Wizard

A tool that guides you through a series of steps and dialog boxes to determine the types of tables and fields your database will contain.

One of the easiest ways to create a table is to use the Table Wizard. The **Table Wizard** walks you through a series of dialog boxes that help you choose the types of tables your database will contain and the fields present in each table. You can change table names and field names and properties as you proceed through the wizard. The wizard also makes it easy to create a primary key for your table and to establish relationships between the new table and other tables in the database.

TIP   You can select fields in the order you want them to appear in the table. In the Sample Fields
list, you can choose the fields you want to include in your table in the order you choose.

Use the Table Wizard to Create a Table

1. In the Database window, click **Tables** on the Objects bar.

2. Double-click the **Create table by using wizard** icon. The Table Wizard dialog box opens.

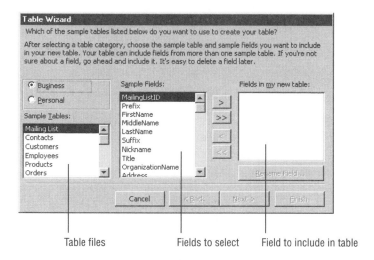

Table files   Fields to select Field to include in table

3. Click the **Business** or **Person** option button, and then click the table that best matches your needs.

4. Double-click each field you want to include in the table, and then click the **Next** button to continue.

5. Type a new name for the table, or accept the suggested name.

251

6. Click the **Yes** option button to have the Table Wizard assign the primary key, or click the **No** option button to assign your own primary key. Click the **Next** button to continue.

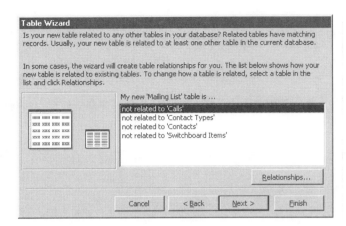

NOTE The Table Wizard prompts you to define how the table you are creating will relate to other tables in the database. Review the relationships of this new table with the other tables in the database before making any changes.

7. If your database already contains at least one table and you want to make changes, select the relationship you want to change, click the **Relationships** button, specify the new table relationships, click the **OK** button, and then click the **Next** button to continue.

8. In the final wizard dialog box, click one of the option buttons to modify the table design (in Design view) before entering data, enter data right away (in Datasheet view), or to enter data in a form that the wizard creates for you.

9. Click the **Finish** button to complete the wizard and create the table.

TIP When you want to enter data to create a new table, in the Database window, click Tables on the Objects bar. Double-click the Create Table By Entering Data icon, and enter the data. Close the Table window, click the Yes button to save the table, enter a table name, and then click the OK button.

Working with a Table in Design View

Most Access objects can be displayed in Design view, which allows you to work with the underlying structure of your tables, queries, forms, and reports. To create a new table in Design view, you define the fields that will comprise the table before you enter any data. You can create any field you choose.

TIP To insert a new field into a database, click the row selector for the field that will be below the inserted field, and then click the Insert Rows button on the Table Design toolbar.

NOTE When you need to delete a field, in Design view, click the row selector for the row you want to delete, click the Delete Rows button on the Table Design toolbar, click the Yes button to confirm you want to continue, or click the No button to cancel the deletion.

Create or Modify a Table in Design View

1. In the Database window, click **Tables** on the Objects bar.

2. Double-click the **Create Table In Design View** icon, or click the table you want to modify, and then click the **Design** button 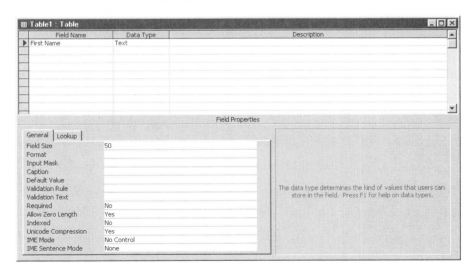.

3. Type a field name for the first column you want to create in the Field Name column, and set properties for the field.

4. Press the Tab key on the keyboard, click the **Data Type** drop-down arrow ![icon] that appears, and then click the data type you want to assign to the field you just created.

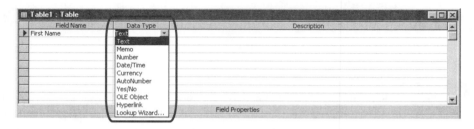

5. Press the Tab key on the keyboard, and then type a description of the field's properties and purpose.

6. Press the Enter key on the keyboard to go to the next row.

7. Repeat steps 3 through 6 as necessary to add new fields to the table.

8. Click the **Close** button ![X] in the Table window.

9. Click the **Yes** button to save the table, enter a table name, and then click the **OK** button.

Specifying Data Types and Field Properties

Data types
A format for fields that designates the types of data that can be entered in the field — text, number, date and time, currency, and so forth.

Access provides 10 different **data types**, field formats that define the kind of data the field can accept, which cover a wide variety of data. When you choose a data type for a field, Access will accept data entered only in the format specified by the data type. Selecting the appropriate data type makes it easier for users to enter and retrieve information in the database tables. It also acts as a check against incorrect data being entered. For example, a field formatted to accept only numbers removes the possibility that a user will erroneously enter text into the field.

You can change the data type for a field even after you have entered data in it. However, you might need to perform a potentially lengthy process of converting or retyping the field's data when you save the table. If the data type in a field conflicts with a new data type setting, you may lose some or all of the data in the field.

Once you've selected a data type, you can begin to work with field properties. A **field property** is an attribute that defines the field's appearance or behavior in the database. The number of decimal places displayed in a numeric field is an example of a property that defines the field's appearance. A property that forces the user to enter data into a field rather than leave it blank controls that field's behavior. In Design view for tables, Access provides a list of field properties, called the **properties list**, for each data type.

The following table describes the available data types.

Data Type	Description
Text (default)	Text or combinations of text and numbers, as well as numbers that don't require calculations, such as phone numbers. Limited to 255 characters.
Memo	A lengthy text or combinations of text and numbers. Limited to 64,000 characters.
Number	Numeric data used in mathematical calculations.
Date/Time	Date and time values for the years 100 through 9999.
Currency	Currency values and numeric data used in mathematical calculations involving data with one to four decimal places. Values are accurate to 15 digits on the left side of the decimal separator.
AutoNumber	A unique sequential number (incremented by 1) or random number Access assigns whenever you add a new record to a table. AutoNumber fields can't be changed.
Yes/No	A field containing only one of two values (for example, Yes/No, True/False, On/Off).
OLE Object	An object (such as a Microsoft Excel spreadsheet) linked to or embedded in an Access table.
Hyperlink	A link that, when clicked, takes the user to another file, a location in a file, or a site on the World Wide Web.
Lookup Wizard	A wizard that helps you to create a field whose values are chosen from the values in another table, query, or list of values.

Field Property

Is an attribute that defines the field's appearance or behavior within the database.

Properties list

Is a list of field properties for each data type.

Planning Table Relationships

Table Relationships
A way of determining how data in a table relates to data in another table.

When you place data into separate tables, you need some way of merging this data together for forms and reports. You can do this by establishing **table relationships**, which indicate how data in one table relates to data in another.

Specify Common Fields

Common field
The same field that appears in two or more tables and which allows you to match records from one or more tables.

Data from several different tables is related by common fields. A **common field** is a field existing in two or more tables, allowing you to match records from one table with records in the other tables. For example, the Customers table and the Orders table might both contain a Customer ID field, which functions as the primary key that identifies a specific customer. Using Customer ID as a common field allows you to generate reports containing information on both the customer and the orders the customer made. When you use a primary key as a common field, it is called a **foreign key** in the second table.

Foreign key
The designation of the primary key when it is used as a common field in a second table.

Build Table Relationships

Once you have a way of relating two tables with a common field, your next task is to express the nature of that relationship. There are three types of relationships: one-to-one, one-to-many, and many-to-many. Each type of relationship is described in the following table.

Type	Description
One-to-one	Each record in one table is matched to only one record in a second table, and vice versa.
One-to-many	Each record in one table is matched to one or more records in a second table, but each record in the second table is matched to only one record in the first table.
Many-to-many	Each record in one table is matched to multiple records in a second table, and vice versa.

A table containing customer names and a second table containing customer addresses exist in a one-to-one relationship if each customer is limited to only one address. Similarly, a one-to-many relationship exists between the Customers table and the Orders table because a single customer could place several orders. In a one-to-many relationship like this, the "one" table is called the **primary table**, and the "many" table is called the **related table**.

Finally, if you allow several customers to be recorded on a single order (as in the case of group purchases), a many-to-many relationship exists between the Customers and Orders tables.

Maintain Referential Integrity

Table relationships must obey standards of **referential integrity**, a set of rules that control how you can delete or modify data between related tables. Referential integrity protects your data by preventing users from erroneously changing data in a primary table required by a related table. You can apply referential integrity when

- ❖ The common field is the primary table's primary key.
- ❖ The related fields have the same format.
- ❖ Both tables belong to the same database.
- ❖ Referential integrity places some limitations on you.
- ❖ Before adding a record to a related table, a matching record must already exist in the primary table.
- ❖ The value of the primary key in the primary table cannot be changed if matching records exist in a related table.
- ❖ A record in the primary table cannot be deleted if matching records exist in a related table.

Access can enforce these rules by cascading any changes across the related tables. For example, Access can automatically copy any changes to the common field across the related tables. Similarly, if a record is deleted in the primary table, Access can automatically delete related records in all other tables. As you work through these issues of tables, fields, and table relationships, you will create a structure for your database that will be easier to manage and less prone to data-entry error.

Primary table
The main table in a one-to-many tables relationship.

Related table
The one-to-many table that is related to the main or primary table in a table relationship.

Referential integrity
A set of rules that control how information can be deleted or modified within related tables.

Defining Table Relationships

You can define table relationships in several ways. When you first create tables in your database using the Table Wizard, the wizard gives you an opportunity to define table relationships. You can also define relationships in the Database window or in Design view. This method gives you more control over your table relationships and a quick snapshot of all the relationships in your database.

> **TIP** To print the Relationships window, open the Relationships window you want to print, choose File ➤ Print Relationships, select the print settings you want, and then click the OK button.

Define Table Relationships

1. In the Database window, click the **Relationships** button on the Database toolbar. If relationships are already established in your database, they appear in the Relationships window. In this window, you can create additional table relationships.

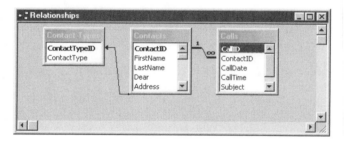

2. If necessary, click the **Show Table** button on the Relationship toolbar to display the Show Table dialog box.

3. Click the **Tables** tab.

4. Click the table you want.

5. Click the **Add** button. The table or query you selected appears in the Relationships window. Repeat steps 4 and 5 for each table you want to use in a relationship

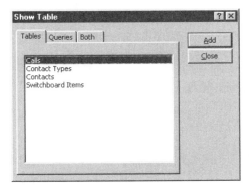

6. Click the **Close** button.

NOTE   You can view the relationships of tables. Click the Show Direct Relationships button on the Relationship toolbar to see tables that are directly related to each other. Click the Show All Relationships button on the Relationship toolbar to see all the relationships between all the tables and queries in your database.

7. Drag the common field in the first table to the common field in the second table. When you release the mouse button, the Edit Relationships dialog box opens, in which you can confirm or modify the relationship.

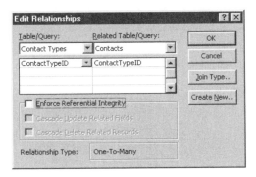

TIP   You can delete a table relationship at any time. In the Relationships window, select the line that joins the tables that you no longer want related to one another. Choose Edit ➤ Delete. In the message box, click the Yes button to confirm the deletion.

8. Click the **Join Type** button if you want to specify the join type. Click the **OK** button to return to the Edit Relationships dialog box.

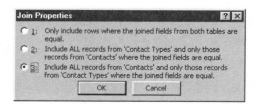

9. Click **Create** to create the relationship. A line appears between the two tables, signifying that they are related.

Managing Data with Access

Once you've created a database, you'll want to be able to manage the records and information within that database. Microsoft Access 2002 gives you a multitude of ways to manage the information you store in its databases.

Some of the techniques you might utilize to manage your databases could include filtering certain records out of a database for a special mailing to certain clients, creating queries to help you retrieve specific information about particular customers, creating forms and reports based on the information you have in your databases, creating Web pages of database information, and creating mailing labels from records in your database.

Filtering Out Records

Filter

A filter isolates items or files that match specifications that you set.

Instead of displaying all the records in a table, you can use a **filter** to display only those records that you want to see. You can display records based on a specific value in one field, or on multiple values in multiple fields. You can filter by selecting the field value on which to base the filter in Datasheet view, or by using the Filter By Form feature to help you create more complex filters involving multiple field values. After you apply a filter, Access displays only those records that match your specifications. You can remove a filter at any time to return the datasheet to its original display.

> **TIP** You can save a filter as a query. Display the filtered table in Datasheet view, and then choose Records ➢ Filter ➢ Advanced Filter/Sort. Click the Save As Query button on the Filter/Sort toolbar, type a name, and then click the OK button.

Filter a Table by Selection

1. Display the table in Datasheet view.

2. Right-click the field value on which you want to base the filter.

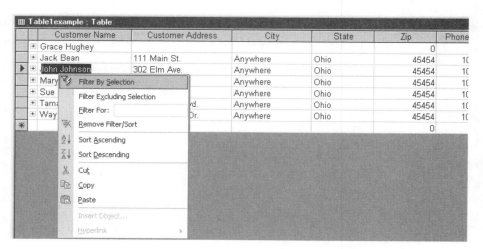

3. Click **Filter By Selection**. The bottom of the Table window tells you the number of records matching your filter criteria. In addition, the notation FLTR in the status bar indicates that a filter is currently in effect.

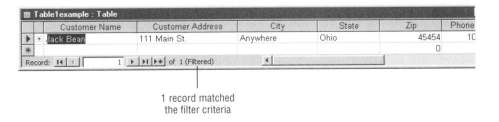

1 record matched
the filter criteria

TIP To clear a filer from a table, display the table with the filter in Datasheet view, select the filtered table, and then click the Remove Filter button on the Table Database toolbar.

Understanding the Different Types of Queries

To locate and retrieve information in a table (or in multiple tables) you create a query. A **query** is simply a question that you ask a database to help you locate specific information. For example, if you want to know which customers placed orders in the last six months, you can create a query to examine the contents of an Order Date field to find all the records with a purchase date within the last six months. Access retrieves the data that meet the specifications in your query and displays that data in table format. You can sort that information or retrieve just a subset of its contents with still more specific criteria, so that you can focus on exactly the information you need—no more or less. As with most database objects you create in Access, there are several ways to create a query. You can create a query from scratch or use a wizard to guide you through the process of creating a query.

Query
A simple question you ask a database to help you locate specific information within the database.

Select query

A query that retrieves and displays records in the Table window in Datasheet view.

Crosstab query

A query that displays summarized values (sums, counts, and averages) from one field in a table, and groups them on the datasheet.

Action query

A query that performs operations (delete queries, update queries, append queries and make-table queries) on the records in one or more tables that match your criteria.

Parameter query

A query that allows you to prompt for a single piece of information to use as selection criteria in the query.

Access offers several types of queries that help you retrieve the information you need. A **select query** displays the records that match your criteria in Datasheet view. A **crosstab query** calculates data and displays it compactly. An **action query** can be one of four types: delete queries, update queries, append queries and make-table queries. A **parameter query** prompts you for specific criteria in its own dialog box.

Creating a Query Using a Wizard

With the Query Wizard, Access helps you create a simple query to retrieve the records you want. When you create a query with the Query Wizard, you can specify the kind of query you want to create and type of records from a table or existing query you want to retrieve. The Query Wizard guides you through each step; all you do is answer a series of questions, and Access creates a query based on your responses.

> **TIP** To include fields from another source (database or table), click the Tables/Queries drop-down arrow if you want to include a field from another source.

Create a Simple Query Using the Query Wizard

1. In the Database window, click **Queries** on the Objects bar, and then double-click the **Create Query by Using Wizard** icon.

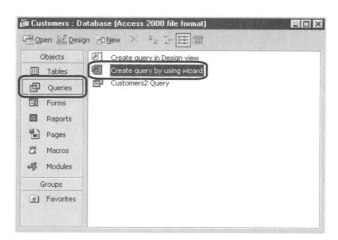

2. Select a table or an existing query.

3. Click the arrow buttons to select the fields that you want included in the query.

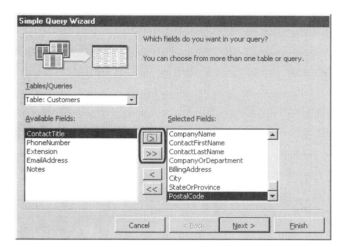

4. Click the **Next** button to continue.

5. If you selected numeric or date fields in step 3, indicate whether you want to see detail or summary information. If you choose Summary, click **Summary Options** to specify the calculation for each field, and then click the **OK** button.

6. Click the **Next** button to continue.

7. In the final wizard dialog box, type the name of the query.

8. Choose whether you want to view the results of the query or modify the query design in Design view.

9. Click the **Finish** button.

Getting Information with a Query

Access saves and lists the queries you create on the Queries tab in the Database window. You can double-click a query to run it and display the results. When you run a query, the query results show only the selected fields for each record in the table that matches your selection criteria.

Open and Run a Query

Dynaset

A window that displays the records that meet a query's specifications you established.

1. In the Database window, click **Queries** on the Objects bar.

2. Click the query you want to run.

3. Click the **Open** button ⬛ Open . The query opens in a table called a **dynaset**. The dynaset displays the records that meet the specifications set forth in the query.

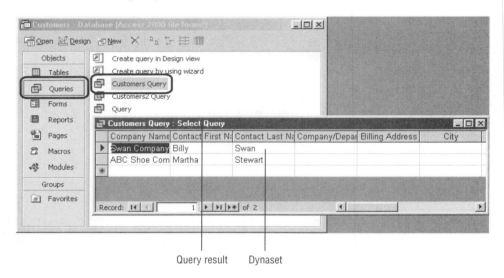

Query result   Dynaset

Modifying a Query in Design View

Once you have completed a query, you can further customize it in Design view. However, you can also create a query in Design view without using the wizard. Queries are not limited to a single table. Your queries can encompass multiple tables as long as the database includes a field or fields that relate the tables to each other.

Create or Modify a Query in Design View

1. In the Database window, click **Queries** on the Objects bar.

2. Double-click the **Create Query In Design View** icon, or click the query you want to modify and click the **Design** button ⬛ Design . If you're modifying a query, skip steps 3 through 5.

3. Select the table or existing query you'll use.

4. Click the **Add** button, and then click the **Close** button.

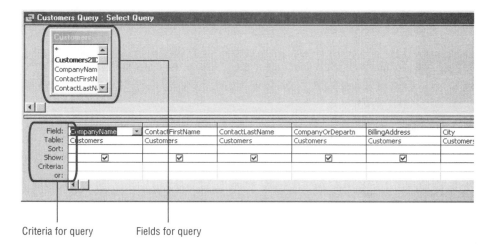

Criteria for query   Fields for query

5. As an alternative, repeat steps 3 and 4 for additional tables or queries, and then click the **Close** button.

6. Double-click or drag each field you want to include in the query from the field list.

7. In the design grid, enter any desired search criteria in the Criteria box.

8. Click the **Sort** drop-down arrow 🔽, and then specify a sort order.

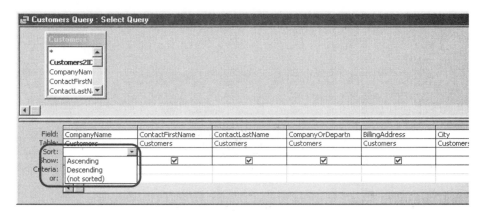

9. Click the **Save** button 💾, type a name for the query, and then click the **OK** button.

TIP To sort the query results in either ascending or descending order, display the query in Datasheet view, select the field in which you want to sort, and then click the Sort Ascending or Sort Descending button on the Table Datasheet toolbar.

 TIP To hide or delete a field from a query, display the query in Design view. To hide a field, click to clear the Show check box. To delete a field, select the field, and then press the Delete key on the keyboard.

Creating a Data Access Page Using a Wizard

Data Access Pages

Pages let you create Web pages out of your databases without the need for a Web server.

Data access pages allow you to create dynamic Web pages without the need of a Web server, unlike an Active Server Page (ASP) file. You can format data access pages, using many of the same tools you use when creating Access forms. Access organizes the data access pages in a separate object group in the Database window. Unlike other data objects, however, a data access page is stored in a file separate from the database file. One of the easiest ways to create a data access page is by using the Page Wizard.

Create a Data Access Page Using a Wizard

1. In the Database window, click **Pages** on the Objects bar.

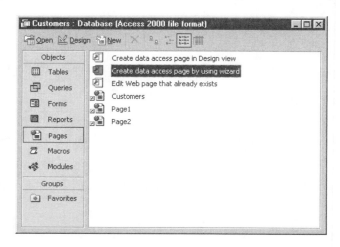

2. Double-click the **Create Data Access Page by Using Wizard** icon.

3. Select the table and fields that you want to appear in the data access page, and then click the **Next** button to continue.

4. If necessary, select any fields you want to act as group levels in the Web page, and then click the **Next** button to continue.

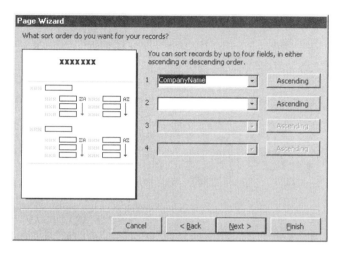

5. Select the fields in which you want to sort the records, and then click the **Next** button to continue.

6. Enter a title for the data access page.

7. Indicate whether you want to open the page in Access or to modify its design in Design view.

8. Click the **Finish** button.

TIP You can export data access pages to Web formats. Choose File ➢ Export, click the Save As Type drop-down arrow, click Microsoft Access Data Access Page, HTML Document, or Microsoft Active Server Pages, and then click the Save button or the Save All button.

Working with a Data Access Page in Design View

If you want to create a data access page without the Page Wizard, you can create it in Design view. Design view allows you to choose the tables, fields, and other objects that you want to appear on the Web page. You can format the appearance of the page using the same techniques you apply when you create Access forms.

Create or Modify a Data Access Page in Design View

1. In the Database window, click **Pages** on the Objects bar.

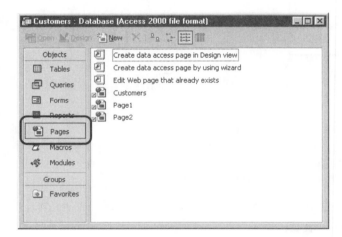

2. Double-click the **Create Data Access Page In Design View** icon, or click the page you want to modify, and then click the **Design** button ![Design]. Click the **OK** button when Access displays an alert box that tells you that if you create a data access page in Design view, you won't be able to open it in design view, you'll have to open it in Page view.

3. If necessary, click the **Field List** button ![icon] to display the list of tables and queries in the database.

4. Double-click the **Tables** or **Queries** folder, depending on which item you want to base your page.

5. Locate the table or query on which you want to base your page.

6. Drag a table or query icon from the field list to the Unbound section of the data access page.

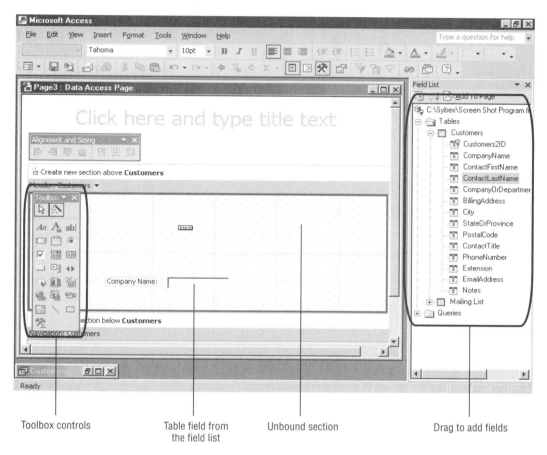

Toolbox controls

Table field from the field list

Unbound section

Drag to add fields

7. Click the **Close** button, click the **Yes** button when prompted to save your work, and then enter a filename for the resulting Web page.

> **TIP**
>
> To group data together on a data access page, display the data access page in Design view, select a field that will act as the grouping field, and then click the Promote button on the Page Design toolbar. Click the Demote button to ungroup the data.

Creating a Form Using a Wizard

To create a simple form in Access, you can use one of the AutoForm wizards. These wizards quickly arrange the fields from the selected table or query as an attractive form. In a form created with the AutoForm: Columnar Wizard, you see each record's data displayed vertically. With the AutoForm: Tabular Wizard, you see each record's data horizontally. With the AutoForm: Datasheet Wizard, the form displays the records in Datasheet view. After you create a form, you can save and name it so that you can use it again. Access lists any form you save on the Forms tab of the Database window.

Create a Form Using the AutoForm Wizard

1. In the Database window, click **Forms** on the Objects bar, and then click the **New** button ⊞ New .

2. Click **AutoForm: Columnar** (to display records in a column), **Auto-Form: Tabular** (to display records in rows), or **AutoForm: Datasheet** (to display records in Datasheet view).

3. Click the drop-down arrow ▼, and then click the name of a table or query on which to base the form.

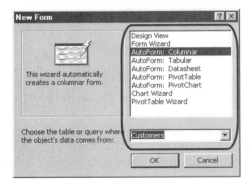

4. Click the **OK** button. After a moment, Access creates a form and displays it in Form view.

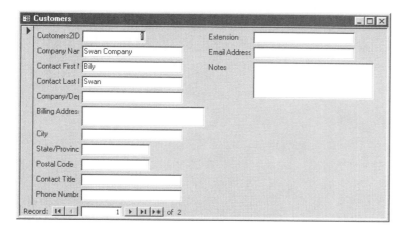

TIP To save a new form, click the Save button on the Form View toolbar while the new form is displayed, type the name of your form in the Save As dialog box, and then click the OK button.

Modifying a Form in Design View

You can create a form without the help of a wizard, as long as you have a good idea of how you want the form to look. You can create, modify, move, and format controls to create the exact form you want.

1. In the Database window, click **Forms** on the Objects bar, and then click the **New** button ▣ New or click a form and click the **Design** button ◩ Design. If you're modifying a form, skip step 2.

2. In the New Form dialog box, click **Design View**, select the table or query with the data you want to use, and then click the **OK** button.

3. If necessary, click the **Field List** button ▥ on the Form Design toolbar to add a bound control.

4. Select the field you want to add to the form.

5. Drag the field to the location in the form where you want the field to appear, and then release the mouse button to position the field.

6. Use the Toolbox to create new controls as needed. Click the Toolbox control, and then drag to create a control. Double-click the control to change the properties.

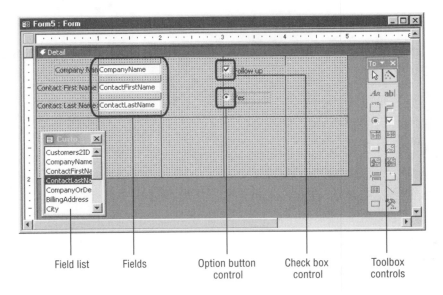

Field list   Fields   Option button control   Check box control   Toolbox controls

7. Use the Formatting toolbar to format the text in the form, as needed.

8. Click the **Save** button 🖫 on the Form Design toolbar to name the form and save it in the database.

Entering and Editing Data in a Form

Database designers often display data in forms that mimic the paper forms used to record data. Forms facilitate data entry and record viewing. They can also contain buttons that allow you to perform other actions, such as running macros, printing reports, or creating labels. The options that appear on a form depend on what features the database designer included.

A form directs you to enter the correct information and can automatically check your entries for errors. Access places the data you've entered in the form into the proper table or tables.

You can open a form in Form view or Design view. Form view allows you to view all the information associated with a record; Design view allows you to modify the form's design.

Enter and Edit Data in a Form

1. In the Database window, click **Forms** on the Objects bar, click the form you want to use, and then click the **Open** button 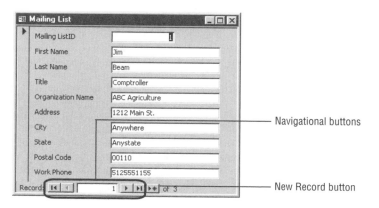.

2. Click the **New Record** button to enter a new record, or click a navigational button to display the record you want to edit.

Navigational buttons

New Record button

3. Enter or edit the data for a field.

4. Press the Tab key on the keyboard to move to the next field, hold down the Shift+Tab keys to move to the previous field, or click the insertion point in a field.

TIP To delete a record from a form, open the form, display the record you want to delete, click the Delete Record button on the Form View toolbar, and then click the Yes button.

Creating a Report Using a Wizard

After you have retrieved and organized only the specific information you want, you can display and print this information as a **report**. In Access, you can create a simple report that displays each record's information, or you can customize a report to include calculations, charts, graphics, and other features to go beyond the numbers and really emphasize the information in the report.

You can print a report, a table, a query, or any data in a single step using the Print button, in which case Access prints a single copy of all pages in the report. If you want to print only selected pages or if you want to specify other printing options, use the Print command on the File menu.

You can also enter data into a table or query in the same way you enter data into a form. When you enter data, some fields accept only certain kinds of information, such as numbers or text.

Report
A means of presenting data from a table, query or form in a printed format.

275

Create and Save a Report Using the AutoReport Wizard

One of the features you can use to create a simple report in Access is the AutoReport Wizard, which arranges data in a selected table or query as a formatted report.

The AutoReport: Columnar Wizard displays each record's data vertically, while the AutoReport: Tabular Wizard displays the data for each record horizontally. You can also create a report using the Report Wizard, which allows you to select the fields and information you want presented, and to choose from available formatting options that determine how the report will look.

> **TIP** You can create a report snapshot. In the Database window, click the report you want to use, choose File ➤ Export, click the Save As Type drop-down arrow, select Snapshot Format, enter a filename, and then click the Save button.

1. In the Database window, click **Reports** on the Objects bar, and then click the **New** button ⬚ New .

2. Click **AutoReport: Columnar** (to display records in a column), or click **AutoReport: Tabular** (to display records in rows).

3. Click the drop-down arrow ⬛, and then click a table or query on which to base the report.

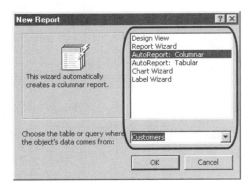

4. Click the **OK** button. Access displays the form in Print Preview, but you can switch to Design view, save, print, or close the report.

5. Click the **Save** button ⬚ on the toolbar, type a name for your report, and then click the **OK** button.

Create and Save a Report Using the Report Wizard

1. In the Database window, click **Reports** on the Objects bar, click the New button ![New], and then click **Report Wizard**.

2. Click the drop-down arrow ![arrow], select the table or query on which to base the report, and then click the **OK** button.

3. Select the fields you want to include, indicating the source of any fields you want to include from other tables or queries, and then click the **Next** button to continue.

4. If necessary, specify any groupings of the records, choosing any or all of the selected fields (up to 10), and then click the **Next** button to continue.

5. Specify the order of records within each group, sorting by up to four fields at a time, and specify ascending or descending order, and then click the **Next** button to continue.

6. Determine the layout and orientation of your report, and then click the **Next** button to continue.

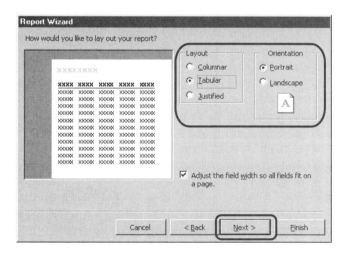

7. Specify the style of the report, which affects its formatting and final appearance, and then click the **Next** button to continue.

8. Name your report, indicate whether you want to preview or display it in Design view, and then click the **Finish** button.

You can create an instant report with the AutoReport command. In the Database window, select the table or query that contains the data you want, and then choose Insert ➤ AutoReport.

Modifying a Report in Design View

When you create a report from scratch in Design view, three sections appear: Page Header, Detail, and Page Footer. Other boxes might appear: the Field List box and the Toolbox. You can hide or view these boxes by clicking their corresponding buttons on the Report Design toolbar, Once you create the report, you need to populate it with data. You can add one or more **bound controls**— fields of data from a table or query—directly from the Field List, or you can add other types of **unbound controls**—text boxes, labels, pictures, buttons, and so on—from the Toolbox. In Design view, you see two parts for every control: the control itself and its corresponding label. When you move a control within a report, its corresponding label moves with it.

Bound Controls

Fields of data from a table or query in your Access database.

Unbound Controls

Items from the Toolbox, such as text boxes, labels, pictures, button, and so on.

> **TIP** The ruler and grid provide guides to help you arrange your controls. To display or hide the ruler and grid, choose View ➢ Ruler or Grid.

Modify a Report in Design View

1. In the Database window, click **Reports** on the Objects bar, and then click the **New** button ⬛ New , or click a report and click the **Design** button 🖊 Design (if you click Design, skip step 2).

2. In the New Report dialog box, click **Design View**, select the table or query on which to base the report, and then click the **OK** button.

3. To add a bound control, drag the selected field or fields to the section in which you want the field to appear. Two boxes appear for each field: one containing the label and one for the field values.

4. To add an unbound control, click a control button, such as a text box, a horizontal line, or a shape, on the Toolbox, and then drag to draw a box in the location where you want the control to appear. If you choose to add a list box, a list box wizard appears.

5. To view or hide headers and footers, choose **View** ➤ **Report Header/Footer** or **Page Header/Footer**. Add bounded or unbounded controls as needed.

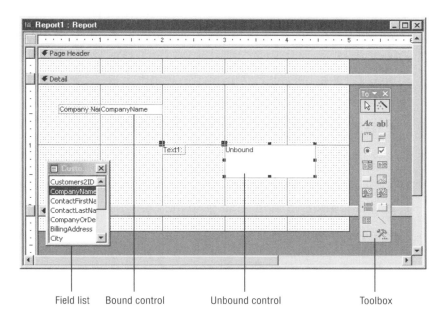

Field list   Bound control   Unbound control   Toolbox

Modify Properties

1. Display the report in Design view, double-click the object (control, section, or form) to open the object's property sheet.

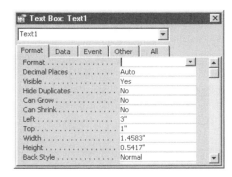

2. Enter the property information you want to change, and then click the **Close** button ✕ in the property sheet.

Formatting a Form or Report

A fast way to format a form or report is with the **AutoFormat** button, available in Design view. When you click this button on the Form Design toolbar, you can select and preview a variety of layouts and styles. After you make your selections, Access consistently formats the entire report or form for you. After using AutoFormat, you can always make additional changes to the formatting.

Format a Report or Form with AutoFormat

1. Display the report or form you want to format in Design view.

2. Click the **AutoFormat** button on the Report or Form Design toolbar. The AutoFormat dialog box opens.

3. Click the style option you want.

4. Click the **OK** button.

Printing Information

You can print a report, a table, a query, or any data in a single step using the Print button, in which case Access prints a single copy of all pages in the report. If you want to print only selected pages or if you want to specify other printing options, use the Print command on the File menu.

Print Data

1. Display the report, form, table, query, or any data you want to format in Design view.

2. Choose **File** ➢ **Print**. The Print dialog box opens.

3. If necessary, click the **Name** drop-down arrow ▼, and then select the printer you want to use.

4. To print selected pages in the report, click the **Pages** option button, and then type the first page in the **From** box and the ending page in the **To** box.

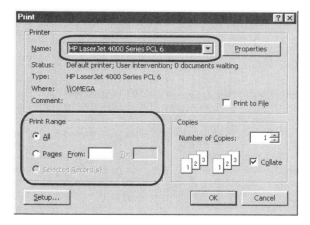

5. Click the **OK** button.

Creating Mailing Labels

Access provides a Label Wizard to help you create mailing labels quickly. The wizard supports a large variety of label brands and sizes. You can create labels by drawing data from any of your tables or queries. In addition to data values, labels can also include customized text that you specify.

NOTE If you are creating mailing labels for a dot-matrix printer, you might have to adjust the page size settings. See Access's online Help for special instructions regarding working with dot-matrix printers.

Create Mailing Labels

1. In the Database window, click **Reports** on the Objects bar, and then click the **New** button 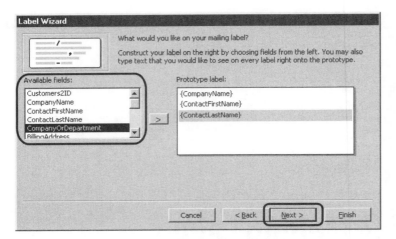.

2. Click **Label Wizard**, select the table or query that will be used in the mailing labels, and then click the **OK** button.

3. Select the type of mailing label you're using, and then click the **Next** button to continue.

4. Specify the font style and color for the label text, and then click the **Next** button to continue.

5. Double-click the field names in the Available Fields list to place them on your mailing labels. Type the text that you want to accompany the field values, and then click the **Next** button to continue.

6. Select a field to sort your labels by, if necessary, and then click the **Next** button to continue.

7. Enter a name for your mailing labels report and choose whether to preview the printout or modify the label design.

Communicating and Scheduling with Outlook

If, like many people, you're juggling a schedule, an address book, and an e-mail address list, and you're cluttering your desk and computer with reminder notes and to-do lists, help is here—Microsoft Outlook 2002.

Outlook, a messaging and personal information manager, integrates all the common messaging, planning, scheduling, organization, and management tools into one simple and flexible system. Whether you send e-mail messages, schedule meetings, or just need a personal information manager (PIM), Outlook provides the necessary tools for your information management needs.

Setting Up Outlook

E-mail service

A connection to an e-mail server where you store and receive e-mail messages.

E-mail is communication that you send or receive through an electronic messaging program, such as Outlook, over the Internet or a company network, known as a LAN (local area network). When you start Outlook for the first time, a setup wizard appears to step you through the process of setting up an **e-mail service**. You can get an e-mail service by contacting an Internet service provider (ISP). An ISP provides access to the Internet so that you can send and receive e-mail, communicate in chat rooms, or browse the World Wide Web.

Before you can create an e-mail account in Outlook, you need to obtain certain information from your ISP, including the type of e-mail account, name of the incoming and outgoing mail server, your user name, your e-mail address (for example: *username@ISPname*.com), and your password. The following table describes the common types of e-mail accounts.

You can connect to the Internet through your ISP over phone or cable lines using a modem or through a LAN. If you are connecting through a modem, your ISP can supply you with the phone number if necessary, modem settings, and network protocols required. If you are connecting through a LAN, your network administrator can provide you with your account information and the network protocols required to gain access to the mail server.

Configure Outlook for the First Time

1. Click the **Start** button ![Start], point to **Programs**, and then click **Microsoft Outlook** to start the program for the first time. The E-mail Accounts dialog box opens.

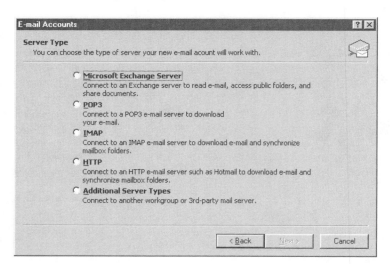

2. Click a server type option button, and then click the **Next** button.

3. Enter the e-mail account information supplied by your ISP or network administrator, and then click the **Next** button.

4. Click the **Finish** button in the last wizard dialog box.

Modify or Add E-mail Accounts

You can add several e-mail accounts. For example, you can add a Microsoft Exchange Server account to handle your business e-mail and an Internet e-mail account (known as POP3 or IMAP) or a Web-based e-mail account (known as HTTP), such as Hotmail, to handle your personal e-mail. You can access all your accounts from Outlook.

1. Choose **Tools** ➢ **E-mail Accounts**. The E-mail Accounts dialog box opens.

2. Click the **View or Change Existing E-mail Accounts** option button, and then click the **Next** button.

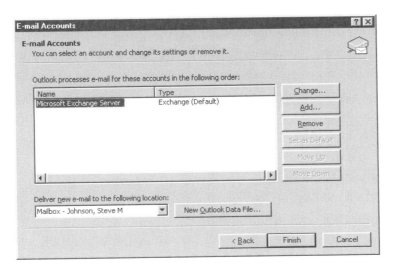

3. Click the **Change** button to modify an e-mail account, or click the **Add** button to add a new e-mail account.

> TIP To remail account, select the account you want to delete, and then click the Remove button in the E-mail Accounts dialog box.

4. Read and follow the setup wizard instructions to modify or add an e-mail account.

5. Click the **Finish** button in the last wizard dialog box.

> TIP If you add more than one e-mail account, you can choose which account to use as you send the message. To choose an e-mail account in a message, click the Accounts button, and then select the account you want to use from the list. The default account (set in the E-mail Accounts dialog) appears first in the list.

Moving Around Outlook

With Outlook, you get several tools to help you manage your busy life. As you work, you'll often need to switch between different activities and to create new **items** such as tasks, contacts, messages, and appointments. A typical session in Outlook might involve revising your list of tasks, calling an associate, adding a new contact to your contact list, sending an e-mail message, and scheduling a meeting. To keep track of all this activity in Outlook, you can move among Outlook's folders—**Inbox**, **Contacts**, Calendar, Tasks, Notes, and Journal—with a single click Outlook organizes folders into groups—click a group button on the Outlook Bar to display related folder icons.

> NOTE You can also add a Web page shortcut icon to the Outlook Bar. Display the Web toolbar, open the Web page you want, choose File ➤ New ➤ Outlook Bar Shortcut to Web Page.

Items
An item in Outlook is a basic element that holds information and is similar to a file in other programs.

Inbox
The Inbox receives and stores your incoming messages.

Contacts
The Contacts folder replaces your standard card file and stores multiple street addresses, phone numbers, e-mail and Web addresses, and any personal information you need about each contact.

View the Outlook Window

When you start Outlook, the Outlook program window opens and displays either Outlook Today or the Inbox, depending on your preference settings.

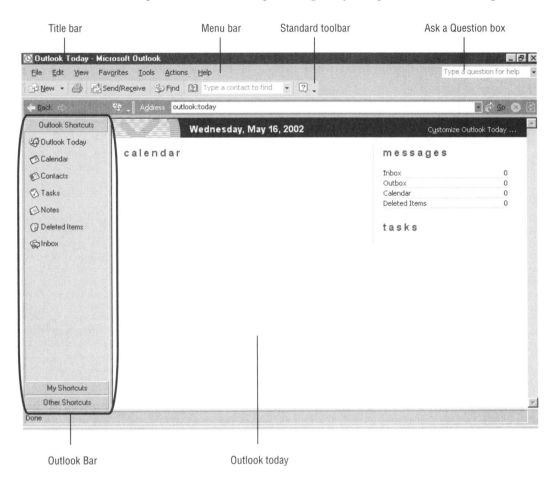

Title bar   Menu bar   Standard toolbar   Ask a Question box

Outlook Bar   Outlook today

TIP   You can import information from other PIM programs. Choose File ➣ Import and Export, and then follow the wizard instructions to import information you want.

Display Folder Icons and Open a Folder

1. Click a group button on the Outlook Bar.

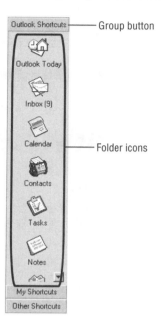

2. If necessary, click the scroll arrow to display the folder icon you want.

3. Click a folder icon that you want to open.

> **TIP** To create a new item for any folder, click the New button drop-down arrow on the Standard toolbar, and then click the item you want to create. The New button on the Standard toolbar changes to identify the kind of item you can create in the current folder. For example, if the Inbox is open, Outlook creates a mail message.

Using Outlook Today

If you like seeing all your appointments, tasks, and upcoming events in one summary view without having to switch between different views, you'll enjoy using Outlook Today. Outlook Today displays information using the style of a Web page, which makes it easy to open any piece of information by simply clicking it. You can easily customize Outlook Today, including options for how Outlook displays e-mail messages, calendar items, tasks, and Web page links.

> **NOTE** Outlook Today is defined using HTML, which allows you to create your own Outlook Today view as you would a Web page. The Outlook Today view could include specific company or workgroup information.

View Outlook Today

1. Click **Outlook Today** on the Outlook Bar.

2. Click any item to view it in more detail or to change it.

Customize Outlook Today

1. Click **Outlook Today** on the Outlook Bar.

2. Click **Customize Outlook Today**.

3. Set the options you want. When you customize Outlook today, you can choose any or all of the following options:

- ◆ Display the Outlook Today page at startup

- ◆ Display message folders

- ◆ Set the number of days in the Calendar

- ◆ Display and sort tasks

- ◆ Choose the page style

4. Click **Save Changes**.

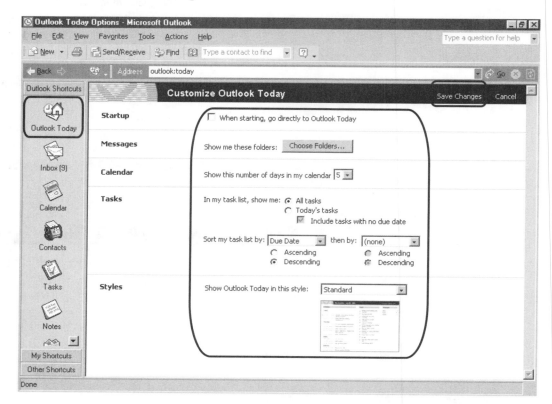

Creating a Contact

A **contact** is a person or company with whom you want to communicate. One contact can have several mailing addresses, various phone and fax numbers, e-mail addresses, and Web sites. You can store all this data in the Contacts folder along with more detailed information, such as job titles, birthdays, and anniversaries. When you double-click a contact, you open a dialog box in which you can edit the detailed contact information. You can also directly edit the contact information from within the Contacts folder. If you send the same e-mail message to more than one person, you can group contacts together into a distribution list.

TIP To change Contacts views, click Contacts on the Outlook Bar, choose View ➢ Current View, and then click the view you want (By Category, By Company, By Location, or By Follow-up Flag).

Create a New Contact

1. Click the **New** button drop-down arrow 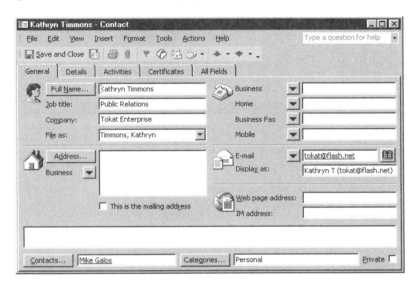 on the Standard toolbar, and then click **Contact**.

2. Fill in information on the **General** tab. You can enter names, addresses (postal, e-mail, and Web page), phone numbers, and comments.

3. If you want, click the **Categories** button to organize the contact, and then click the **OK** button.

4. Click the **Save and Close** button Save and Close.

| TIP | To open and update an existing contact, click Contacts on the Outlook Bar, double-click the contact you want to update, use the normal editing commands to update the information, and then click the Save and Close button. |

| TIP | To delete a contact, click Contacts on the Outlook Bar, click the contact you want to delete, and then click the Delete button on the Standard toolbar. Any journal entries that refer to that contact remain intact. |

When you create an e-mail message, the name you type in the Display As box in a Contact window appears in the To box instead of the actual e-mail address. Instead of typing an e-mail address, you can type the name as shown in the Display As box.

Create a Distribution List from Contacts

1. Click **Contacts** on the Outlook Bar.

2. Choose **Actions** ➤ **New Distribution List**. The Untitled Distribution List window opens.

3. In the **Name** box, type a name for the distribution list.

4. Click **Select Members**. The Select Members dialog box opens.

5. Select the members you want, click the **Members** button, and then click the **OK** button when you're done selecting names.

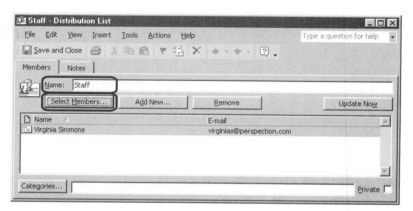

6. Click the **Save and Close** button.

Creating and Sending an E-Mail Message

Sending mail messages is a quick and effective way to communicate with others. Mail messages follow a standard memo format in which you specify the recipient of the message, the subject of the message, and the message. To send a message, you need to enter the recipient's or recipients' complete e-mail addresses.

Create and Send an E-Mail Message

1. Click the **New** button drop-down arrow on the Standard toolbar, and then click Mail Message.

An e-mail address is not case-sensitive (that is, capitalization doesn't matter), but an e-mail address cannot contain spaces.

2. In the **To** box, type the e-mail address (use a semicolon to separate two or more addresses), or click the **To** button to open the select Names dialog box.

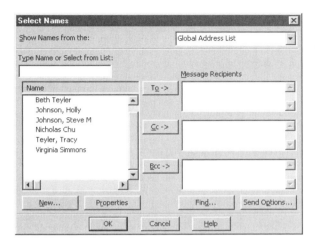

As you start typing an e-mail address in a message, Outlook displays a list of names that match people you've already sent messages.

As you type your message, Outlook uses Microsoft Word to detect and correct misspelled words with the AutoCorrect feature.

3. Click the **Show Name From The** drop-down arrow ▾, and then select an Address Book.

4. Click a name. To select multiple names, hold down the Ctrl key on the keyboard while you click other names.

5. Click the **To** button, the **Cc** button, or the **Bcc** button. (To sends the message to the selected names; Cc sends a courtesy copy; Bcc sends a blind courtesy copy.)

6. When you're done selecting names, click the **OK** button.

7. In the **Subject** box, type a brief description of your message.

8. Type the text of your message.

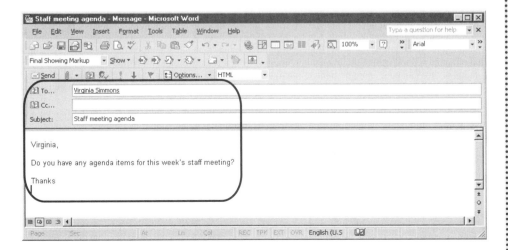

9. Click the **Options** button, specify the message settings you want, and then click the **Close** button.

10. Click the **Send** button.

Using Stationery

There is no reason to limit your mail messages to a black and white color scheme. Give your mail messages a dramatic appearance by writing them on stationery. Outlook comes with a variety of stationery, which includes background images and borders. You can customize the stationery to reflect your creative spirit or create your own stationery from scratch.

Create a Mail Message Using Stationery

1. Click **Inbox** on the Outlook Bar.

2. Choose **Actions** ➤ **New Mail Message Using**.

3. Click the stationery you want to use. If none is available, click **More Stationery**, click the stationery you want, and then click the **OK** button.

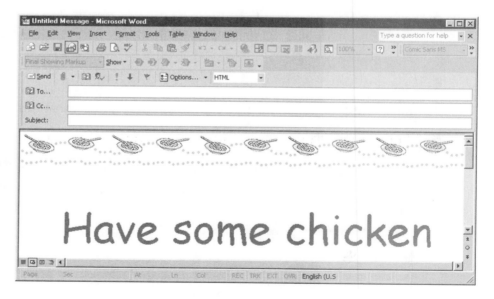

TIP To create stationery, choose Tools ➤ Options, click the Mail Format tab, click the Compose in this format drop-down arrow, click HTML, click the Stationeyr Picker button, click the New button, and then follow the Wizard instructions.

Creating a Signature

Give your message a personal touch by ending it with your unique signature. A **signature** is any file (a text file, graphic file, or a file that is a scanned image of your handwritten signature) that you choose to use in the closing of a mail message. A **business card** is your, or someone else's, contact information that comes directly from the Address Book.

Create a Signature and Attach a Business Card

1. Choose **Tools ➤ Options**, and then click the **Mail Format** tab. The Options dialog box opens.

2. Click the **Signatures** button, and then click the **New** button. The Create New signature dialog box opens.

3. Enter a name for your signature, and then click the **Next** button to continue. The Edit Signature dialog box opens.

4. In the **Signature text** box, type your signature text.

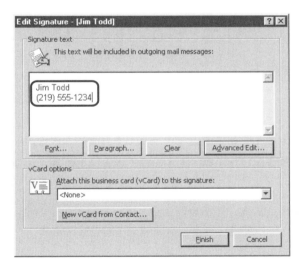

5. Click the **Font** button and the **Paragraph** button to further customize the text.

6. To attach a business card, click the **Attach This Business Card (vCard) to this signature** drop-down arrow , and then select a contact.

Signature

A signature is a file containing an image that represents your handwritten signature, used in the closing of an e-mail message.

Business Card

Contact information about yourself or someone else that comes directly from the Address Book.

7. To create a new business card, click **New vCard from Contact**, click a contact, click the **Add** button, and then click the **OK** button.

8. Click the **Finish** button, and then click the **OK** button. The Options dialog box appears.

9. Click the **Signature for New Messages** drop-down arrow ▼, and then select a signature. If you want, click the Signature for replies and forwards drop-down arrow, and then select a signature.

10. Click the **OK** button.

> **TIP** To switch between signatures, right-click the existing signature in the e-mail message, and then select the name of the signature you want to use.

Reading and Replying to an E-Mail Message

Flag
A flag indicates a specific level of importance or sensitivity on an e-mail message.

You can receive an e-mail message anytime, day or night, even when your computer is turned off. New mail messages (which are displayed in bold text) appear in the Inbox along with mail messages you haven't yet stored or deleted. A **flag** next to a mail message indicates a specific level of importance or sensitivity. The message's flag, along with the sender's name and subject line, can help you determine which message you want to open, read, and respond to first. Whenever you reply to or forward a mail message, Outlook adds a note indicating when you replied or forwarded the mail message.

> **NOTE** Below the list of messages in the Inbox is the Preview pane. Within the Preview pane, you can open file attachments, follow a hyperlink, respond to meeting requests and display status information and the text for the selected message.

> **NOTE** The moment you receive new e-mail messages, the New Mail icon appears next to the clock on the taskbar. You can double-click the icon to switch to your Inbox. Depending on your e-mail service, you might have to log on to a network or dial in to an Internet Service Provider (ISP) to receive your new e-mail messages.

Preview and Open an E-Mail Message

1. Click **Inbox** on the Outlook Bar.

2. Choose **View** ➢ **Preview Pane** or **AutoPreview** (or both).

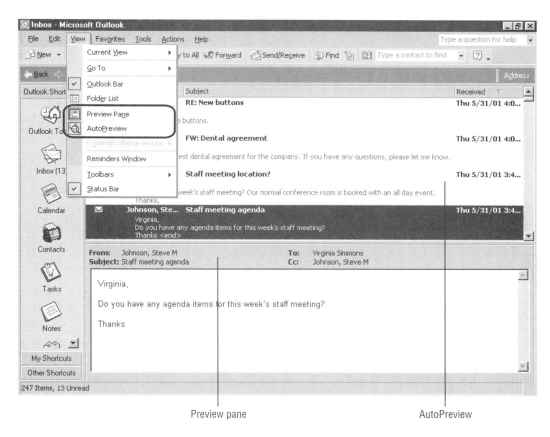

Preview pane   AutoPreview

3. Click the message header to preview the message in the Preview pane, or double-click the message you want to open.

Reply to an E-Mail Message

1. Click **Inbox** on the Outlook Bar.

2. Click the message to which you want to respond.

3. Click the **Reply** button 🖳 Reply to respond to only the message's sender, or click the **Reply to All** button 🖳 Reply to All to respond to the sender and all other recipients of the original mail message.

4. Type your message at the top of the message box.

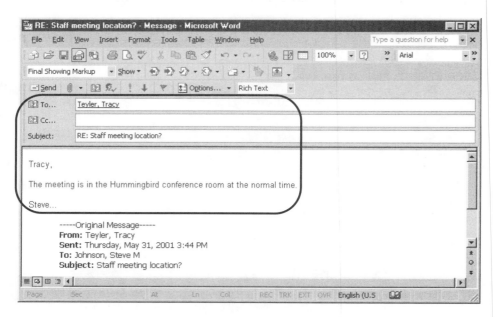

5. Click the **Send** button ☑ Send .

To add an e-mail address to your contact list, open the e-mail message, right-click the e-mail address you want, click Add to Contacts on the shortcut menu, enter any additional information, and then click the Save and Close button.

Forward an E-Mail Message

1. Click **Inbox** on the Outlook Bar.

2. Click the message you want to forward.

3. Click the **Forward** button 🔄 Forward on the Standard toolbar.

4. Click the **To** button or **Cc** button, and then select recipients for this mail message.

5. Type new text at the top of the message box.

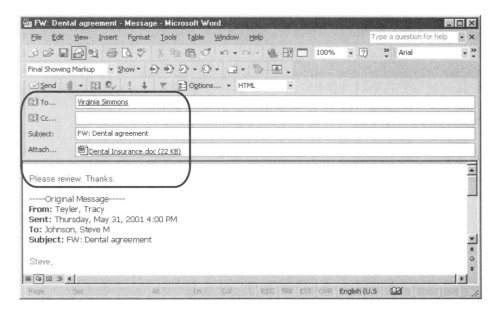

6. Click the **Send** button ⌐⁼ Send .

Managing E-Mail Messages

Instead of scrolling through your Inbox to find a particular mail message, you can use the Find button on the Standard toolbar. To avoid an overly cluttered Inbox, remember to routinely clear the Inbox of mail messages that you have read and to which you have responded. You can delete mail messages you no longer need or move them to other folders. Storing your mail messages in other folders and deleting unwanted mail messages makes it easier to see new mail messages and to clear your computer's resources for new activities.

Find E-Mail Messages

1. Click **Inbox** on the Outlook Bar.

2. Click the **Find** button 🔍 Find on the Standard toolbar.

3. In the **Look For** box, enter the information you want to find in a message.

4. Click the **Search In** button, and then click where you want to search.

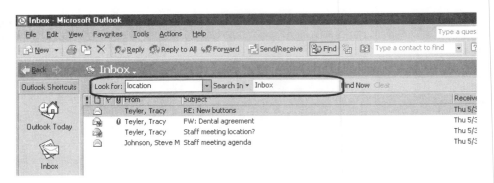

5. Click the **Find Now** button.

6. Click the **Find** button 🔍 Find on the Standard toolbar to return to the Inbox.

> **NOTE** You can sort items within a folder. If available, click a column button to sort items in the folder by that column in either ascending or descending order.

Deleting Unwanted Messages

If you no longer need a mail message, you can delete it. To delete unwanted messages, select the mail message or messages you want to move to the Deleted Items folder, and then click the Delete button on the Standard toolbar. You can retrieve mail messages from the Deleted Items folder. Items remain in the Deleted Items folder until you empty it. To retrieve mail messages from the Deleted Items folder, click the My Shortcuts group button on the Outlook Bar, and then click Deleted Items. Drag an item to the Inbox or to any other folder icon on the Outlook Bar. To empty the Deleted Items folder and permanently delete its contents, right-click Deleted Items on the Outlook Bar, click Empty "Deleted Items" Folder, and then click the Yes button to confirm the deletion.

Create a New Folder

1. Choose **File ➢ Folder ➢ New Folder**. The Create New Folder dialog box opens.

2. In the **Name** box, type a name for the new folder.

3. Click the **Folder Contains** drop-down arrow 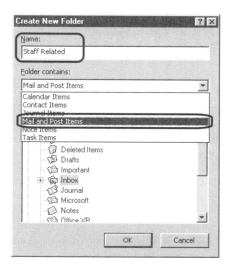, and then click the type of item you want to store here.

4. Click the folder in which you want to file this subfolder.

5. Click the **OK** button.

Move E-Mail Messages to a Different Folder

1. Click **Inbox** on the Outlook Bar.

2. Select the mail message or messages you want to move.

3. Click the **Move To Folder** button 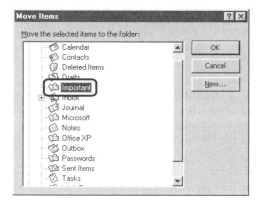 on the Standard toolbar, and then click **Move To Folder**. The Move Items dialog box opens.

4. Click the folder where you want to move the mail messages.

5. Click the **OK** button.

> **TIP** You can also drag an e-mail message to a folder on the Outlook Bar to quickly move the message to a different folder.

Attaching a File to an E-Mail Message

File sharing is a powerful feature of e-mail. You can attach one or more files, such as a picture or a document, to a mail message. For example, suppose you are working on a report that a colleague needs to present today in another part of the country. After you finish the report, you can attach the file to a mail message and send the message with the attached file directly to your colleague. When the recipient of the mail message opens the attachment, the file opens in the program in which it was created.

> **TIP** You can save attachments to your hard drive. Open the e-mail message with the attachment, choose File ➣ Save Attachments, select the location where you want to save the file, and then click the Save button.

Attach a File to an E-Mail Message

1. Compose a new message. The Untitled Message window opens.

2. Click the **Insert File** button 📎 on the Standard toolbar.

> **TIP** To attach an Outlook item, such as a contract or e-mail message, click the Insert File button drop-down arrow, click Item, click the folder and item you want to insert, and then click the OK button.

3. Click the **Look In** drop-down arrow ▾, and then select the drive and folder that contains the file you want to attach.

4. Click the file you want to attach to the message.

5. Click the **Insert** button.

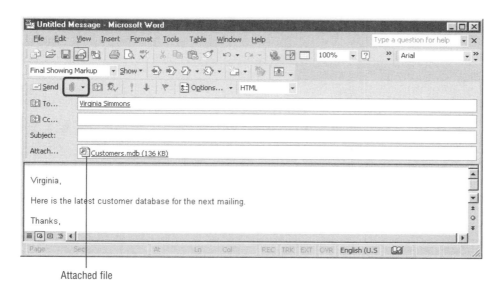

Attached file

6. Send the mail message, or save it to send later.

Viewing the Calendar

The **Calendar** is an electronic version of the familiar paper daily planner. You can schedule time for completing specific tasks, meetings, vacations, holidays, or for any other activity with the Calendar. You can adjust the current view to display different Calendar options. From the View menu, you can display your schedule in a planner format: daily, weekly, or monthly. With AutoPreview turned on, you see the first three lines of the appointment. You can view all the appointments and meetings scheduled from the current day forward, or view current and future events, including those that occur only once a year. You also can view all appointments that take place regularly. In addition, you can display all appointments by category.

Change the Calendar View

The Calendar displays your schedule in a typical daily planner format or in list format. You can change the Calendar view in several ways.

◆ Choose **View** ➢ **Current View**, and then click the view option you want.

◆ Click one of the Calendar view buttons on the Standard toolbar.

Calendar

An electronic version of a paper calendar or organizer, where you can record appointments, tasks, events, activities, and meetings.

◆ Click the left arrow or right arrow on the Date Navigator to change the current month.

◆ Click a date on the Date Navigator to view that day's schedule. The date highlighted in red is today's date.

Appointment area   Calendar view   Date Navigator   TaskPad

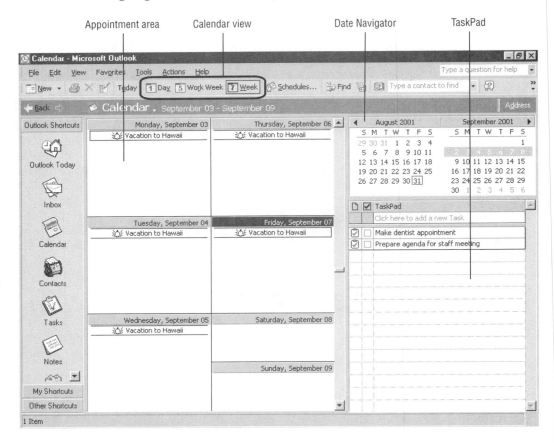

To customize the Calendar view, choose Tools ➤ Options, click the Preferences tab, click the Calendar Options button, select the options you want, and then click the OK button twice.

Appointment
An activity you schedule which doesn't include other people or resources within your organization.

Event
An appointment that lasts more than one day, such as a seminar, conference, or vacation.

Scheduling an Appointment and Event

In Outlook, an **appointment** is any activity you schedule that doesn't include other people or resources. An **event** is any appointment that lasts one or more full days (24-hour increments), such as a seminar, a conference, or a vacation. You can mark yourself available (free or tentative) or unavailable (busy or out of the office) to others during a scheduled appointment or an event. You enter appointment or event information in the same box; however, when you schedule an event, the All Day Event check box is selected; the check box is cleared when you schedule an appointment.

TIP To edit an appointment or event, click Calendar on the Outlook Bar, double-click the appointment or event, make changes, and then click the Save and Close button.

TIP To cancel an appointment or event, click Calendar on the Outlook Bar, click the appointment or event, and then click the Delete button on the Standard toolbar.

Schedule an Appointment or Event

1. Click **Calendar** on the Outlook Shortcut Bar.

2. If you want to schedule an appointment, drag to select a block of time in the appointment area.

3. Right-click the selected block, and then click **New Appointment** or click **New All Day Event**.

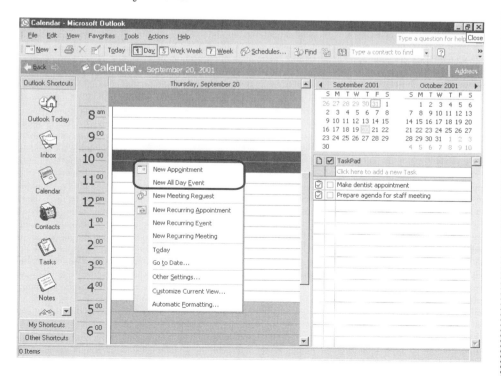

> **TIP** To change an event to an appointment or vice versa, click the All Day Event check box to clear it or select it.

4. In the **Subject** box, type the subject.

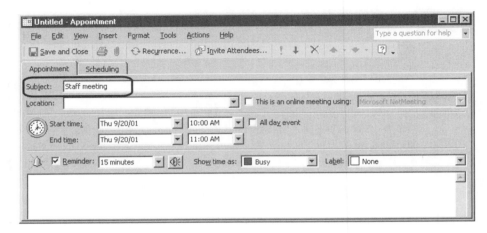

5. In the **Location** box, type the location, or click the drop-down arrow [▼], and then select a location from the list.

6. Specify the start and end times.

7. Type any notes or details regarding the event, or attach a file if necessary.

8. To help you sort, group, or filter your appointments, click the **Categories** button, select the options you want, and then click the **OK** button.

9. If you want a reminder notice, click the **Reminder** check box to select it, specify an amount of time before the event that you want to be notified.

10. Click the **Save and Close** button ![Save and Close].

> **TIP** You can schedule a recurring appointment. In Calendar, select a block of time, choose Actions ➢ New Recurring Appointment, fill in the appointment times and recurrence information, click the OK button, and then click the Save and Close button.

Reschedule an appointment or event quickly by dragging it to a new time on the Time Bar or to a new day in the Date Navigator in Day/Week/Month view.

14 Managing Information with Outlook

Microsoft Outlook 2002 provides an easy and efficient way to track and organize all the information that lands on your desk. You can use Outlook tools for your personal information management needs. With Outlook, you can organize and manage your day-to-day information, from e-mail and calendars to contacts and tasks. It's easy to share information with others, and organize and view your schedule and communications in one place.

Managing Information

Group

Within Outlook, a group is a set of items with something in common, such as e-mail messages from the same sender, or tasks with the same due date.

Field

An element for storing certain types of information.

Newsgroup

An area on the Internet that contains messages and posts on particular subjects.

Task Request

The process of assigning a task to another individual.

You can use Outlook to create a to-do list and assign the items on the list to others as needed from Tasks. Rather than cluttering your desk or obscuring your computer with sticky pad notes, use Notes to jot down your immediate thoughts, ideas, and other observations. With everything related to your work in one place, you can always locate what you need—files, notes for a project, or even the time of a phone call with a certain contact. Just check the Journal timeline to find it.

To help organize and locate information, Outlook allows you to group, sort, and filter items. **Group** organizes items based on a particular **field** (an element for storing a particular type of information). Sort arranges items in ascending or descending order according to a specified field. Filter shows items that match specific criteria, such as "High Priority." You can group, sort, and filter by more than one field at a time.

If you are interested in communicating with people around the world about things that interest you, you will have fun with newsgroups. A **newsgroup** is a forum where people can share common interests, communicate ideas, ask and answer questions, and comment on a variety of subjects. You can find a newsgroup on almost any topic, from the serious to the lighthearted, from educational to controversial, from business to social.

Managing Tasks

A common Monday chore is creating a list of activities that you should accomplish that week. Outlook Tasks is more efficient than a traditional to-do list, because you can track a task's status and progress, estimated and actual hours, mileage, and other associated billing costs. You can create a to-do list with deadlines and cross off items as you complete them. Overdue tasks remain on your list until you finish them or delete them. You can also delegate a particular task to someone by sending a **task request**, complete with deadlines and related attachments. You can see an outstanding task in the Calendar TaskPad and in the tasks list until you check it off or delete it.

Create a New Task

1. Click the **New** button drop-down arrow ⊞ New ▼ on the Standard toolbar, and then click **Task**. The Task window opens.

2. In the **Subject** box, type a description of the task.

3. Set the time frame, status, priority, alarm, categories, or any other option.

4. Type any relevant notes, or attach related files.

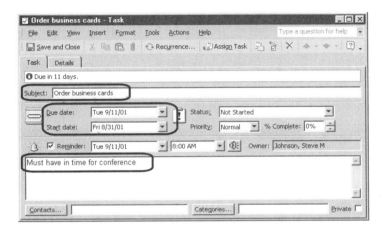

5. Click the **Save and Close** button .

Assign a New Task to Someone Else

1. Click the **New** button drop-down arrow on the Standard toolbar, and then click **Task Request**. The Task window opens.

2. Type the name or e-mail address of the person you are assigning the task to, or click the **To** button and select a recipient from the list.

3. Type the subject, and then set the time frame, status, priority, alarm, categories, or any other option.

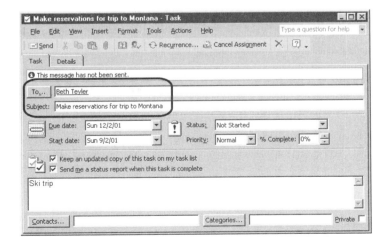

4. Click the **Send** button ⊟ <u>S</u>end .

Delete a Task from the Task List

1. Click **Tasks** on the Outlook Bar.

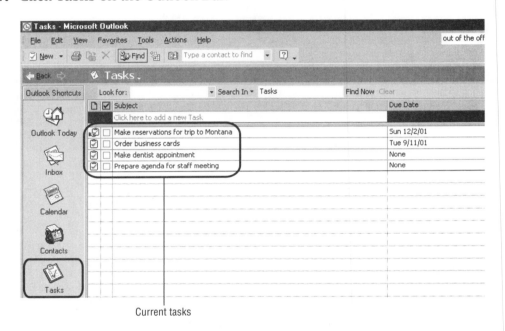

Current tasks

2. Click the task you want to delete.

3. Click the **Delete** button ✕ on the Standard toolbar.

Recording Items in the Journal

The Outlook Journal is a diary of all the activities and interactions from your day. With everything organized on a timeline, you can see an overview of what you accomplished and when and how long certain activities took. The Journal also provides an alternate way to locate a particular item or a file. You can have the Journal automatically record entries of your phone calls, e-mail messages, meeting requests and responses, tasks, faxes, and documents on which you've worked. You must record tasks, appointments, personal conversations, and existing documents manually.

Automatically Record New Items and Documents

1. Choose **Tools** ➢ **Options**. The Options dialog box opens.

2. Click the **Journal Options** button. The Journal Options dialog box opens.

3. Click to select the check boxes for the items you want to record in the Journal automatically.

4. Click to select the check boxes of the contacts for whom you want to record the selected items.

5. Click to select the check boxes of the programs that you want recorded.

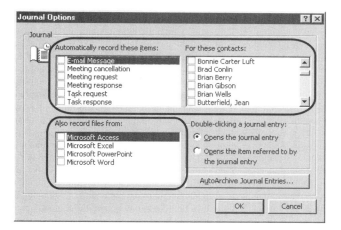

6. Click the **OK** button to close the Journal Options dialog box.

7. Click the **OK** button.

Manually Record an Activity

1. Click the items or the files you want to record.

2. Choose **File** ➢ **New** ➢ **Journal Entry**. The Untitled Journal Entry window opens.

3. In the **Subject** box, type a description of the journal entry.

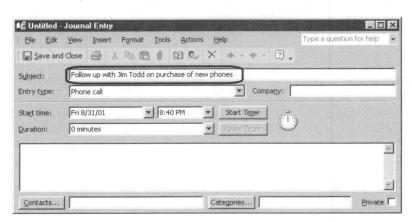

4. In the **Company** box, type a company, select a start time and duration, and enter any notes.

5. Click **Contacts**, select a contact, and then click the **OK** button.

6. Click **Categories**, select one or more categories, and then click the **OK** button.

7. Click the **Save and Close** button .

TIP To manually record an activity for a contact, Click Contacts on the Outlook Bar, and then double-click an existing contact, choose Actions ➤ New Journal Entry for Contact, fill in the journal entry information, and then click the Save and Close button.

Working with Journal Entries

Timeline
A timeline in Outlook is a simple way to view the time due order of recorded items, documents and activities in your Journal.

A **timeline** is an easy way to view the chronological order of recorded items, documents, and activities in the Journal. Each item appears next to the date and time it originated. A solid bar indicates the duration of any activity. You can move items and documents by changing the start time. You can also change the time scale to see items by day, week, and month.

Journal entries and their related items, documents, and contacts are easy to open, move, and even delete. When you modify a journal entry, its associated items, documents, or contacts are not affected. Likewise, when you modify an item, document, or contact, any existing related journal entries remain unchanged. If you no longer need a journal entry, you can select the entry and press the Delete key on the keyboard or click the Delete button to remove it.

To create a new journal entry quickly, double-click the white area below the Entry Type bar. Fill in the Journal Entry window as usual.

Open a Journal Entry and Its Recorded Item

1. Click the **My Shortcuts** group on the Outlook Bar.

2. Click **Journal** on the Outlook Bar.

3. To change the way items display in the Journal, click one of the time scale buttons (**Go To Today** button Today, **Day** button 1 Day, **Week** button 5 Work Week, or **Month** button 31 Month) on the Standard toolbar.

4. If necessary, click the plus sign (+) or double-click the **Entry Type** bar to display its items.

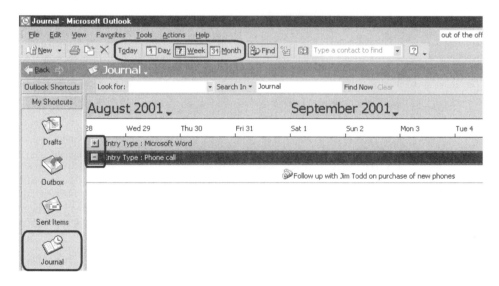

5. Double-click the journal item, document, or contact name you want to open.

6. Change the time frame, status, priority, alarm, categories, or any other option.

7. Click the **Save and Close** button ⊟ Send.

> **TIP** When you switch to the Journal to view recorded items, some types of entries might be expanded to show all items and others might be collapsed to hide all items. You can easily switch between expanded and collapsed views by double-clicking the Entry Type bar.

View Journal Entries for a Contact

1. Click **Contacts** on the Outlook Bar.

2. Double-click a contact name. The Contact window opens.

3. Click the **Activities** tab.

4. Click the **Show** drop-down arrow ▼, and then click **Journal**.

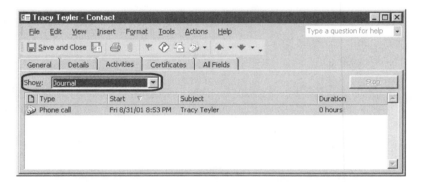

5. Read the entries for the selected contact.

6. Click the **Save and Close** button 🖫 Save and Close .

Organizing Information by Categories

Category
A category is a keyword or keywords you give to items so you can find them later, or sort, or filter them.

A **category** is one or more keywords or phrases you assign to items so you can later find, group, sort, or filter them. Categories provide additional flexibility in how you organize and store items and files. By using categories, you can store related items in different folders or unrelated items in the same folder, and still compile a complete list of items related to a specific category. Outlook starts you off with a *Master Category List* of some common categories, but you can add or remove them to fit your purposes.

> **TIP** You can export a specific category of contacts using Microsoft Word's Mail Merge to create a mailing list.

Assign and Remove Categories to and from an Outlook Item

1. Click any Outlook item to select it.

2. Choose **Edit ➤ Categories**. The Categories dialog box opens.

3. Click to select or clear check boxes to assign or remove categories.

TIP To add or remove a master category, and then click the Master Category List button in the Categories dialog box. To add a category, type a new category name, and then click the Add button. To remove a category, click the category you want to remove, and then click the Delete button.

4. Click the **OK** button.

Sorting Items

Sometimes you'll want to organize items in a specific order—for example, tasks from high to low priority or in alphabetical order by category. A **sort** arranges items in ascending (A to Z, lowest to highest, recent to distant) or descending (Z to A, highest to lowest, distant to recent) alphabetical, numerical, or chronological order. You can sort items by one or more fields; you can also sort grouped items. Items must be in a table view in order for you to sort them.

Sort
Arranging items in ascending or descending order.

TIP You can print categorized items. Sort items by categories or find a particular category. Select one or more items, and then print.

Sort a List of Items

1. Open the list of items you want to sort.

2. Choose **View** ➤ **Current View** ➤ **Customize Current View**. The View Summary dialog box opens.

3. Click the **Sort** button. The Sort dialog box opens.

4. Click the **Sort Items By** drop-down arrow , and then click a field.

5. Click the **Ascending** or **Descending** option button.

6. Click the **Then By** drop-down arrow , and then click a second sort element and order, if necessary.

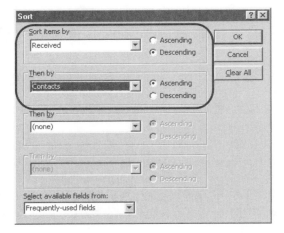

TIP To remove a sort, click the Clear All button in the Sort dialog box.

7. Click the **OK** button to close the Sort dialog box.

8. Click the **OK** button.

Viewing Specific Files Using Filters and Rules

A **filter** isolates the items or files that match certain specifications, such as all appointments with a certain contact or any documents you created last week. If you select two or more filter criteria, Outlook lists only those items and files

Filter
A filter isolates items or files that match specifications that you set.

that meet all the criteria are listed. "Filter Applied" appears in the lower-left corner of the status bar as a reminder that you filtered the items and files you are viewing.

> **TIP** You can filter for any or all of the options available in the Filter dialog box. For example, you might want to filter for a specific word in a certain field, for all items with a particular status, or for all items received from or sent to someone on a specific day.

Set a Filter to Show Certain Items and Files

1. Open the list of items and files in which you want to apply a filter.

2. Choose **View ➢ Current View ➢ Customize Current View**. The View Summary dialog box opens.

3. Click the **Filter** button. The Filter dialog box opens.

4. In the **Search for the word(s)** box, type a word to search for.

5. Click the **In** drop-down arrow ▾, and then select where you want to search.

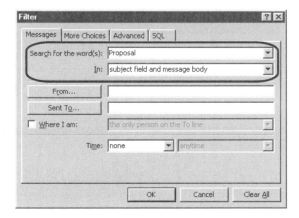

6. Click the **From** button to select the sender, click the **Sent To** button to select the recipient, and click the **Time** drop-down arrow ▾ to specify a time frame as necessary.

> **TIP** To remove a filter, click the Clear All button in the Filter dialog box.

7. Click the **OK** button to close the Filter dialog box.

8. Click the **OK** button.

Organizing Folders

Rules

Rules are a specific set of criteria you set to help you organize your e-mail messages.

As you become more familiar with using e-mail for communicating, you will need to logically organize the volumes of e-mail messages that you receive. Outlook provides a way to organize each of your folders using specific criteria, known as **rules**, which you set. For example, you can set your Inbox to store incoming messages from a particular organization in an existing folder (such as Important), or in a folder that you create. You can even specify a way to identify the junk mail that comes into your Inbox.

> **TIP** You can organize folders by color. Click the Organize button on the Standard toolbar, click Using Colors, and then make the color selections you want.

Organize Your Inbox Folder

1. Click **Inbox** on the Outlook Bar.

2. Click the **Organize** button on the Standard toolbar.

3. Click an e-mail message in the Information viewer.

4. Click **Using Folders**.

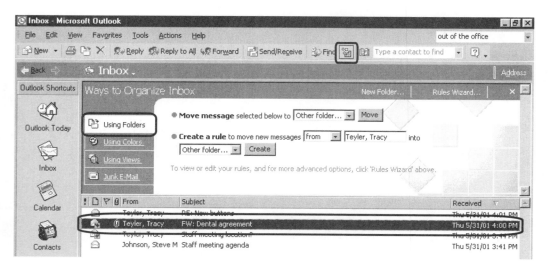

5. To move the selected message, click the **Move Message Selected Below To** drop-down arrow ▼, click a folder in the folder list, and then click the **Move** button.

6. To create a rule to move new messages, click the **Into** drop-down arrow ▼, click a folder in the folder list, and then click the **Create** button. You can also use the Rules Wizard to set criteria for incoming messages. Choose **Tools ➢ Rules Wizard**, or click the **Rules Wizard** button 🗒 when the Organize feature is on.

7. Click the **Yes** button or the **No** button to apply the rule to the current contents of the folder.

8. Click the **Organize** button 🔲 on the Standard toolbar to remove the organize pane.

TIP You can use the Rules Wizard to set criteria for incoming messages. Choose Tools ➢ Rules Wizard, or click the Rules Wizard button when the Organize feature is on.

TIP To archive all folders using AutoArchive, choose Tools ➢ Options, and then click the Other tab, click AutoArchive, set the archive duration, select the location in which to save the archive, and then click the OK button. To archive a single folder, choose File ➢ Archive.

File Junk E-Mail

1. Click **Inbox** on the Outlook Bar.

2. Click the **Organize** button 🔲 on the Standard toolbar.

3. Click **Junk E-Mail**.

4. Click the first **Automatically** drop-down arrow , and then select **Color** or **Move**.

5. Click the **Turn On** button, and then click the **OK** button to create a Junk E-Mail folder.

6. If necessary, click the **Yes** button or click the **No** button to create a shortcut icon on the Outlook Bar.

7. Right-click an e-mail message, point to **Junk E-Mail**, and then click **Add To Junk Senders List**.

> **TIP** To add to the junk senders list, click the e-mail message you want to add to the junk senders list, choose Actions ➤ Junk E-mail ➤ Add To Junk Senders List or Add To Adult Content Senders List.

Flag an E-Mail Message for Follow Up

1. Click the e-mail message you want to flag.

2. Choose **Actions** ➤ **Follow Up**. The Flag for Follow Up dialog box opens.

3. Click the **Due By** drop-down arrow , and then select a date.

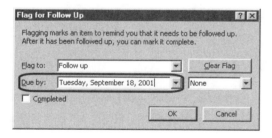

> **TIP** Click the Completed check box to select when the follow-up is complete or click the Clear Flag button to remove the flag in the Flag for Follow Up dialog box.

4. Click the **OK** button.

Writing Notes

Notes replace the random scraps of paper on which you might jot down reminders, questions, thoughts, ideas, or directions. Like the popular sticky notes, you can move an Outlook note anywhere on your screen and leave it displayed as you work. Any edits you make to a note are saved automatically. The ability to color-code, size, categorize, sort, or filter notes makes these notes even handier than their paper counterparts.

Notes
Notes in Outlook are electronic versions of paper sticky notes.

TIP   To change the note color, size, font, and display, choose Tools ➤ Options, click the Notes Options button, select the options you want to change, and then click the OK button twice.

Write and Open a Note

1. Click **Notes** on the Outlook Bar.

2. Click the **New** button ![New] on the Standard toolbar. A new note opens.

3. Type the text of the note.

You can delete a note. Select the note or notes you want to delete, and then click the Delete button on the Standard toolbar.

You can write a note anywhere in Outlook. Click the New button drop-down arrow on the Standard toolbar, and then click Note.

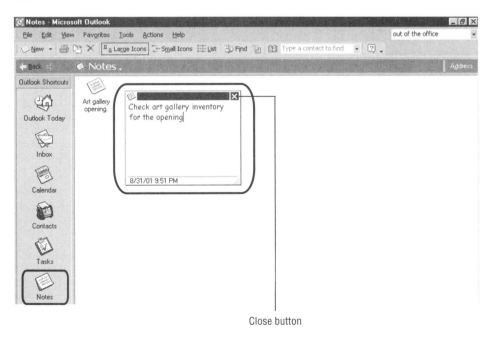

Close button

4. Click the **Close** button ![X].

321

TIP To open a note, click Notes on the Outlook Bar, double-click the note you want to open and read.

Printing Items from Outlook

You can print any item in Outlook. By clicking the Print button on the Standard toolbar, you can print a selected item using the default print settings. The default or preset printing style is different for each view depending on what type of information you are printing. There are other printing options available in table, calendar, and card views. To choose a printing option, use the Print command on the File menu. You cannot print from a timeline or an icon view.

TIP You can preview your print results. Choose File ➢ Print Preview. Use the Print Preview toolbar buttons to preview your print results, and then click the Close button.

Print an Item or View

1. Click the item or display the view you want to print.

2. Choose **File ➢ Print**. The Print dialog box opens. Printing options change depending on the item and view. Refer to the following table for information on the printing options available for different views.

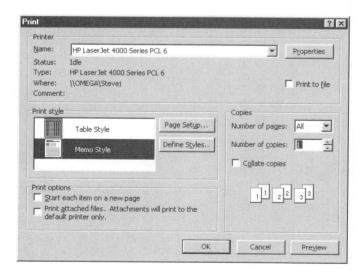

3. If necessary, click the **Name** drop-down arrow ⬛, and then select a printer.

4. Select a print style.

   If you want, click the **Define Styles** button to specify the print style settings you want.

5. Click the **Number of pages** drop-down arrow ⬛, and select **All**, **Odd**, or **Even**.

6. Specify print options or a print range. Options vary depending on the item you selected.

7. Click the **OK** button.

Subscribing to a Newsgroup

Before you can participate in a newsgroup, you need a **newsreader program**, such as Outlook Newsreader, that allows you subscribe to newsgroups. **Subscribing** to a newsgroup places a link to a group in the Folder list, providing easy access to the newsgroup. Before subscribing to a newsgroup, read some messages (called **articles**) and get a feel for the people and content. If you like what you read and want to participate regularly in the series of conversations related to specific topics (called **threads**), you can subscribe to that newsgroup.

TIP To set up Outlook newsgroup account, choose View ➢ Go To ➢ News. The first time you access the Newsreader, the Internet Connection Wizard opens. Otherwise, on the Outlook Newsreader start page, click Setup a Newsgroup account, and then follow the wizard instructions.

View and Subscribe to a Newsgroup

1. Choose **View** ➢ **Go To** ➢ **News**. The Outlook Newsreader window opens.

2. Click **Newsreader** in the Folder list.

3. Click the **Newsgroup** button. The Newsgroups Subscriptions dialog box opens.

Newsreader Program
Program that lets you access newsgroups and read the messages posted there.

Subscribing
Link in your folders list for easy access to the newsgroup.

Articles
The individual messages posted to a newsgroup.

Threads
A series of posts or messages related to a certain topic within a newsgroup.

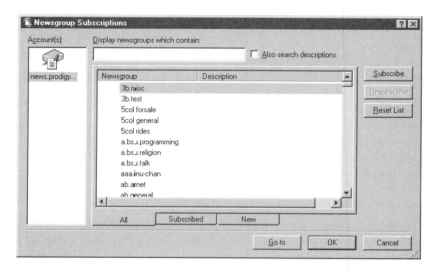

4. Click a Newsgroup you want to view.

5. If you want to subscribe, click the **Subscribe** button.

6. Click the **Go To** button. Newsgroup messages appear in the Outlook Express window.

TIP To unsubscribe to a newsgroup, right-click the newsgroup to which you want to unsubscribe, and then click the Unsubscribe button on the shortcut menu.

TIP To delete a newsgroup, click the newsgroup in the folder list, and then click the Delete button.

Reading and Posting News

Conversation thread

The original message about a specific topic along with any responses to the original message.

Once you have subscribed to a newsgroup, you will want to retrieve new newsgroup messages (or at least the message headers), open the messages, and read them. If you want, you can save a message to your hard disk drive or network drive for future reference. Part of the fun of newsgroups is that you can participate in an ongoing discussion, respond privately to a message's author, or start a new conversation thread yourself by posting your own message on a topic. A **conversation thread** consists of the original message on a topic along with the responses that include the original message title preceded by *RE:*.

Open and Read News Messages

1. Choose **View** ➤ **Go To** ➤ **News**. The Outlook Newsreader window opens.

2. Click the news server icon in the folder list.

3. Click the newsgroup whose messages you want to read.

4. If necessary, click the plus sign (**+**) to the left of a message header to display all the reply headers for that message.

5. When you see a message or reply you want to read, click its header in the message list.

Folder list   Folder bar   Message list

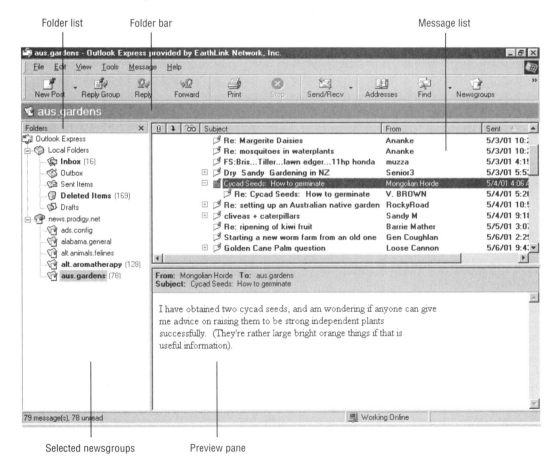

Selected newsgroups   Preview pane

6. Read the message in the preview pane.

Post a New Message

1. Choose **View** ➤ **Go To** ➤ **News**. The Outlook Newsreader window opens.

2. Select the newsgroup to which you want to post a message.

3. Click the **New Post** button on the toolbar. The New Message window opens.

4. In the **Subject** box, type a subject for your message.

5. Type your message.

6. Click the **Send** button on the toolbar.

Sending and Receiving Instant Messages

Instant Messaging is a service on the Internet that lets you send text messages to other people who also use the same Instant Messaging service and are online at the same time that you are. Using Instant Messaging, you can chat in real-time with co-workers, friends, and family. It is as close as you can get to face-to-face conversation without using an Internet phone or video conferencing service. Outlook offers you an Instant Messaging service called the MSN Messenger Service.

Instant Messaging is enabled by default in Outlook. If Instant Messaging gets disabled or isn't enabled when you try to use it the first time, choose Tools ➤ Options, and then click the Other tab. Click the Enable Instant Messaging in Microsoft Outlook check box to select it, click the Options button, fill in the appropriate boxes in the Personal and Preferences tabs if you haven't already set up Instant Messaging before, and then click the OK button twice.

Once you have set up the Instant Messenger Service you will need to add the people with whom you wish to chat to the address book of the Instant Messenger Service.

Add a Name to the Contacts List in Instant Messaging

1. Double-click the **Instant Messaging** icon  on the taskbar to open it.

2. Click the **Add** button. The Add a Contact dialog box opens.

3. Select an option for adding a contact, either by e-mail address or sign-in name, and then click the **Next** button.

4. Enter the name and other pertinent information about the contact, and then click the **Next** button.

5. If your contact doesn't have Instant Messaging, you can click the **Send E-mail** button and Instant Message will send that person a invitation to install Instant Messaging. If your contact does have Instant messaging, click the **Finish** button, or click the **Next** button to add more contacts.

Send an Instant Message

1. Double-click the **Instant Messaging** icon   on the taskbar to open it, if necessary.

2. Click the name of the contact in your Contacts list that you wish to send an Instant Message to, and click the **Send** button. The Message window opens.

3. Type your message, and then click the **Send** button.

4. The message window remains open and your contact's responses appear in the upper pane. To respond, click in the lower pane, type your response, and then click the **Send** button.

> **NOTE** There are times when you are working on a special project and don't want to be disturbed by anyone. Instant Messaging gives you the option to set your status to let others know that you're busy or unavailable. Left-click your name in the Instant Message window, and then select an option from the list.

15 Creating Web Pages with Office XP Programs

World Wide Web technology is now available for all your Microsoft Office XP programs. You can add hyperlinks (graphic objects or text you click to jump to other Office documents and intranet or Internet pages) to your Office documents. Office XP makes it easy to create a Web page without learning HTML, the coding system used to format Web pages. The Web Page Wizard walks you through the process one step at a time. Office also provides several templates to get you started. In addition, you can save any document as a Web page to your hard drive just as you would save an Office document. You can also preview how your document will look as a Web page in your Office program or in your browser. Without ever leaving an Office XP application, you can turn a document into a Web page. Office XP allows you to work with people around the world as if they were around a conference table.

Designing Web Pages

Web pages are multi-media documents that contain links to other documents on the Internet, an intranet, a local network, or a hard drive. These **links**—also called hyperlinks, hypertext, or hypermedia—are highlighted text or graphics that you click to follow a pathway from one Web page to another. Linked Web pages, known collectively as a Web site, are generally related by topic.

Hypertext Markup Language (HTML) is the standard format for posting and viewing data on a Web site. A Web browser, such as Microsoft Internet Explorer, interprets HTML code to determine how to display a Web. Different codes mark the size, color, style, and placement of text and graphics, and mark the words and graphics as hyperlinks and the files to which they link.

Because many businesses create intranet and Internet Web sites—both of which use HTML documents—the ability to create, read, open, and save HTML documents directly from Office becomes an important business function.

HTML and Office XP

In Office XP, Word, Excel, PowerPoint, Access, and Publisher all can save and read HTML documents. Office recognizes the .html filename extension as accurately as it does those for its own programs (.doc, .xls, .ppt, .mdb, and .pub). In other words, you can use the familiar Office tools and features to create and share Web documents. Any user with a browser can view the Web documents you create in Office.

Converting Documents to Web Pages

In addition to creating Web pages from scratch in Office programs, you can also save an existing document as a Web page to your hard drive, intranet, or Web server. These HTML documents preserve such features as styles, revision marks, PivotTables, linked and embedded objects, and so on. If HTML cannot convert an item in your document exactly, a dialog box explains how HTML will change the item.

When you save an Office file as an HTML file, Office creates a folder with the same name and in the same location as the original file. The folder contains several files that support and relate to the HTML file. For example, HTML creates a separate file for each graphic, worksheet, or slide.

Opening Web Pages

After saving an Office document as a Web page, you can open the Web page, in HTML format, in an Office program. This allows you to quickly and easily switch from HTML to the standard program format and back again without losing formatting or functionality. For example, if you create a formatted chart in a PowerPoint presentation, save the presentation file as a Web page, and then reopen the Web page in PowerPoint, the chart will look the same as the original did when you created it in PowerPoint.

Open an Office Web Page

1. Click the **Open** button 🗁 on the Standard toolbar.

2. Click the **Files Of Type** drop-down arrow ▾, and then click **Web Pages**.

3. Click the **Look In** drop-down arrow ▾, and select the folder where the file is located.

5. Click the name of the file.

6. Click the **Open** button. To open an Office Web page in your default Web browser, click the **Open** button drop-down arrow ▾, and then click **Open In Browser**.

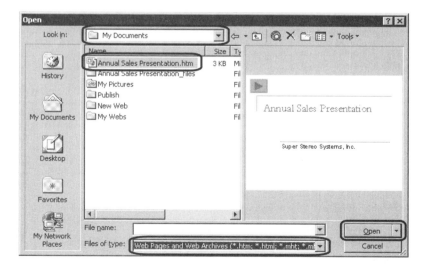

Creating Web Pages the Easy Way

Theme

A pre-designed appearance that remains consistent throughout Web pages.

Use the Web Page Wizard to create your own Web page with minimal effort. The wizard walks you through each step of creating a visually appealing multi-page site. First, you name your site and choose a storage location. Next, you decide if you want to place navigational links in a frame and where to display the frame. Add as many blank pages as you like, based on pre-designed layout templates, or based on your existing files. Reorganize the sequence of the pages (visible in the order of the navigational links). Select a visual **theme**, or pre-designed format, to give the background, text, bullets, and so on a professional and consistent look. Finally, replace the placeholders with your own text and graphics.

Create a Web Page with a Wizard in Word

1. Click the **Start** button 🪟 Start on the taskbar, and then click **New Office Document** from the Start menu, or open Word, choose **File ➤ New**, and then click **General Templates** on the task pane.

2. Click the **Web Pages** tab, and then double-click **Web Page Wizard**.

3. Click the **Next** button.

4. Enter the title of your site, enter the location of your site, and then click the **Next** button.

5. Select the location of your site's navigational links. Click the **Next** button.

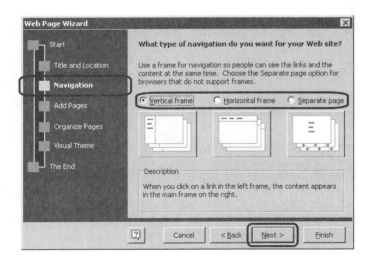

6. Click one of the following buttons to set up the site structure, and then click the **Next** button.

   ◇ The **New Blank Page** button inserts an empty page.

   ◇ The **Add Template Page** button displays the Web Page Templates dialog box. Click a template, preview a sample, and then click the **OK** button.

   ◇ The **Add Existing File** button displays the Open dialog box. Double-click any Office file you want to include.

7. Click the **Next** button. Click the **Remove Page** button to delete a page in the list.

> **NOTE** Word and Access use themes that coordinate with the Microsoft FrontPage Web site creation and management tool; PowerPoint use design templates that are consistent with the themes; and Outlook uses stationery to help you create a consistent-looking Web site.

> **TIP** Office templates often contain placeholders that already contain text or graphics. To replace the placeholder, select the text and type new text, or select the graphic and insert a new image.

8. Click the **Move Up** button or the **Move Down** button to change the order of the links. Click the **Rename** button to rename a page. Click the **Next** button.

9. To add a theme to your site, click the **Add A Visual Theme** option button, click **Browse Themes**, click the theme you want, and then click the **OK** button. Click the **Next** button.

10. Click the **Finish** button. Word creates the Web pages, which may take a few moments depending on the speed of your computer.

11. Select the placeholder text, and then enter your personalized text.

Create a Web Page from a Template in Word

1. In Word, choose **File ➢ New**. The New Document task pane opens.

2. Click **General Templates**. The Templates dialog box opens.

3. Click the **Web Pages** tab, and then click a Web page template icon.

4. Click the **OK** button to create the selected Web page.

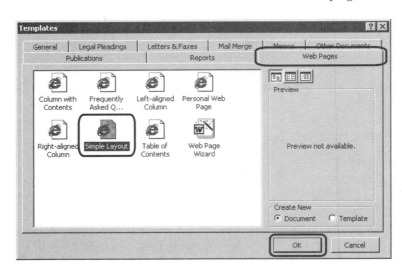

5. Select the placeholder text and graphics, and then add your personalized text.

Inserting Hyperlinks

Traditionally, when you reference information that was included earlier in a document, you had to duplicate the material or add a footnote. Now you can create a hyperlink—a graphic object or colored, underlined text that you click to move (jump) to a new location (the destination). The destination can be in the same document, another file on your computer or network, or a Web page on your intranet or the Internet.

NOTE Office inserts an absolute link—a hyperlink that jumps to a fixed location—to an Internet destination. Office inserts a relative link—a hyperlink that changes when the hyperlink and destination paths change—between documents. You must move the hyperlink and destination together in order to keep the link intact.

Insert a Hyperlink within a Document

1. Create a bookmark or heading, and then click in the document where you want to insert the hyperlink, or select the text or object you want to use as the hyperlink.

2. Click the **Insert Hyperlink** button 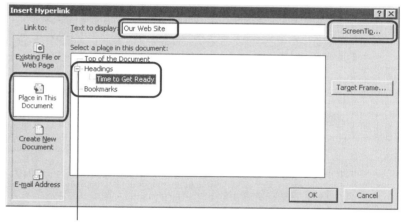 on the Standard toolbar. The Insert Hyperlink dialog box opens.

3. Click **Place In This Document**.

4. Click a destination in the document. The destination can be a Word heading or bookmark; an Excel cell reference or range name; a Power-Point slide, slide title, or custom show; or an Access object.

5. In the **Text to Display** box, type the text that you want to appear as the hyperlink.

6. Click the **ScreenTip** button.

7. Type the text that you want to appear when someone points to the hyperlink, and then click the **OK** button to close the Set Hyperlink ScreenTip dialog box.

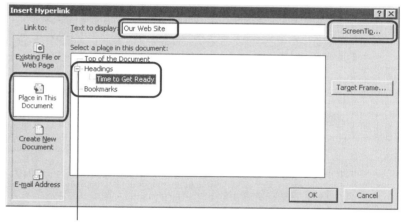

Click Plus symbol to display list of Heading;
click Minus symbol to close list

8. Click the **OK** button.

NOTE You can create a hyperlink to send e-mail. Click where you want to insert the hyperlink, click the Insert Hyperlink button on the Standard toolbar, click E-Mail Address, enter the recipient's e-mail address, enter a subject, enter the hyperlink display text, and then click the OK button.

TIP In Access, a hyperlink appears as a form or report label and uses the Caption property as the display text for the hyperlink.

Insert a Hyperlink Between Documents

1. Click where you want to insert the hyperlink, or select the text or object you want to use as the hyperlink.

2. Click the **Insert Hyperlink** button 🔗 on the Standard toolbar. The Insert Hyperlink dialog box opens.

3. Click **Existing File Or Web Page**.

4. Enter the name and path of the destination file or Web page. You can also click the **File** button, the **Web Page** button, or the **Bookmark** button; select the file, Web page, or bookmark; and then click the **OK** button.

5. In the **Text to Display** box, type the text that you want to appear as the hyperlink.

6. Click the **ScreenTip** button.

7. Type the text that you want to appear when someone points to the hyperlink, and then click the **OK** button to close the Set Hyperlink ScreenTip dialog box.

8. Click the **OK** button.

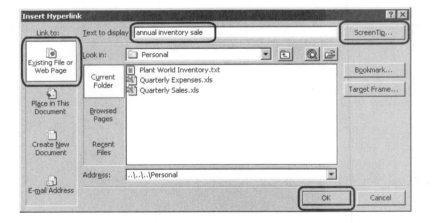

Using and Removing Hyperlinks

Hyperlinks connect you to information in other documents. When you click a hyperlink for the first time (during a session), the color of the hyperlink changes, indicating that you have accessed the hyperlink. You can easily update or remove a link.

To display the Web toolbar, choose View ➢ Toolbars ➢ Web.

Use a Hyperlink

1. Position the mouse pointer (which changes to a hand pointer) over any hyperlink. In Word, you also need to hold down the Ctrl key.

2. Click the hyperlink. Depending on the type of hyperlink, the hyperlink will perform one of the following:

❖ Jump to a new location within the same document.

❖ Jump to a location on an intranet or Internet Web site.

❖ Open a new file and the program in which it was created.

❖ Open Outlook and display a new e-mail message.

3. Navigate between open hyperlinked documents with the Web toolbar.

❖ Click the **Back** button ← or the **Forward** button → to move between documents.

❖ Click the **Start Page** button 🏠 to go to your home page.

❖ Click the **Search The Web** button 🔍 to go to a search page.

You can change the look of a hyperlink. Right-click the hyperlink, click Select Hyperlink, and then click the Bold button, Italic button, Underline button, Font button, or Font Size button on the Formatting toolbar.

Edit a Hyperlink

1. Right-click the hyperlink you want to edit, and then click **Edit Hyperlink**. The Edit Hyperlink dialog box opens.

2. If you want, change the display text.

3. If you want, click the **ScreenTip** button, edit the custom text, and then click the **OK** button.

4. If necessary, change the destination in the Address box.

5. Click the **OK** button.

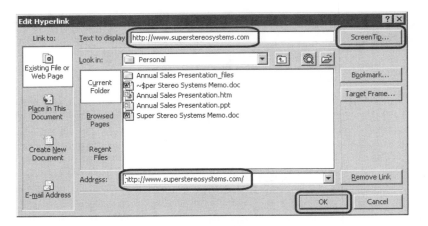

TIP   To remove a hyperlink, right-click the hyperlink you want to remove, and then click Remove Hyperlink.

Enhancing Web Pages

A basic Web page usually includes text, graphics, and hyperlinks. You can change the look of your Web site by selecting a theme—a pre-designed visual layout that changes text formatting (such as font type, size, format, and color), as well as bullets, backgrounds, colors, and horizontal lines to create a specific tone. Each theme has two color variations: default and vivid. Some themes include animations.

You can make your Web site easier to navigate by adding frames—separate panes that contain unique content and scroll independently. For example, you might place navigation links in one frame and a home page link in another frame.

Use Themes to Add a Color Scheme in Word or Access

1. Open the Word document or the Access data access page in Design view to which you want to add a theme.

2. Choose **Format ➤ Theme**. The Theme dialog box opens.

3. Click a theme to view a sample.

4. Click the **Vivid Colors** check box to select it. The new colors appear on the Web page in the sample area.

5. Click the **OK** button.

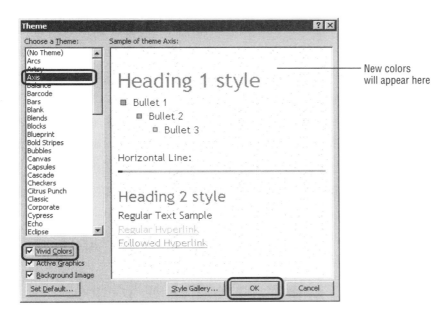

New colors will appear here

Add or Remove Frames in Word

1. Open the Word document to which you want to add or remove a frame.

2. Right-click any toolbar, and then click **Frames** to display the Frames toolbar.

3. Click the appropriate button to add a frame. To remove a frame, click the frame you want to remove, and then click the **Delete Frame** button ⊟.

Delete Frame button

Previewing Web Pages

Web Page Preview

Allows you to view unsaved Web pages using your browser.

After you create a Web page, you should preview it in a Web browser or in the Office program to make sure that your Web page displays the way you want. **Web Page Preview** displays the open file in your default browser even if you haven't saved it yet. **Web Layout View** shows you how a document will be displayed on the Web, but does not use your browser. If the document includes formatting or layouts that HTML cannot match exactly, Word uses an HTML layout that matches the original as closely as possible.

Web Layout View

Office feature that shows you how your Web pages will look on the Internet.

Preview a Web Page in a Browser

1. In an Office program, open the Web page that you want to preview.

2. Choose **File ➢ Web Page Preview**. Your default Web browser starts and displays the Web page.

3. Scroll to view the entire page, click hyperlinks to test them, and so on.

Preview a Web Page in Word

1. Open the Word document that you want to preview.

2. Click the **Web Layout View** button  located next to the horizontal scroll bar. The document appears just as it would on the Web.

Saving Documents as Web Pages

You can save your document as a Web page in any Office program. After you save it as a Web page, you can continue to work with the file in its original Office program. The Office document that you save as a Web page consists of an HTML file and a folder that stores supporting files, such as graphics, worksheets, slides, and so on, or a Web archive file that saves all the elements of an Office document, including text and graphics, into a single file with the MHT format.

Save an Office Document as a Web Page

1. Open the document that you want to save as a Web page.

2. Choose **File ➤ Save As Web Page**. The Save As dialog box opens. If you want to change the title of your Web page, click the **Change Title** button, type a new title, and then click the **OK** button.

3. Select the drive and folder in which to store the file.

4. In the **File Name** box, type a name for the file.

5. Click the **Save** button. Office saves the Web page in the selected folder, and includes the supporting graphics and related files.

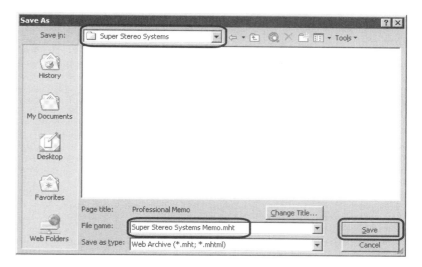

TIP You can save a your Calendar in Outlook as a Web page. Switch to the Calendar view you want to save, choose File ➤ Save As Web Page, select the duration and publishing options you want, enter a title and filename, and then click the Save button.

NOTE Data Access pages are HTML files designed in Access and stored outside the database so you can display your data as forms and reports on the Web or e-mail them. Access updates changes made to these pages over the Web in your database.

Save an Excel Worksheet as an Interactive Web Page

1. Open the Excel workbook that you want to save as a Web page.

2. Choose **File ➢ Save As Web Page**. The Save As dialog box opens.

3. Select the drive and folder in which to store the file.

4. Select an option button to save the entire workbook or the just the selection.

5. Click the **Add Interactivity** check box to select it if you want others to be able to edit the file.

6. Type a name for the file. If you want, click the **Change Title** button to type a new title for the Web page, and then click the **OK** button.

7. Click the **Save** button. Excel saves the Web page in the selected folder, and includes the supporting graphics and related files.

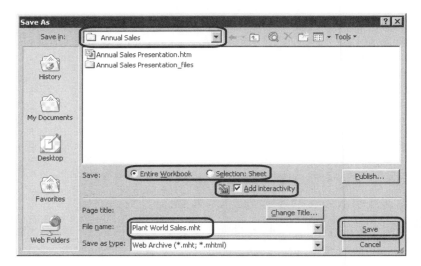

Publishing Web Pages

At times, you'll want to publish a copy of your current Office document in HTML format directly to a **Web server** so that others can view and manipulate your data. Publishing to a Web server is as simple as saving a file. You can elect to let anyone interact with your data from Excel or Access as long as they use the Internet Explorer 4.01 or later Web browser. When you publish a Web page, you move the Web page and graphic images to a Web server.

Publish PowerPoint Slides as a Web Page

1. Open the presentation with the item that you want to publish.

2. Choose **File ➤ Save As Web Page**. The Save As dialog box opens.

3. Click the **Publish** button. The Publish as Web Page dialog box opens.

4. Select the options that you want to include in the Web page.

5. Select the browsers that you want others to be able to use to view your Web page.

6. If you want, click the **Change** button, type a title for the Web page, and then click the **OK** button.

7. Type the folder and filename for the published Web page, if necessary.

8. If you want, click the **Open Published Web Page In Browser** check box to select it and preview the page in a browser.

9. Click the **Publish** button.

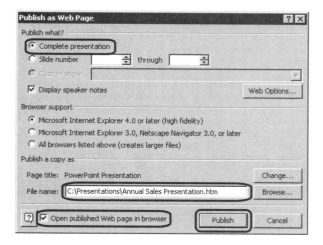

Publish Excel Worksheet Items as a Web Page

1. Open the workbook with the item you want to publish.

2. Choose **File ➢ Save As Web Page**. The Save As dialog box opens.

3. Click the **Publish** button. The Publish As a Web Page dialog box opens.

4. Select the items you want to include in the Web page.

5. Select the Viewing options you want.

6. If you want, click the **Change** button, type a title for the Web page, and then click the **OK** button.

7. Type the folder and filename for the published Web page, if necessary.

8. If you want, click the **AutoRepublish Every Time This Workbook Is Saved** check box to select it.

9. If you want, click the **Open Published Web Page In Browser** check box to select it and preview the page in a browser.

10. Click the **Publish** button.

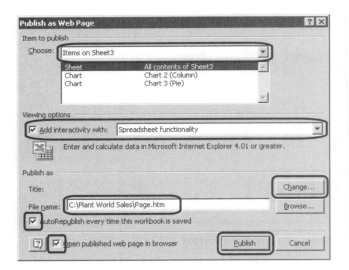

16

Sharing Information Between Office XP Programs

Microsoft Office XP has the power and flexibility to share information between programs. You can create, store, and manage information in the program that works best for you, and then move that information to another program.

Completing a successful project in Office XP is not always a solitary venture; sometimes you may need to share data with others or obtain data from other programs. In many offices, your co-workers (and their computers) are located across the country or around the world. You can merge information from different programs into a single document, and you can link data between programs. You can create one seamless document that includes data from several programs.

Sharing Information Between Programs

Object linking and embedding (OLE)
A technology that allows you to move text or data between programs.

Importing
Creating a file with the same or different program in another file.

Exporting
Converts a copy of the open file into a different program's file type.

Embedding
Inserts a representation of a file created in one program file into the file of another program.

Linking
Information connected to and displayed in one program that was created in another program.

Hyperlink
Text or graphic image in a Web page that you can click to jump to another page. Also known as a link.

Office XP programs can convert data or text from one format to another by employing a technology known as **object linking and embedding (OLE)**. In this case, an object can be text, data, or a graphic image. OLE allows you to move text or data between programs in much the same way that you move them within a program. The familiar cut and paste or drag and drop methods work between programs just as they do within a document. You can use techniques such as **importing**, **exporting**, **embedding**, **linking**, and **hyperlinking** to move information from one program to another. The method you use to edit or update the information depends on the technique you choose.

Consider an example. Sarah coordinates her local school district's soccer teams. She sends out monthly newsletters that list the scheduled dates and times for practices and games, as well as a brief summary of scores and highlights from the previous month's games. In Access, she creates a database of team members and their relevant information—names, addresses, phone numbers, emergency numbers, and team positions. Using Excel workbooks, she tracks the year-to-date expenses and plans the tentative schedules between teams. Every month, Sarah writes the newsletter in Word, imports the upcoming schedule from Excel, and then merges the newsletter with the Access database to create a mailing list. This is just one scenario—as you work with Office programs, you'll find many ways to share information.

The following table describes the terms associated with sharing objects among Office programs.

term	definition
Source program	The program you used to create the original object
Source file	The file that contains the original object
Destination program	The program into which you insert the object
Destination file	The file into which you insert the object

Deciding Which Method to Use

Office provides several methods to use to share information. To decide which method is best for your needs, use the following decision guide.

1. Do you want to display the contents of another file in the open document?

   No. Create a hyperlink.

   Yes. Go to question 2.

2. Do you want to edit the content of the file from within the open document?

   No. Embed the file as a picture.

   Yes. Go to question 3.

3. Is the source program (the program used to create the file) available on your computer?

   No. Import the file. See "Importing and Exporting Files" on page 358.

   Yes. Go to question 4.

4. Do you want to use the source program commands to edit the file?

   No. Import the file.

   Yes. Go to question 5.

5. Do you want changes you make to the file to appear in the source file (the original copy of the file)?

   No. Embed the file.

   Yes. Link the file.

Importing and Exporting Files

Importing and exporting information are two sides of the same coin. Importing copies a file created with the same or another program into your open file. Exporting converts a copy of your open file into the file type of another program. For example, you might import an Excel worksheet into a Word document, or you might want to export part of an Excel worksheet to a PowerPoint slide. The information becomes part of your open file, just as if you created it in that format. However, not all formatting and program-specific information may translate from program to program.

Import a File

1. Click where you want to insert the imported file.

2. Perform one of the following commands.

   ◆ In Word, choose **Insert** ➤ **File**.

   ◆ In Excel, choose **Data** ➤ **Import External Data** ➤ **Import Data**.

   ◆ In Publisher, choose **Insert** ➤ **Text File**.

   ◆ In PowerPoint, choose **Insert** ➤ **Slides From Files** ➤ **Browse**.

   ◆ In Access, choose **File** ➤ **Get External Data** ➤ **Import**.

TIP You can insert into a Word document a bookmarked section of a Word document or a specific range in an Excel worksheet. Click the Range button in the Insert File dialog box, enter a bookmark name or range, and then click the OK button.

3. Click the **Files Of Type** drop-down arrow ▼, and then select All Files.

4. Click the **Look In** drop-down arrow ▼, and then select the drive and folder of the file you want to import.

5. Double-click the name of the file you want to import, or click the **Insert** button.

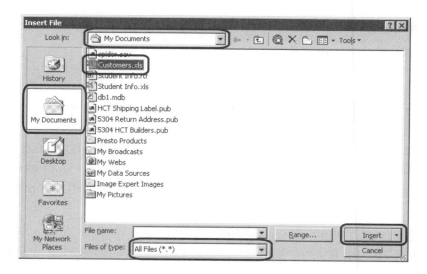

If you want to move only part of a file into your document, copy the information you want to insert, and then paste the information in the file where you want it to appear.

6. In PowerPoint, click the **Display** button if necessary, click the slides you want to import, click the **Insert** button, and then click the **Close** button. In Access, follow the **Import Spreadsheet Wizard** instructions to set up an Excel data as an Access table.

7. Edit the imported information with the open program's commands.

Export a File to Another Program

1. Choose **File ➢ Save** As. The Save As dialog box opens.

2. If necessary, click the **Save In** drop-down arrow 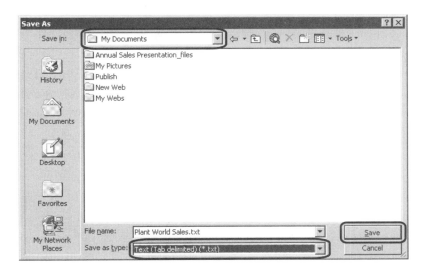, and then select the drive and folder where you want to save the file.

3. Click the **Save As Type** drop-down arrow , and then select the type of file you want. You can save each file as some form of text file, an html file, or another file format for the current program (although this varies from program to program).

4. If necessary, type a new name for the file.

5. Click the **Save** button.

6. Edit the file from within the new program.

Embedding and Linking Information

Embedding inserts a copy of a file created in one program into a file created in another program. The original file is called the source file; the file in which it is embedded is called the destination file. Unlike imported files, you can edit the information displayed in embedded files with the commands and toolbar buttons from the program that you used to create the original file. When you change the embedded object in the destination file, you change that object only, not the information in the original source file.

Linking maintains a connection between the information stored in one document (the source file) and displayed in another (the destination file). For example, you might link an Excel chart to a Word document and a PowerPoint slide so you can update the chart from any of the files. You can edit the linked object from either Word or Excel; the changes are stored in the source file. As you work, Office updates the linked object to ensure that you always have the most current information, and keeps track of all the drive, folder, and filename information for a source file. However, if you move or rename the source file, you will break the link between the files and the object will become embedded, not linked.

Another effective way to share information between programs is to create a hyperlink—a term borrowed from World Wide Web technology. A hyperlink is an object (either colored, underlined text or a graphic) that you click to jump to a different location in the same document or to a different document.

TIP   If you break the link between a linked object and its source file, the object becomes embedded. Breaking a link varies slightly from program to program. To break a link in Excel, open the linked file, choose Edit ➢ Links, and then click the link you want to break, click the Break Link button, and then click the Yes button.

Embed an Existing Object

1. Click where you want to embed the object.

2. Choose **Insert ➢ Object**. The Insert Object dialog box opens.

3. Click the **Create From File** tab or option button.

4. Click the **Browse** button, and then double-click the file you want to embed.

5. Click the **OK** button.

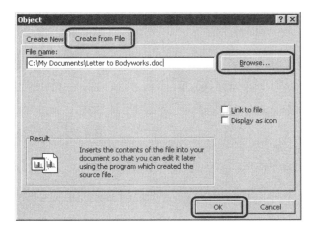

Embed a New Object

1. Click where you want to embed the object.

2. Choose **Insert** ➢ **Object**.

3. Click the **Create New** tab or option button.

4. Double-click the type of object you want to create, or click the object type and then click the **OK** button.

5. Enter information in the new object using the source program's commands and toolbars.

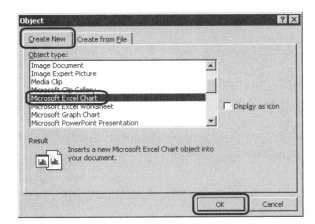

TIP To view the linked file as an icon instead of viewing the entire file, click the Display As Icon check box to select it.

NOTE If you want to link or embed only part of a file, copy the information, and then click where you want to link or embed the copied information. Choose Edit ➢ Paste Special, click the Paste option button to embed the data, or click the Paste Link option button to link the data, select a format, and then click the OK button.

Link an Object Between Programs

1. Click where you want to link the object.

2. Choose **Insert ➢ Object**.

3. Click the **Create From File** tab or option button.

4. Click the **Browse** button, and then double-click the object you want to link.

5. Click the **Link To File** check box to select it.

6. Click the **OK** button.

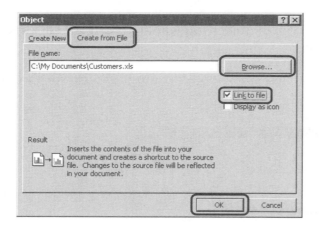

Edit an Embedded or Linked File

1. Double-click the linked or embedded object that you want to edit to display the source program's menus and toolbars.

2. Edit the object in the source program window using the source program's commands and toolbars.

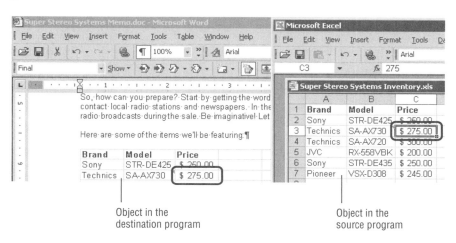

Object in the
destination program

Object in the
source program

3. When you're done, click outside the object to return to the destination program.

Creating a Word Document with Excel Data

You can create a Word document that includes Excel data. You can also pair other Office programs to efficiently create a document that contains the information you need and displays it in the way you want. For example, as you write a sales report, explain a budget, or create a memo that shows the distribution of sales, you may want to add existing spreadsheet data and charts to your text. Instead of re-creating the Excel data in Word, you can insert all or part of the data or chart into your Word document.

TIP If you plan to insert part of an Excel worksheet in a Word document, be sure to name the range. This is easier to recall than the specific cell references.

353

Copy an Excel Worksheet Range to a Word Document

1. Click in the Word document where you want to copy the Excel range.

2. Choose **Insert** ➢ **File**. The Insert File dialog box opens.

3. Click the **Files Of Type** drop-down arrow 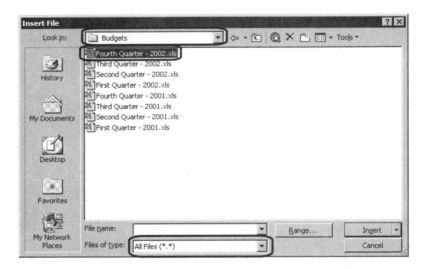, and then select **All Files**.

4. Click the **Look In** drop-down arrow , and then select the drive and folder that contains the workbook you want to copy.

5. Double-click the filename of the workbook you want to copy.

6. Click the **Open Document In Workbook** drop-down arrow, and then select the worksheet you want.

7. Click the **Name Or Cell Range** drop-down arrow, and select the range or range name you want to copy.

8. Click the **OK** button.

Embed an Excel Chart in Word

1. Open the Excel worksheet that contains the chart you want to use.

2. Click the Excel chart you want to embed.

3. Click the **Copy** button on the Standard toolbar.

4. Click the Word document where you want to embed the chart.

5. Click the **Paste** button on the Standard toolbar.

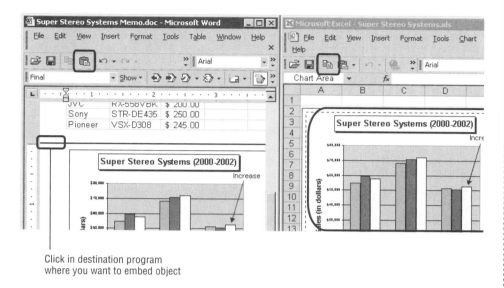

Click in destination program
where you want to embed object

Inserting Excel Data in an Access Database

You can create a customized form in Access and then use the form to enter, find, or delete data in Excel. Access forms provide greater layout and formatting flexibility than Excel data forms.

> **TIP** To drag Excel data to Access tables, open and tile the Excel workbook and the Access database table you want to use. Drag the Excel data to the database table.

Create an Access Form with Excel Data

1. Click a cell in the Excel worksheet that contains data you want in the Access form.

2. Click the **Save** button 🖫 on the Standard toolbar to save the workbook.

3. Choose **Data** ➢ **Microsoft Access Form**. If Microsoft Access Form doesn't appear, you need to install the AccessLinks add-in program from the Web (choose Help ➢ Office on the Web).

4. Click the **New Database** option button. To create an Access form from an existing database, click the **Existing Database** option button, click the **Browse** button and then double-click the database you want to use.

5. Click the **OK** button.

6. Follow the instructions in the Microsoft Access Form Wizard.

7. If necessary, click **Forms** on the Objects bar, and then double-click the form.

8. Use the form to enter data into Excel.

Creating a PowerPoint Presentation with Word Text

PowerPoint presentations are based on outlines, which you can create using either PowerPoint or the more extensive outlining tools in Word. You can import any Word document into PowerPoint, although only paragraphs tagged with heading styles become part of the slides. Edit the slides using the usual PowerPoint commands. You can also copy any table you created in Word to a slide.

| TIP | You can create slides from a Word outline and insert them into an existing PowerPoint presentation. In PowerPoint, display the slide after which you want to insert the new slides. Choose Insert ➢ Slides from Outline, and then select the Word document you want. |

Create PowerPoint Slides from a Word Document

1. Open or create a Word document with heading styles.

2. Choose **File ➢ Send To ➢ Microsoft PowerPoint**. PowerPoint creates a new slide whenever it encounters a Heading 1 style. Heading 2 becomes the first level of indented or bulleted text, and so on. If a document contains no styles, PowerPoint uses the paragraph indents to determine a slide structure.

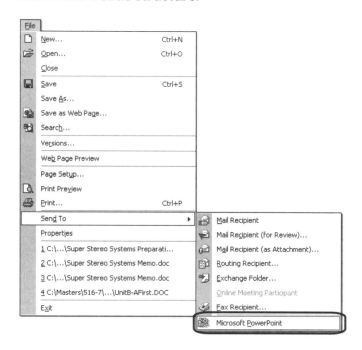

3. Save the presentation, and then edit it by adding slides, changing slide layouts, and applying a design template.

Create a Word Outline from a PowerPoint Presentation

1. Open the PowerPoint presentation you want to use as a Word document.

2. Choose **File ➢ Send To ➢ Microsoft Word**. The Send To Microsoft Word dialog box opens.

3. Click the **Outline Only** option button.

4. Click the **OK** button to save the slide text as a Word file, start Word, and open the file.

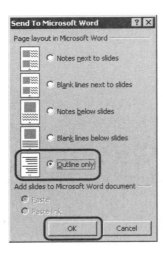

Using an Access Database to Create Word Documents

Merge

Process of combining database records with Word documents.

Access is a great program for storing and categorizing large amounts of information. You can combine, or **merge**, database records with Word documents to create tables or produce form letters and envelopes based on names, addresses, and other Access records. For example, you might create a form letter in Word and personalize it by inserting names and addresses from an Access database.

Insert Access Data into a Word Document

1. In the Access Database window, click the table or query you want to use.

2. Click the **OfficeLinks** button ![OfficeLinks icon] on the Database toolbar.

3. Click **Merge It With Microsoft Word**.

4. Click the linking option button you want to use. If you choose to insert data into an existing document, double-click the name of the file in the Select Microsoft Word Document dialog box.

5. Click the **OK** button, and then follow the steps in the Mail Merge Wizard.

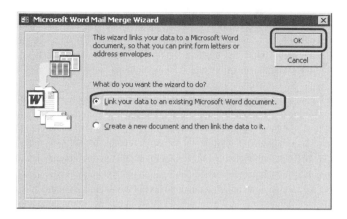

6. In Word, enter text and format it as needed.

7. To add fields, click the **Insert Merge Fields** button on the Mail Merge toolbar, and then click the field you want to insert.

Create a Word Document from an Access Database

1. In the Access Database window, click the table, query, report, or form you want to save as a Word document.

2. Click the **OfficeLinks** button ![OfficeLinks icon] on the Database toolbar.

3. Click **Publish It With Microsoft Word** to save the data as a Word file, start Word, and then open the document.

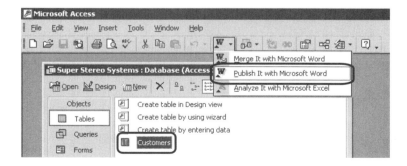

4. Edit the document using Word commands and toolbars.

Analyzing Access Data in an Excel Workbook

Before you can analyze Access data in a workbook, you must convert it to an Excel file. You can use the Analyze It With MS Excel command to export Access data as an Excel table file.

TIP To drag Access objects to Excel, open and tile the Excel workbook and the Access database you want to use. Drag the database object (tables, queries, and so on) from the Database window to the Excel worksheet.

Export an Access Table into an Excel Workbook

1. In the Access Database window, click the table you want to analyze.

2. Click the **OfficeLinks** button on the Database toolbar.

3. Click **Analyze It With Microsoft Excel** to save the table as an Excel file, start Excel, and open the workbook.

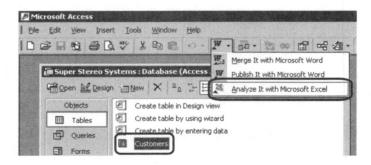

4. Use Excel commands to edit and analyze the data.

Glossary

Action button

An onscreen object that users can click to control a presentation.

Action query

A query that performs operations (delete queries, update queries, append queries and make-table queries) on the records in one or more tables that match your criteria.

Active cell

A selected cell in the datasheet that has a heavy border around it.

Active sheet

The sheet on which you are currently working.

Animation schemes

Animated effects designed by Power-Point and installed with the program.

Antonyms

Words with opposite meanings.

Appointment

An appointment is an activity you schedule which doesn't include other people or resources within your organization.

Argument

The cell references or values in a formula that contribute to the result. Each function uses function-specific arguments, which may include numeric values, text values, cell references, ranges of cells, and so on.

Articles

Articles are the individual messages posted to a newsgroup.

Attributes

Effects that change the appearance of characters.

AutoComplete

A feature that finishes entering your text entries based on the entries you previously entered in a column. AutoComplete does not work with numbers, dates, or times.

AutoCorrect

A feature that automatically corrects misspellings and incorrect capitalization, and changes abbreviations as you type.

AutoFill

A feature that fills in data based on entries in adjacent cells.

AutoFit

A feature that automatically resizes a column or row to the width/height of its largest entry.

AutoFit Text

A feature that adjusts the size of characters or the spacing between lines to make text fit within a text box.

AutoFormat

A quick and easy way to format text and data.

AutoLayout

A feature that makes it easy to arrange objects consistently on your slides.

AutoShape

A collection of pre-designed shapes that you can easily insert in a slide.

Automatic page breaks

A control that Excel automatically inserts to begin a new page.

Bound Controls

Fields of data from a table or query in your Access database.

Business Card

Contact information about yourself or someone else that comes directly from the Address Book.

Calendar

An electronic version of a paper calendar or organizer, where you can record appointments, tasks, events, activities, and meetings.

Category

A category is a keyword or keywords you give to items so you can find them later, or sort, or filter them.

Cell

The intersection of a row and column in a table or spreadsheet.

Character Styles

A group of format settings, font, size, effect (bold, italic etc.) that can be selectively applied to any block of text at the user's discretion.

Chart

A graphical representation of the data in the datasheet.

Chart boxes

Individual boxes into which individual's within an organization are entered.

Chart objects

Individual items within a chart that you can select and modify.

Chart Options

Augmentations and enhancements that you can add to a chart.

Chart Title

Text you can insert to clarify the purpose of the chart.

Chart Wizard

A series of dialog boxes that require your input in order to create a chart.

Clip art

Graphic art that comes with Office or you create and insert in a file.

Color scheme

Eight professionally coordinated colors that PowerPoint uses throughout a presentation.

Comments

Text you insert that is tagged with your initials. A comment is visible only when you place the mouse pointer over your initials.

Common field

The same field that appears in two or more tables and which allows you to match records from one or more tables.

Contact

A person or company with whom you correspond and exchange information

Contacts

A folder that replaces your standard card file and stores multiple street addresses, phone numbers, e-mail and Web addresses, and any personal information you need about each contact.

Content template

A template that includes visual elements and suggested text.

Contiguous

Adjacent, or touching, cells.

Conversation Thread

The original message about a specific topic along with any responses to the original message.

Crop

Hide areas within an image without eliminating them from the image file.

Crosstab query

A query that displays summarized values (sums, counts, and averages) from one field in a table, and groups them on the datasheet.

Custom animations

Animated effects created by you or others.

Custom slide show

A presentation in which you have specified which slides will be used and their order of appearance.

Data Access Pages

Pages let you create Web pages out of your databases without the need for a Web server.

Database Window

A window that displays the database objects.

Data Point

A single value in a data series.

Data series

A group of related data points in a datasheet or worksheet.

Datasheet

A place to store chart data that is composed of individual cells in rows and columns.

Data type

A format for fields that designates the types of data that can be entered in the field—text, number, date and time, currency, and so forth.

Design template

A template that includes visual elements, such as colors and graphics.

Detect and Repair
A feature that allows Office to fix missing or corrupted program files.

Diagram
A collection of shapes that illustrates conceptual material.

Dialog box
A window that displays onscreen that you use to enter or select information.

Directory
Any document that contains recurring fields that are suitable for a merge, such as an inventory list, parts list, or catalog.

Docked
A toolbar that is attached to one edge of the window.

Document
The file you create that contains text and graphics.

Drag-and-drop editing
A method of copying or moving selections without using the Windows Clipboard or the Office Clipboard.

Dynaset
A window that displays the records that meet a query's specifications you established.

Edit mode
Status bar state indicating that you can edit the contents of a cell.

E-mail service
A connection to an e-mail server where you store and receive e-mail messages.

Embedding
Inserts a representation of a file created in one program file into the file of another program.

Event
An event is an appointment that lasts more than one day, such as a seminar, conference, or vacation.

Exporting
Converts a copy of the open file into a different program's file type.

Field
An element for storing certain types of information.

Field Property
Is an attribute that defines the field's appearance or behavior within the database.

Fill handle
A tool that copies cell data or fills in a series of cells. When you select a cell, the fill handle is a small black box. When you point to the fill handle, it changes to a black plus sign.

Filter
A filter isolates items or files that match specifications that you set.

Flag

A flag indicates a specific level of importance or sensitivity on an e-mail message.

Floating

A toolbar that has a visible title bar and that you can move.

Font

A collection of characters, numbers, and symbols in the same letter design.

Footers

Text and art that appear at the bottom of pages within a document.

Foreign key

The designation of the primary key when it is used as a common field in a second table.

Format

Cosmetically enhance the appearance of label and values in a worksheet.

Formula

A series of values, cell references, and mathematical operators that results in a calculation.

Functions

Built-in formulas that make it easy to create complex calculations that involve one or more values, performing an operation, and returning one or more values.

Gridlines

Horizontal or vertical lines of a specified width and interval that aid in a chart's readability.

Group

Within Outlook, a group is a set of items with something in common, such as e-mail messages from the same sender, or tasks with the same due date.

Gutter

Additional blank space inserted into the margins of alternating left and right pages to allow for binding those pages without concealing any of the body text of the document.

Handles

Small circles or squares that surround an object when it is selected.

Header buttons

Buttons at the top of each column and to the left of each row that you can click to select an entire column or row.

Headers

Text and art that appear at the top of pages within a document.

Horizontal alignment

Aligning cell contents relative to the left and right edge of the cell.

Horizontal or vertical page breaks

Controls that let you determine where a new page will begin.

Hyperlink

Text or graphic image in a Web page that you can click to jump to another page. Also known as a link.

Hypertext Markup Language (HTML)
Coding instructions used to create Web pages that are interpreted by a browser program.

Importing
Creating a file with the same or different program in another file.

Inbox
The Inbox receives and stores your incoming messages.

Insert Function
Feature that organizes Excel's functions and makes it easy to create a complex calculation.

Insertion point
The blinking cursor that indicates where PowerPoint will place the text that you enter.

Items
An item in Outlook is a basic element that holds information and is similar to a file in other programs.

Journal
An area within Outlook that lets you record actions relating to contacts and place them in a timeline view.

Label
Cell text used in titles and column or row headings, and not included in calculations.

Leader
A line in the table of contents that connects an entry to its page number.

Legend
An identifier that matches colors or patterns in the chart with data.

Link
Text or graphic image in a Web page that you click to jump to another page. Also known as a hyperlink.

Linking
Information connected to and displayed in one program that was created in another program.

List
A collection of related records in an Excel worksheet.

List AutoFill
A feature that automatically extends the list's formatting and formulas to adjacent cells.

Macro
A sequence of commands and entries that can be activated collectively by clicking a toolbar button, clicking a menu command, typing a key combination, or clicking the Run command in the Macros dialog box.

Mail Merge
A process that combines a main document, such as a form letter, with a list, database, or other data document to create a new custom document.

Margins

The blank space between the edge of a page and the text. The blank area at the top, bottom, left, and right of the page.

Masters

Slides designed for specific uses throughout a presentation.

Menu

A list of associated commands or options, located beneath the title bar (at the top of the window).

Merge

Process of combining database records with Word documents.

Multiple Document Interface

An optional file management setting that allows the user to shift between multiple documents in a single Word window.

New page break

Inserts a page break below and to the right of the selected cell.

Newsgroup

An area on the Internet that contains messages and posts on particular subjects.

Newsreader Program

A program that lets you access newsgroups and read the messages posted there.

Noncontiguous

Cells that are not adjacent, or touching.

Notes

Notes in Outlook are electronic versions of paper sticky notes.

Notes page

A page that contains a miniature version of a slide and speaker notes.

Numeric formats

A way to display values in different formats, such as changing the number of decimal places or whether currency symbols appear.

Object

A picture or graphic image you can insert in a file.

Object linking and embedding (OLE)

A technology that allows you to move text or data between programs.

Office Clipboard

A temporary area that holds up to 24 pieces of copied information and is available from within any Office program.

Organization chart

Series of boxes that depicts an organization's structure.

Orientation

The appearance of cell text, which can be level or tilted or rotated horizontally up or down.

Page break

A command that stops flowing text on the current page and proceeds to the top of a new page.

Page break preview

A feature that lets you move page breaks as you view your work.

Page orientation

Determines how the worksheet data is arranged on the page when you print it—vertically or horizontally.

Pane

An individual window within the PowerPoint screen.

Paper size

The physical dimensions of the paper on which data is printed.

Paragraph Styles

A group of format settings, font, size, indent, spacing and so forth, that can only be applied to all of the text within a paragraph.

Parameter query

A query that allows you to prompt for a single piece of information to use as selection criteria in the query.

Pick From List

A feature that lists previous field entries for you to use to enter information in a field.

Primary key

Fields that have a unique value for each record in the table.

Primary table

The main table in a one-to-many tables relationship.

Print area

The specific range you want to print.

Print Preview

A miniature view of the entire document that shows you how your document will look when it is printed.

Print scaling

Resizes text and graphics to fit a specific paper size.

Print titles

Columns and rows that Excel prints on each page.

Properties list

A list of field properties for each data type.

Query

A simple question you ask a database to help you locate specific information within the database.

Range

One or more cells that you've selected.

Range reference

The cell address that displays in the name box.

Record

Data that is stored for a single entity, such as a customer's information or product information.

Referential integrity

A set of rules that control how information can be deleted or modified within related tables.

Related table

The one-to-many table that is related to the main or primary table in a table relationship.

Report

A means of presenting data from a table, query or form in a printed format.

Rules

A specific set of criteria you set to help you organize your e-mail messages.

ScreenTips

Descriptive text that displays when you hold the mouse pointer over a button.

Section break

A document within a document that uses a different layout for the text that follows the break.

Select

Highlighting text so that you can modify it.

Select query

A query that retrieves and displays records in the Table window in Datasheet view.

Set

Establish a specific range you want to print.

Shortcut menu

A menu that lists commands when you right-click a word or object. To customize shortcut commands, choose Tools ➢ Customize ➢ Toolbars.

Signature

A signature is a file containing an image that represents your handwritten signature, used in the closing of an e-mail message.

Single document interface

The default file management setting that opens a new window for each document and displays an icon for the window on the taskbar.

Slide Finder

A feature that makes it easy to find a specific slide by letting you view miniature versions of each slide.

Slide meter

Feature that helps you set the timing for each slide in a presentation.

Slide transitions

Effects applied to individual slides that determine how one slide advances to the next.

Sort

Arranging items in ascending or descending order.

Spreadsheet program

A type of software you can use to enter, evaluate, manipulate, and communicate quantitative information.

Style

A collection of formatting settings saved with a name.

Subscribing
Link in your folders list for easy access to the newsgroup.

Switchboard
A window that gives easy access to the most common actions a database user might need to take.

Synonyms
Words with similar meanings.

Tab
A location in a paragraph to align text.

Tab stop
A predefined stopping point along the document's typing line.

Table
A structure that organizes information into rows and columns.

Table of contents
An outline of the main topics and page location in a document.

Table Relationships
A way of determining how data in a table relates to data in another table.

Table Wizard
A tool that guides you through a series of steps and dialog boxes to determine the types of tables and fields your database will contain.

Task pane
An expanded display area to the right of the main window that displays groups of related commands and wizards.

Task Request
The process of assigning a task to another individual.

Tasks
A personal or work related errand you want to track through completion.

Template
A file that defines the styles, fields, formatting, and layout of a document.

Text placeholder
An empty text box used to simulate where actual text would appear.

Theme
A pre-designed appearance that remains consistent throughout Web pages.

Threads
Threads are a series of posts or messages related to a certain topic within a newsgroup.

Thumbnail
A miniaturization of the current slide or image.

Timeline
A timeline in Outlook is a simple way to view the time due order of recorded items, documents and activities in your Journal.

Toggle switch
A button you click to turn them on and off.

Toolbar
A collection of buttons that represent tools and that have equivalent commands on a related menu.

Unbound Controls
Items from the Toolbox, such as text boxes, labels, pictures, button, and so on.

Value
The number you enter in a cell that is in calculations.

Vertical alignment
Aligning cell contents relative to the top and bottom edge of the cell.

Washout
A grayscale or pale hue version of an image that appears in the background of a page.

Web Layout View
Office feature that shows you how your Web pages will look on the Internet.

Web pages
Documents on the Web that provide information and contain links to other pages.

Web Page Preview
Allows you to view unsaved Web pages using your browser.

Web server
A computer on the Internet or intranet that stores Web pages.

Window
An onscreen box that contains a title bar, menus, toolbars, and a work area.

Wizard
A series of dialog boxes that guide you through a task.

WordArt
Program that lets you enhance text by stretching, skewing, and applying special effects to it.

Word processing program
A type of software you can use to create a letter, memo, or report.

Workbook
The file you create that contains one or more worksheets.

Worksheet
A page from a workbook that contains lines and grids.

Index

SPECIAL CHARACTERS

' (apostrophe), numeric label prefix, 144
= (equal sign), formula prefix, 164
+ (plus sign), in pointer box, 26
(pound signs), cell contents display, 155

NUMERALS

3-D effects, adding to objects, 53–54

A

abbreviations, entering words as, 30
absolute hyperlinks, 334
Access (Microsoft), 239–282
    startup options, 244
    Web page operation, 333
    See also Access databases
Access data
    analyzing in Excel worksheets, 360
    creating Word documents from, 359
    inserting into Word documents, 358–359
    printing, 280–281
Access databases, 239–282
    closing, 22
    creating, 240–243
    data. *See* Access data
    data processing methods, 261–282
        See also data access pages; filters;
            forms; mailing labels; queries;
            reports
    elements. *See* fields, in Access databases;
        records, in Access databases; tables, in
        Access databases
    inserting Excel data into, 355–356
    opening, 240
    planning, 247–248
    relational. *See* table relationships
Access window, 243
action buttons, 218–220, 362
    inserting on slides, 218, 219
    linking to slides, 219–220
    testing, 219
    See also hyperlinks
action queries, 264, 362
actions, undoing/redoing, 28, 31
active cell, 66, 362
active sheet, 150, 362
active window, 14
activities. *See* appointments; events; meetings;
  tasks
addressing envelopes, 111
aligning objects, 53
aligning tables, in Word documents, 132

aligning text
    in Word documents, 96–97
        in headers/footers, 116
    in table cells, 134
    in worksheet cells, 158–159, 366, 372
animating objects. *See* animations
animating text
    on slides, 227–228, 229
    in Word documents, 94
animation schemes, 224, 225, 362
animations (on slides), 224–230
    bulleted lists, 227, 228
    charts, 227
    custom animations, 224, 226–227
    modifying the order, 229–230
    pre-designed schemes, 224, 225, 362
    previewing, 224, 225–226
    removing, 226
    text objects, 227–228, 229
    timing, 227
antonyms, finding (in Word), 84
apostrophe ('), numeric label prefix, 144
appointments, 304–305, 362
    displaying, 286, 288–290, 303–304
    scheduling/canceling, 305–306
arguments (of formulas), 164, 362
arithmetic operators (in Excel), order of
  precedence, 165
arrows, drawing, 53–54
articles. *See* news messages
Ask a Question, 17
attaching business cards to e-mail messages,
  295–296
attaching files to e-mail messages, 302–303
attaching templates to Office documents, 114
AutoComplete, 28, 143, 362
    enabling, 145
    entering words/phrases, 30
    entering worksheet labels, 143, 144–145
AutoContent Wizard (PowerPoint), 193–195
AutoCorrect, 28–30, 46, 362
AutoFill, 362
    copying worksheet cell contents, 146–147, 166
AutoFit, 362
    adjusting column widths/row heights,
      155–156
AutoFit Text, 362
    entering text in text boxes, 200
AutoForm Wizard (Access), 272–273
AutoFormat, 362
    formatting Access forms/reports, 280
    formatting worksheet cells, 161–162
AutoLayouts, 198–200, 363
automatic page breaks, 183, 363
automating routines. *See* macros